Cunningly Clever $elling
Outsell Everyone!
Easily & Ethically

Andrew Wood

Legendary Marketing
www.CunninglyClever.com
800-827-1663

Price: $39.95
Published by Select Press
Novato, California
ISBN 978-189077-23-4
10 9 8 7 6 5 4 3 2 1

Printed in Korea

Some Other Books by Andrew Wood

Cunningly Clever Marketing

Cunningly Clever Entrepreneurship
(coming soon)

The Golf Marketing Bible

Traits of Champions
(with Brian Tracy)

Making It Big in America

Summary Contents

(A detailed Table of Contents follows on page vii.)

Detailed Contents

Section 3

Section 4

Section 7

Section 10

Section 12

Section 13

Section 14

INTRODUCTION

To win one hundred victories in one hundred battles is not the highest skill. To win without fighting at all, that is the highest skill.
—Sun Tsu

Cunningly Clever Selling is unlike any sales book you have ever read before. It discussess the usual sales topics, but covers them from a very different angle—the perspective of a street-smart veteran who combines traditional ideas with proven cutting-edge concepts you simply won't get anywhere else.

Part story, part sales system, part answer book, *Cunningly Clever Selling* is NOT about tricking people into buying things they don't want!

Instead it's about selling SMARTER, much smarter: more effective prospecting, quicker rapport building, and instant qualifying.

It's about crafting well-thought-out sales stories about your products and services and presenting them in a way that captures your prospects' immediate attention!

It's about removing objections, closing deals, and making money!

Cunningly Clever Selling is also about YOU—breaking mental barriers, using your time wisely, and staying motivated through the normal highs and lows that are the world of professional selling!

Sales is by far the most financially rewarding profession in our country. Yet many people—even those already in sales for many years—are often uncomfortable selling. They lack the confidence to ask strangers to part with their money. They feel awkward when rejected and often fail to ask for the order a second or third time when success is easily within their grasps.

Your rewards for becoming a superstar salesperson are many and varied. Top salespeople are financially secure and always in demand. They can pick where they work, where they live, and for whom they work. They can set their own hours and prioritize other important aspects of living, such as time spent with their families.

In short, being a good salesperson means freedom—the freedom to live life more or less on your own terms. The key to enjoying this freedom is learning to sell with confidence.

Let me ask you a few questions:

1. How much money did you take home last year?
2. Was it enough to live your life the way you want to? Unconditionally?
3. Are you the best salesperson in your company? —region? —industry?
4. Do you wonder why some salespeople make $250,000 while others make $36,000?

Continually Enhance Your Sales Skills and You'll Enhance Your Income, Opportunities, and Lifestyle!

I used to ask myself the questions in the previous section frequently. I also used to think about what I needed to do in order to come up with the right answers.

Success in sales, as in most endeavors, stems from extensive preparation. This means knowing all there is to know about your prospect, your product, and your profession. In this book you will learn how to be an expert in all aspects of sales so you can sell with confidence and raise your career and income to new heights.

Like superstar athletes, superstar salespeople must prepare for the game; whether rookies or veterans, they must train and keep training to keep their edge.

Commit to continued sales training. Even if you're a veteran who doesn't need to be told, you can still use some reminders. And, frequently, all it takes is one new way of looking at something to propel you to that next level.

Commit to practice, commit to goal setting, commit to excellent time management, commit to self-motivation, and commit to surpassing your previous success. Your destiny is in your hands. Remember, the past doesn't equal the future! Past success is no guarantee of future success any more than past failure prevents the achievement of success!

Abraham Lincoln said, "If I was given six hours to chop down a tree, I should spend four of them sharpening my axe." Sharpening your selling axe will quickly give you an edge in your career no matter how long you have or haven't been selling!

Almost Everything I Learned About Sales I Learned in a Karate School!

I first learned about sales while running my own karate school. After I got my second karate school off the ground and was doing quite well, I started to give sales serious consideration. If, on average, I was signing up approximately seven people a week for lessons, why couldn't I sign up 20 students a week? I could have if I had known then what I know now. It is actually possible to double or triple your annual sales figures astonishingly quickly if you follow the advice you will find in these pages.

Believe me, if you can sell karate lessons, you can sell anything. Why do I say this? For several reasons:

First, karate instruction is an intangible service because, despite what you may think, most people don't study karate for self-defense purposes. They do it to increase confidence, self-esteem, flexibility, and self-satisfaction. The tough part of selling any of these qualities is that many people either don't know that's why they are there or don't care to admit it to you. For example, most young adult males don't come into a karate school and blurt out that they have NO self-confidence. They have too much pride to do that. The real reasons that prompted them to come to a karate school must be uncovered with great care and tact to avoid bruising egos.

Second, few people who walk into a karate school have any idea of what they are actually buying. They are often intimidated by the aura of secrecy surrounding the martial arts. They become further intimidated by the noise of students yelling and by the fact that they don't know what's involved. This makes them cautious and hesitant to buy. Additionally, most karate schools require a commitment of at least a year or more, so you are trying to get prospects to sign a year's contract for a service they know little about—well, I'm sure you get the picture. It's not an easy task.

Finally, because a very large part of the market is children, three people are often involved in making the buying decision —the child, the mom, and the dad. To complicate the sales process even further, most karate schools are one- or two-man operations, meaning that the selling must usually be done in the short time between teaching classes, and sometimes even during class. This calls for a quick sales presentation with no room for error.

In spite of these difficulties, the karate business was very good to me. While I was still in my mid-twenties, I was making around $120,000 a year from a small, 1200-square-foot school in a suburban shopping center!

Shortly after I opened my first karate school, I graduated to running a small chain of schools and had to deal with the problem of training others to sell. This led me to expanding my area of interest beyond my own schools. I soon found myself teaching other school owners how to get the most from their businesses. I quickly found that the techniques I had learned while selling karate lessons were equally effective when selling my own sales manuals and videos, offering consulting services, and conducting seminars.

When I published my own magazine, these techniques worked just as well in selling advertising space. Later the same principles allowed me to sell to licensees and ultimately to build a national franchise of over 400 schools.

If You Learn to Sell One Thing Really Well, You Open the Opportunity to Sell Anything—Sales Is Sales!

After I sold my schools I went on to develop and sell a leading website/software package and advertising services of all kinds through my ad agency Legendary Marketing. Along the way I have sold, or taught people how to sell, golf memberships, meeting space, real estate, vacations, cars, consumer products, and a host of other products and services. Today our Legendary sales and marketing division trains thousands of people a year in a variety of industries to sell products, large and small, and services, tangible and intangible.

In short, good sales techniques are good sales techniques, regardless of what you are selling. I proved to myself that the better your fundamentals, the more confidence you gain and the more sales you make!

I learned that if you go into a sale prepared and excited it's not hard to get others emotionally involved in your product or service. Follow up this excitement by dealing with any objections they may have, then ask for the sale and they will buy. Seal the deal by making buyers feel good about buying and they will keep coming back to buy more. People love to feel they have made a smart decision, especially when it involves spending their hard-earned money. If you make a point of showing them how to justify their purchases to themselves and feel good about it, they will tell their family and friends about you and you will soon have all the business you will ever need.

GREAT salespeople are always in demand because they know how to deal with problems. They understand that in the heat of battle, success or failure is entirely in their hands. Using this knowledge, they make more money than their peers. Confident salespeople seem to attract luck and, on top of all this, they enjoy life more because they have achieved a state of balance between working and playing.

Here's to your cunningly clever success!

Andrew Wood

1

Sales Alchemy

CHAPTER 1

The Real Reason Why Most Businesses Ultimately Fail to Reach Their True Potentials

Recently I visited several prospective clients, including a golf school, a new resort, and a couple of semi-private golf clubs. All were struggling for business, but the golf school in particular reminded me of my days in the karate business: several talented technicians with the latest equipment and years of teaching experience in an exquisite, brand-new facility. Like the karate instructors, the golf pros can talk shop all day long, exchanging the latest techniques in their quest for perfection. Unfortunately, as in the karate business, their facility, talent, and experience mean NOTHING if they can't sell!

It's the entrepreneurial curse on steroids. A mechanic fixes cars but has no clue how to attract and maintain customers—sales just sort of happen. I'd say 99% of all small business owners fall into the trap of focusing on what they do rather than running a business. In every business, from IBM to single person lawn-care services, there are five key departments that must be run with more or less equal efficiency:

- accounting
- marketing
- sales

- research & development
- operations

Almost every business, large or small, spends some time paying bills but little time budgeting or forecasting; spends some time thinking of ads but no time developing a complete year-long marketing plan. Sales are made only when people ask to buy. Research and development is almost nonexistent and 95% of the time is spent on operations: fixing cars, baking pies, or running the store.

Contrary to what most people might think—or wish—the most successful business are *not* the ones with the best product or service. Those are the exception not the rule (think Microsoft). The most successful businesses are the ones with a decent marketing plan for generating leads and the best sales strategy for closing them.

In the late Seventies and early Eighties, Chuck Norris was a world karate champion and a fledgling movie star, yet all three of the karate studios he started quickly went bankrupt! I asked him once why he thought that was and he replied, "I was the world karate champion and I thought everyone who came to my school would want to be a world champion as well."

In other words, he built schools and thought customers would come. The few that did come were taught like boot-camp recruits to make them tough. Instead of getting tough, they quit! Meanwhile a bunch of mediocre instructors (like me!) raked in millions by realizing that being able to sell karate lessons was far more important than being world champion!

This is a difficult concept for most people to accept because most business owners don't like to sell! They don't like the thought of being a salesman. They don't like the rejection. So instead they tinker with their produce or service. They talk about their experience, their philosophy, their quality, or the price of coffee in Bolivia. In fact they talk and do anything they can to fill their day, other than pick up the phone and SELL!

These people never measure success in financial terms. They can't—it's too painful to accept that someone with their skills could be struggling through life in a five-year-old Buick Regal. You can talk about the economy, the Middle East, the weather, or the competition down the street, but there is only one reason businesses fail: lack of sales!

That's not much of a shock. The question is why do businesses put so little emphasis on sales. Why don't they design a sales manual? Take sales training? Buy sales audios? Hire people who can sell rather than talk?

Now there's an idea!

The first step in any business that wants massive growth is to develop a sales culture!

CHAPTER 2

Double Your Income in 60 Seconds; Train Your People— ALL Your People—to Sell!

Double your income in 60 seconds! Sounds ridiculous right? I mean, if increasing business was that easy you'd already have thought of it and EVERYONE would be doing it, right?

Actually, no. In fact, you'd be astonished at how easy it is to increase income. It's so simple that no one ever seems to do it!

Before I give you the answer, let me share one old and a couple of recent experiences with you.

Several years ago I toured a very high-end Florida real-estate community with my wife. During the 45-minute tour the salesman on four occasions told us what he thought of "rich" people. (Apparently, as we told him we were looking for only a million dollar house, he did not think us one of the evil rich people!) He trashed the president (Bush), which I know was a popular sport back then, but he should have found out which way I leaned before doing it. To top it all off, at the end of the presentation, he said, "That's it, no high-pressure sales here!"

FINE, and there are no sales happening there either!

Recently, during a membership tour of an expensive golf property in the Midwest, I asked the membership director—who had only been in the position for 12 months—how long it took to play a round of golf. She replied that it took six hours (it should take under four). The owner, who was also in the meeting, rolled his eyes and about dug a hole in the floor. But no one in management had ever offered her sales training, and the saleswoman in question had NEVER read a sales book of any kind! (I asked. And, it's no longer true, I'm glad to say.)

Now, let's stand by the golf pro shop counter in Texas as the phone rings, although it could just as easily be any business anywhere. "How much are your green fees?" says a voice on the other end.

"Fifty bucks," the man at the counter replies.

The prospective player says, "Thanks," and hangs up!

Will he come?

Will he call back?

Will he spend his money with you or are you just going to let him go down the street?

Sales training for ALL your frontline employees may not increase your business 100% but it will increase it significantly, even when just booking greens fees, taking orders, or selling coffee. And the increase will be staggering if you're selling memberships, rooms, real estate, cars, or any high-ticket item!

YOU CANNOT afford not to TRAIN your staff how to sell!

Leads are too precious to waste! Let's look again at our pro shop counter scenario and, instead of merely responding with a price, let's take the conversation in a different direction. As a good salesperson, YOU, not the customer, MUST take control of the conversation.

Caller: *How much are your green fees?*

Golf Pro: *My name is Andrew. Sir, may I ask yours?*

Caller: *Fred.*

Golf Pro: *Fred, have you played our course before?*

Caller: *No.*

Golf Pro: *Well, let me ask you something, Fred. Do you like fast, smooth greens?*

Caller: *Yes.*

Golf Pro: *Well-manicured tees and fairways?*

Caller: *Yes.*

Golf Pro: *And a challenging layout that allows you to use every club in your bag, with five different sets of tees so you can pick the ones you'll most enjoy?*

Caller: *Yes.*

Golf Pro: *Great. Then I know you are going to love playing here at Wounded Frog. Were you looking for a morning or afternoon time?*

Caller: *Afternoon.*

Golf Pro: *Great. I have a 12:30 slot—or would 1:50 be better for you?*

Caller: *Err, 1:50.*

Now, does changing the 60-second conversation to something like that produce more green fee revenue? YES; at least 20%–30% more and possibly significantly more!!

Notice that once you engage the customer in a conversation, price is not asked again. This will work in upwards of 30% of your calls (of course, there are other scripts that get you beyond price).

Is this approach for everyone?

No; it's only for those businesses that want to thrive and prosper even in a down economy, those businesses that know they must do more to get their share of the market and who realize that discounting alone is a path of doom!

Sure, sometimes callers will go back to asking the price, but if you build some rapport and add some value before you tell them the price, sales will rise dramatically!

Change your focus from simply quoting a price to something that builds rapport or value first!

CHAPTER 3

How 98% of All Retail Sales Are Killed in Just Four Words!

You have just walked into a clothes shop, antique store, golf pro shop, or specialty market because something in the window caught your attention, or perhaps just because you are bored. You might be looking for a gift. You might be looking for an item for yourself. But unless you are in the store with a very specific purpose in mind, you don't expect to really buy anything.

You go to the nice blue shirt and fumble around for the price tag when a friendly young girl comes up to you with a big smile and says those fatal four words that have killed more sales than any in history: "Can I help you?" (or "May I help you?")

Your immediate response 98% of the time (when you are not on a gift deadline) has been preprogrammed since birth: "No thanks; I'm just looking!"

This response kills any conversation, bonding, rapport, or further questions DEAD in their tracks!

Instead the shop girl could have said, "Do you like blue?" or "We have that style in several sizes—what size are you looking for?" The best opener is often "Have you shopped here before?" If shoppers say yes, you can welcome them back and say you're available if they need you. If they say no, welcome them and offer any help they need.

Just about any question would be a better conversation starter then the killer words "Can I help you?"

The cunningly clever salesperson knows that one's choice of words can make the difference between massive success and dismal failure.

Since prospects are preprogrammed to say "no thanks," don't EVER ask them a question to which "no thanks" is an answer and your sales will be sure to rise!

CHAPTER 4

Just Because the Prospect Asked a Question Doesn't Mean You Are Obligated to Answer It!

There is an old story about a Hollywood screenwriter who, after years of trying, finally gets to see the biggest studio boss in Hollywood. When he enters the elaborate office, the boss looks up from his desk, asks for the script, and then dismisses the writer almost at once, telling him to come back at the same time in two weeks.

Two weeks later the writer knocks on the door at the appointed time and walks into Mr. Big's office. As soon as Mr. Big sees the writer walking towards him, he starts hurling a string of abuse: "This is the worst script I have ever seen in twenty years. The audience will hate it; they will walk out after five minutes..."

The crestfallen writer turns and walks towards the door without a word.

"Now," says Mr. Big, "if you were to kill the hero on page 92 instead of page three, it will be the best movie I have ever made!"

The writer turns, utterly confused…

Mr. Big looks at him, "You can't kill the hero in the first scene. No one cares about him that early in the movie; but, by the end of the movie, they LOVE him!"

Very often prospects will interrupt your sales presentation with a question. The natural tendency, the polite thing to do, is to respond to that question as soon as it's asked, but this impulse is very often the wrong one and must be resisted. You have to build value into your product or service before you answer certain questions like price!

If it's a question that helps your sale, by all means answer it. But if not, if it's a question better answered further into your presentation, you can say something like:

> *That's a good question—I'll get back to that in just a minute.*

Or

> *I am sure you will have a lot of questions, which I'll be glad to answer at the end of the presentation.*

Another option is to counter with a question of your own, one that leads back to your presentation.

Resist the temptation to answer certain questions before you have built value!

CHAPTER 5

Don't Burst the Prospect's Bubble

It's the strangest thing, but every prospect who ever walked into one of my karate studios had a bubble over his head, just like you see in comic strips when people are dreaming of something. My job was to find out what was in that bubble. Here's the problem. When I first meet someone, I can't see what's on the inside of the bubble on account of the fog! I know what is in there though—it's the alter ego of the person right under the bubble!

The big question is how does the young man who just walked into my studio see himself in that bubble. Is he Bruce Lee, Chuck Norris, or Jean Claude van Damme throwing bad guys out of ten-story windows? If it's a child, the person in the bubble might be the Karate Kid, a Ninja Turtle, or a Mighty Morphin Power Ranger. The child's parents also have bubbles above their heads filled possibly with A's on a report card or a vision of little Erica taking out the trash and cleaning up her room.

When prospects walk into a karate school, they already have preconceived notions of how the end result of taking lessons will benefit them in their daily lives. The 13-year-old boy anticipates a transition from being weak and fearful to being strong and confident. The woman in her thrities sees herself no longer as twenty pounds overweight but as a lean and mean athletic machine. The parent sees that no one will ever kick sand in their child's face again; he will be brimming with self-esteem.

Regardless of your business, it is up to you to find out exactly what's in each prospect's bubble. Only then will you be able to convey to the prospect just how he can metamorphose into that vision of himself by buying your product or service. In short, get the prospect to paint a vivid, colorful, exciting picture in the bubble.

Use all your power to enhance the picture and, whatever else you do, avoid jumping right in there with a pin and bursting the bubble!

Don't burst the prospect's bubble; find out what image it holds and tailor your presentation to paint that picture!

CHAPTER 6

Customers Buy What They Want, Not Always What They Need

When dealing with people, remember you are not dealing with creatures of logic, but with creatures of emotion, creatures bristling with prejudice, and motivated by pride and vanity.
—Dale Carnegie

Occasionally a prospect will have a clear vision in his "mind bubble" of what he wants that is comparatively easy for you to discern. The trouble is, sometimes you can plainly see that what he wants is probably wrong for him and possibly even dangerous. You would be doing him a disservice not to try and change, or at least modify, his mind. This is not always a painless task.

A few years ago, when the movie *Bloodsport* starring Jean Claude Van Damme was released, a large number of young adults came into my karate school wanting to study kickboxing and full-contact karate (the two styles depicted in the movie.) Now, both kickboxing and full-contact karate are your basic no-holds-barred, fight-to-the-death type arts. Practitioners of these arts are plagued by injuries and poor student retention. (Injured people don't come to class and that means they don't pay you! They also don't learn much when they're not in class.)

One broad-shouldered young man about 20 years old strutted in and announced that he had seen the movie and wanted to learn full-contact karate. I spent several minutes gently trying to move him toward the programs that we offered, but he remained determined. Finally, I decided that I would make the sale, meet his needs, and perhaps change his mind later. I told him that although we did not recommend full-contact karate for beginners, we would make an exception in his case, since he seemed to have such a sincere desire to learn the art.

He paid in full immediately, signed the injury waiver, and I gave him a uniform. He asked when he could start. Since I had a spare half hour, right away seemed like a good time. Once in the training area, I confirmed again that he wanted full-contact karate and he said he did. With that I told him to get on guard and defend himself. As he adopted a defensive stance, I moved in quickly and used a basic move to throw him on his back on the mat; not hard enough to break any bones but hard enough to bruise both his body and his ego.

"What are you doing!" he screamed.

"I'm sorry, but I understood that you wanted full-contact karate," I said calmly.

"Well, I do. But I didn't expect you to slam me on the floor and hurt me," he whined.

"Oh, then what do you think full-contact karate means?" I asked innocently. Then I helped him get back on his feet and took him back into the training area.

"Look," I said, "I can teach you full-contact karate if you'd like, but I think it will be much better for both of us if we start off without the contact until you master basic skills such as blocking and tumbling."

He agreed and never asked about full-contact classes again.

What is more, he stayed with the program for several years, eventually becoming a fine martial artist.

The moral is clear…

Once you have made your best effort to sell the customer what he needs, sell him what he wants. At least you have made the effort and maybe later he will thank you for it!

CHAPTER 7

Understanding the Reasons People Buy—Everyone Likes to Buy, But No One Likes to "Be Sold"

Knowledge is the only instrument of production that is not subject to diminishing returns.
—J.M. Clark

In order to become a cunningly clever salesperson, it is necessary to truly understand why people buy a particular product or service. You must also determine what it is they *think* they are buying, for it's not always the same thing.

People buy only two things. They don't buy cars, computers, or golf lessons.

They actually buy:

- good feelings
- solutions to problems

Let's examine this simple but often-missed idea more closely. People do not buy your service or product. They buy the perception of how they imagine that service or product will make them feel and of what it will do to help them.

Do people buy a lawnmower so they can cut the grass? Not

really. Do they buy a lawnmower so they will have the best looking lawnmower on the block? Of course not! They buy a lawnmower so they can have the best-looking lawn on the block.

Do they buy hammers to pound nails? No! They buy hammers to build things.

People always buy to satisfy their own needs and desires. It is important to understand this concept. It is overlooked all too often. Many a salesperson tries to sell based on features of his company, previous awards, years of experience, and so on—all attributes that he or she thinks will be important to the customer, but which, in reality, are not. Do not make this mistake. You must see your product or service as it is perceived through the eyes of your customer.

In the martial arts business, this mistake was often made as an instructor told a prospect that his particular style dated back to 100 BC, or explained in detail all the different belts and degrees the prospect could achieve in the practice of various styles. But 99.9% of the prospects couldn't care less. In the real-estate business, this mistake manifests itself in statements on brochures and listing presentations like "10 million dollars in sales" or "member of the million dollar club." All I want to know and all the rest of the world wants to know is: What can you do for me? Can you sell my home?

What Have YOU Bought Lately?

Perhaps one of the best—and seldom used—weapons in any salesperson's arsenal is, as the saying goes, to walk a mile in the other person's moccasins. Closely analyze the reasons that you used to rationalize your recent purchase of a particular product or service. Have you bought clothes, a computer, or car? Take a moment to think why you bought the specific style, model, or product. What picture did you have of yourself in your own bubble? You may have bought clothes to keep you warm, but the chances are you also bought them in your favorite colors so you would feel and look good! If you bought a computer, perhaps you said it was so you could save time, increase performance, or educate your children. But instead you bought XYZ model because it was a status symbol. Remember to think like a customer as well as a salesperson.

Prospective customers will gladly sign on the dotted line when they believe your product or service will bring them enjoyment or provide a solution to any problem they may be experiencing. Therefore, to make a successful sales presentation, you must first find out what problems your prospective customers need to have solved, and what emotions they are trying to experience from buying your service or product.

Selling from the prospect's perspective will always produce more sales. Uncover the prospect's desired end result and motivation.

CHAPTER 8

How Buying Motives Are Expressed

Success is turning knowledge into positive action.
—Dorothy Leeds

Often, your prospects will not come right out and tell you their reasons for wanting your product or service. With some prospects, a few carefully worded questions will elicit the information you need. In these cases, you will often hear their motives expressed in some of the following ways:

- I want to feel appreciated.
- I want to feel more secure.
- I want to be more confident.
- I want to have fun.
- I want to improve my self-image.
- I want to solve a particular problem.
- I want to grow or improve.
- I want to improve my appearance.
- I want to be like someone else.
- I have a lot of stress in my life.
- I need to feel important.

- I want to be respected.
- I want to be successful.
- I want to experience something new.
- I want to be liked by others.
- I want to make new friends.
- I want encouragement.

WAIT A MOMENT!

You just scanned though the list didn't you? Take a minute to go back and highlight specific ones that move people to buy your products or services.

With many prospective customers the reasons are not crystal clear and must be pulled from them by a series of very specific questions. By questioning, and listening intently to the reply, you will discover your prospect's true motives. Then you can structure your sales presentation to reinforce your prospect's motives and provide the justifications that will meet his or her objectives.

When prospects can clearly see they have something to gain from what you have to offer, they will gladly buy from you.

CHAPTER 9

Raising the Price Often Brings Sales Success—Strange But True!

One of the best and least-used techniques in sales is to raise the price or size of the deal, not lower it, in order to make a sale!

When most people lose a sale, their immediate reaction is that the prospect wants a cheaper solution and so they go back with a watered-down version of their first proposal. I have often found the very opposite to be true and have frequently gone back to prospects with a much larger, all-encompassing proposal that was far more expensive than the original, but that might have more favorable payment terms or some other element changed in their favor.

I could give you hundreds of examples of this phenomenon in action but here are just a couple of recent ones:

A golf pro I coached in sales techniques offered his members who had not taken lessons in a while unlimited lessons for a year for $5,000 instead of the typical $100 or so per lesson. For that price, he would be their personal swing coach—whenever they needed him they just had to call. Twenty people paid him $5000 and the most lessons anyone took was 22!

Eighteen golfers renewed the deal in year two as they loved the idea of having their own swing coach on call—just like the big boys on the PGA tour!

Last year a real-estate development turned down my $50,000 marketing proposal. I went back with a $150,000 deal which was also turned down. My third proposal was an all-encompassing $250,000 deal that they accepted after I agreed to take some of the payment in lots!

I used the very same strategy a year later to turn a similar proposal from $50,000 to $150,000 to $250,000, and eventually to $400,000 before it was accepted!

Every other vendor is most likely to lower the price to try to get the business. Buck the trend by going up and adding value. Very often you'll be the only vendor that does this, standing out from the others and winning the business.

Just because someone turned down your first proposal does not mean they won't respond to a different one—even if the cost is double or triple that of the original offer!

CHAPTER 10

Uncover the Truth Early—Even If It's Not What You Want to Hear!

No is very often a better answer than maybe, even though it's not what you want to hear.

Reality sometimes bites, but don't hear only what you want to hear: Don't have happy ears!

"I'll get back to you." "We'll talk it over." "We want to read the proposal" (the one you sent two weeks ago). These statements are all convenient ways of saying no without actually saying no.

The majority of salespeople waste 70–80% of their time on following up with prospects who are never going to buy!

They are never going to buy because—pick one of your choice:

- They don't believe your product is the right solution.
- They don't really have the authority to spend the money.
- They are using your proposal to get a better deal from their current vendor.
- They are going bankrupt.
- They forgot to tell you their existing contract is with their brother-in-law! While they told you the truth about

being unhappy with their current provider, they are not about to start a family war by firing him any decade soon!

Dig for the REAL reason for inaction. Sometimes at the end of a potential deal, helping the prospect say NO is your very best option so you can stop wasting your time with phone calls, emails, and letters — so you can reduce your prospect list by one and have more time to go find another prospect you can sell!

Don't pad your prospect list and sales forecasts with dead leads. Be ruthless about grading your potential sales and ruthless about discovering the truth!

It may take several calls, but the quicker you receive a definite YES or NO answer, the more sales you will make. Don't settle for maybe!

Be committed to uncovering the truth as quickly as possibly—weed out the bad prospects.

CHAPTER 11

Learn the 250 Rule

I first read about the 250 rule in Joe Girard's best-selling book *How to Sell Anything to Anyone*. Joe Girard is listed in *The Guinness Book of World Records* as "the world's greatest salesman." He achieved this title not because of some extraordinary innate skill but by a clear understanding of what makes people tick. He also understood a great deal about sales.

His theory is simple and based on the fact that everyone knows about 250 people well enough to invite them to a wedding or a funeral—which means they also know those people well enough to tell them about you and your business, service, or product. Whatever it is you are selling, whether it's yourself or tangible goods, the people you meet will talk about you. Not to 250 people at once, but over the course of a year in the local bar, at college, at work, or wherever, that person comes into contact with others and tells them about you.

If what they have to say about you is good, then when the first 250 people talk to their 250 people, a lot of people are going to be told what a wonderful person you are or what a pleasure it is to do business with you. On the other hand, if all that is mentioned are the bad things about you, then watch out! By this same principle, if you treat one person unfairly, 250 people could find out about it a lot faster than you'd think. Whether you actually did treat that person unfairly does not matter. What matters is the perception, not the reality.

With the advent of the Internet, Twitter, and all the other social media, the word now spreads like wildfire!

Learn the 250 rule; live it; breathe it!

CHAPTER 12

A Word to the Wise on the Technical Aspects of a Sales Presentation

Here are some timeless tips on presenting to groups—from someone who has done it all over the world to audiences big and small—me!

- Play some motivational upbeat music before you start; it really does put people in a better mood.
- Keep the room temperature low; it keeps attendees from dozing off.
- To limit distractions, stand so your prospects are looking at a wall behind you, not the rest of the office or out the window.
- Don't keep the lights out too long for a visual presentation; it puts people to sleep.
- Try to present before lunch time; people pay more attention.
- Bond with at least a couple of people before you start so you can use their names during your presentation.
- Don't pass out key information on handouts until you have made the majority of your main points. This stops people from skipping ahead without the needed foundation in place (and ignoring your speech!).

And, regarding logistics:

- Expect the bulb to go out on your projector.
- Expect a virus to take over your computer.
- Expect the DVD you wanted to play to develop a terminal scratch.
- Expect the Internet to be down at your hotel.
- Expect any equipment you have been promised to be AWOL.
- And if you didn't carry the samples on board the plane with you, they may be in Bangkok by now!

When presenting always expect the worst and be pleasantly surprised when everything works!

Always have a complete paper presentation as back up for your PowerPoint®, DVD, or Internet presentation, with multiple copies for everyone in the group!

CHAPTER 13

The Astonishing Sales Power of Knowledge

Knowledge is power!
—Francis Bacon

I am frequently astonished as a consumer when salesmen know less than I do about the product they are selling. For example, recently at a Corvette dealership the salesman could not tell me the difference between this year's and last year's models, both of which were on the showroom floor!

Knowledge builds trust. Knowledge gives you an edge. Commit to being the most knowledgeable salesperson in your company and you will enjoy a staggering advantage!

Know Your Customers

Know your customers' likes, dislikes, problems, challenges, mind sets, demographics, and psychographics (motivations for buying, fears, and so on).

Know Your Product

Learn every feature, every benefit, and every technical advantage of your product or service. While you may sell using only three or four key benefits, having a greater depth will undoubtedly make you seem more knowledgeable and therefore more trustworthy. Plus when you do get a technically-minded prospect, you win where others will lose out for lack of details.

Know Your Competition

Visit your competitors' websites weekly, subscribe to their newsletters using a clandestine email, download their white papers, request their brochures, read their press releases, talk to their customers. Find their weaknesses, find their strengths—know your competitors as well as you know yourself!

Know Your Market

Keep your ear to the ground for your market in general. Study your prospects' websites, join industry discussion groups, and subscribe to relevant newsletters. Be the first to find out how new rules or regulations will affect prospects' businesses!

Know Your Trade

Adopt the Japanese philosophy of Kaizan for every aspect of your job, career, or business. Read every book, listen to audios, watch DVDs, subscribe to business emails, attend seminars, and continue to hone your skills. Superstars NEVER stop training!

Know Your Industry

Read every publication, newsletter, blog, and email you can find on your chosen industry; 95% of your competitors won't!

Know What's Coming Next

Look outside your industry for ideas and trends you can adapt to yours. Very often the simple act of imitation can bring big dividends. Be an early adopter. Try new things—as the Taco Bell commercial advocates: Think outside the bun!

Learn everything you can about your customers, products or services, competition, market, and industry, and you'll be miles ahead of your competition.

Knowledge is power, but only if you act on it!

CHAPTER 14

Why Prospects Say NO When They Should Say YES!

You just made a great presentation, everyone likes you, and your prospects need and can afford to buy whatever it is you are selling—but they don't buy!

In the face of overwhelming evidence that your product or service is the right one for the prospect, one reason for inaction is fear of embarrassment. Prospects fear looking foolish in front of their spouses, co-workers, friends, or bosses, not for the decision they want to make now, but because it will PROVE beyond all doubt that the previous decision they made was poor and has, in fact, FAILED!

This can be a very powerful force in making prospects procrastinate and needs to be dealt with tactfully.

Provide them with a viable out; remove the embarrassment:

> *Ms. Prospect, I think everyone will understand that when you wanted to re-do your digital marketing last time you were looking for cheap, effective ways to get the ball rolling. I think your current vendor did an admirable job of getting things started but now that your company has a greater understanding of the web and expanded needs, it's certainly time to upgrade. Technology is ever changing and you have to move*

with the times to stay competitive!

Providing prospects with a viable out for their failure in previous decisions can be as important as selling them replacements!

2

Getting Ready

CHAPTER 15

The Awesome, Profitable, and Unbeatable Sales Power of Enthusiasm!

John Paul Getty, at one time the world's richest man, ranked the power of enthusiasm ahead of imagination, business skill, and ambition. Mark Twain, when asked to explain his great success in life said, "I was born excited." Follow their examples. Exude enthusiasm from every pore as you make your sales presentation. Enthusiasm is contagious and will almost always cause your prospects to respond favorably. Enthusiasm builds prospects' confidence in you, your company, and your products or services.

How I Got Started in Sales — and Came to Own My First Business

I started taking karate lessons because I realized it would be a fun way to keep fit. I had no intention of becoming an instructor, let alone a school owner. I was working out at the school one day when my instructor called me to tell me he was sick with the flu and had no one to teach classes for him. He wanted to know if I could look after the school for a few days. At the time I was a green belt (two levels below black, which is generally the level at which someone starts to teach), but I was young and eager and I jumped at the chance. I was ready for action!

There was only one problem. Like a student pilot finding himself at the controls of an F-16 or a sports car enthusiast given the opportunity to drive an Indy car around the track, I didn't know what to do! Oh, I could teach classes; that was easy. The problem was, I did not know how to run the office or the business, and I certainly didn't know how to sell, let alone with confidence. My concern began to turn to panic when the phone rang for the first time. It was a prospect wanting information about classes for her two children. Bubbling with enthusiasm (and babbling like an idiot), I somehow convinced the caller to bring her kids to the school for a trial lesson. During the lesson I was so energized that I continued to babble. In spite of this, when I asked her to sign the children up, she did. Seven more times that week I talked to people on the phone, persuaded them to come down to the office, take a demonstration class, and write a check. One afternoon, I practically dragged two young boys from the parking lot into the school to try a class, and was rewarded when they later returned with their parents who signed them up for lessons.

At the end of the week my instructor, feeling better, stopped by to see how I was getting along. When he opened the top drawer where I kept the money, his mouth fell open.

"What's this?" he asked.

"That's all we made this week," I replied sheepishly, thinking I had let him down.

"Where did it all come from?" he asked, breaking into a huge grin.

I relaxed and smiled back. "Well, I signed up eight new students, collected dues for about 30 people, and renewed one guy on a one-year membership."

He shook his head and looked at me with puzzled eyes. "This is more money that I have ever made in a week and you don't even know what you're doing."

Although I had no idea what to do, I was on fire with enthusiasm.

The following week my instructor asked me to run the office while he taught classes. This arrangement again produced record receipts. The third week, my instructor fell sick again and I ran the entire school. At the end of that week, he came in and threw the keys to the school on the desk.

"Andrew," he said, "I have been struggling in this school for years and I can't seem to make it work. I have a family to support and I just can't do it this way. You've signed up more people in a couple of weeks than I ever have in a month. The school's yours. I want $15,000 for it. I'm moving back east to my old job so I can have some security for my family."

By combining my savings, my wife's savings, and a loan from a friend, I scratched together enough to become the proud owner of my first business. I have never looked back!

At that stage in my career, I had NO sales training, NO sales background, NO technique, NO fancy closes, and NO way of overcoming objections except one—my unlimited enthusiasm for my job, my company, and my product. Corny maybe, but I assure you it's true—enthusiasm sells! As Samuel Goldwyn (of MGM) said, "I have found enthusiasm for work to be the most priceless ingredient in any recipe for success."

In less than ten years, I turned that simple opportunity into a multimillion dollar operation with over 400 locations based on not much more than enthusiasm!

Never underestimate the power of enthusiasm to win people over to your cause!

CHAPTER 16

The Fox, the Rabbit, and the Six Simple Keys to Unlimited Enthusiasm

The Master sat down with his student and posed the question, "Which is faster, the fox or the rabbit?" With little hesitation, the student answered that the fox was faster than the rabbit. The Master pointed out that although, technically, the fox should be faster, it was not. "You see," said the Master, "the rabbit has more enthusiasm. The fox is running for his dinner, but the rabbit is running for his life."

So it is in sales and in life. Even a less-accomplished salesperson can produce great success if he or she is full of real desire, along with the confidence and motivation that results from this state. Remember, nothing happens in sales until someone gets excited. The best sales take place when you *and* your prospect are *both* excited about what you're selling!

6 Simple Keys to Unlimited Enthusiasm

1. Love what you do. If you don't love what you do, get a different job! You have to be excited about what you do or you will never reach your true potential. If you don't like your job, your company, or your product, you will come across as insincere to prospective buyers. The best way to love your job is to seek mastery of your craft! Immerse yourself in the skills and training needed to be cunningly clever at what you do!

2. Be excited about your product or service. List ten reasons why a prospect should want to buy your product or do business with you. Make sure that for each reason you list a clear and positive benefit for the prospect!

	Reason	Benefit
1.	______________________	______________________
2.	______________________	______________________
3.	______________________	______________________
4.	______________________	______________________
5.	______________________	______________________
6.	______________________	______________________
7.	______________________	______________________
8.	______________________	______________________
9.	______________________	______________________
10.	______________________	______________________

3. Be in tune with what you sell. If you sell jet airplanes, then chances are you are not going to own or use the products you sell. If you sell Fords, however, you certainly shouldn't be driving a Toyota, or vice versa. By not using the products you sell, you create a feeling of distrust about your product. After all, would you want to buy stocks from a broker who doesn't put any of his own money in the market? Would you buy one brand of computer when the salesperson proudly tells you he uses another?

There is a famous story in golfing circles about South African pro Gary Player. When he first came to America in the late Fifties, his hero was the great Ben Hogan who had just started his own equipment company. After playing badly one day, he called Hogan for some advice. The call came late at night. Player reverently asked his idol for some advice. Hogan's reply was short and to the point. "Whose logo do you wear on your visor, Mr. Player?" he asked.

"Dunlop," said Player, naming the equipment manufacturer that sponsored him.

"Then call Mr. Dunlop!" replied Hogan and hung up abruptly.

4. Be your own coach. It pays to be your own coach as you work daily to build up your levels of motivation and enthusiasm. Keep testimonial letters from satisfied customers on your office walls and in your day planner. Look at them often, especially when you have to deal with someone who doesn't appreciate your efforts. Keep a library of motivational music to anchor you to positive and exciting feelings. Keep a few humorous CDs in your car so that you can enjoy a relaxing chuckle as you drive to work. In short, gather a locker full of various items to help you coach yourself and keep your attitude, enthusiasm, and motivation high!

DO NOT RELY ON ANYONE ELSE TO MAKE YOU BETTER! Buy books, audios, and courses on how to sell and related topics! If you are not interested in taking personal charge of your career, *JOIN THE ARMY!*

5. Set personal goals and chart your progress. Set personal goals and keep a visual record of your progress. It sounds simplistic to keep a tally of appointment calls and sales wins, but an "official" record is motivating. When you see a goal in sight, you work harder to finish it.

6. Reward yourself. Your company may offer some rewards for good performance. If this is not the case, take matters into your own hands to boost your levels of enthusiasm and motivation.

Constantly remind yourself why you are working. Not just to pay bills but to experience new and exciting places, events, and friends. Each time you achieve a goal, give yourself a weekend trip to the mountains or the ocean as a reward. It can seem silly but even giving yourself little treats can make a difference. Some salespeople literally eat an M&M after each cold call on the phone. Use small rewards to mentally tie your daily work to the bigger rewards it will bring. You will quickly find that your motivation increases. As Henry Ford said, "Enthusiasm is at the bottom of all progress! With it, there is accomplishment; without it, there are only alibis."

Practice increasing your enthusiasm and you WILL increase your sales!

CHAPTER 17

The Critical Importance of a Positive Attitude

If there were just one word I could use to describe a successful person it would be attitude.
—Bart Starr

Getting someone to admit they actually have a bad attitude is about as rare as finding a business that admits to a bad reputation. Over the years I have met thousands of martial arts instructors, but I have never met an instructor who thinks he has a bad reputation. Strangely enough, however, they can always tell me about a competitor down the street who has a terrible reputation. That's the same story I hear from Realtors, insurance agents, mechanics, and people with whom I've consulted in a variety of other occupations. They're never the ones with the bad reputations or attitudes. It's always someone else!

Do you know someone with a bad attitude? I'll bet you do.

What do you think of that person?

Is he a happy, balanced, fun-to-be-around individual? I think not! You can tell a lot about a person's attitude by the way other people relate to him, whether acquaintances greet him with a smile or merely nod in his general direction. Attitude has been defined as "the belief or bearing of an individual as it indicates thoughts, feelings, or actions." Our attitudes and moods determine to a very large degree the actions, beliefs, and moods of our prospects. Your attitude is like a flashing sign telling the world at large exactly what you expect. If it's a happy, cheerful, positive attitude, there is little doubt that is what you will get in return. If it's sullen, dull, and negative, there is likewise little doubt that's what you will get back.

Many products and services are becoming more and more indistinguishable from one another. As costs are brought down in almost every industry, more people than ever before buy goods and services based on their perception of the person they are dealing with rather than the actual product. (This is better than their buying on price alone!) The very first indication of what type of service may be offered by an organization begins with the salesperson or, more specifically, the salesperson's attitude. The delivery of the service begins with the sale.

Success depends not only on your attitude toward others, but also on your attitude toward yourself. The cunningly clever salesperson knows that **attitude, more than aptitude**, has again and again proven to be the most important ingredient to success in any endeavor. Selling is certainly no exception. Attitude is what holds us back or propels us forward. When things seem to be going well, it is easy to have a positive attitude. It is when things are not going so well that keeping a positive attitude really makes a difference.

"The greatest discovery of my generation is that a human being can alter his life by altering his attitude."
—William James

CHAPTER 18

Managing Your Outlook for Sales Success

There is a little difference in people that makes a big difference. The little difference is attitude. The big difference is whether that attitude is positive or negative.

—Clement Stone

Your attitude is like a powerful magnet. A friendly, happy, and light-hearted attitude creates an environment of good luck. It attracts good people and good things to you. But beware, for the reverse is also true. A negative attitude will very often produce negative results. Since your actions reflect your attitudes, you will not be inclined to make strong efforts to accomplish something if your attitude is negative and you do not believe it can be done.

Many people will base their reactions to your offers on their perceptions of you— the person they are dealing with—rather than your actual product or service offered. The very first indication of what type of service may be offered by an organization begins with you or, more specifically, your attitude because the delivery of your service begins with the sale.

Attitude is a way of thinking about, and looking at, the people and things around you, as well as yourself. It includes your point of view of the way things are now as well as your expectation of the way things are going to be. Because a solidly positive attitude is the necessary foundation for success, your attitude is one of your most valuable personal possessions. Protect it from anything that might harm it, just as you would a priceless jewel.

That means, among other things, avoiding negative thoughts, discussions, and people. You know the type of people I mean. The ones who think their lack of success in life can be blamed on the stock market, the prime rate, the economy, or the type of leads they are getting. These people's attitudes can quickly grow in you like a cancer. Disassociate yourself from this type of person at once. Those people are destined to go nowhere. You, however, because of your excellent attitude, have a ticket to the TOP!

Food for Thought

Good attitudes are like health food for the mind. To be successful, you need to feed your mind with positive, healthy thinking. Just as you must continually replenish your body's fuel, so must you continually supply your mind with a positive attitude.

When you begin to feel negative and down, your mind tells you that it is hungry for "nutritious" positive thoughts. Positive thoughts will help you free up your creative energies. If an event occurs that is not very "tasty" or nutritious in terms of positive thinking, add a little spice by turning the situation around. Humor is one of the best ways to turn negative incidents around. It can restore your attitude and help you maintain a healthy outlook on life.

For instance, if you completely blow a presentation and there is nothing you can do to save it, just laugh and tell yourself that the rest of the day has to be better by contrast. (You might even tell prospects that this was the worst job you've ever done in a presentation and they might chuckle with you and tell you what they think you can do to improve.) As my friend and colleague, Brian Tracy, says, "Get up early and eat a dead frog for breakfast; after that everything will seem better!"

What's Your Attitude Today?

What is your attitude today? Chances are that the words of Abraham Lincoln can hold true for you if you let them. To quote him exactly: "Most people are about as happy as they make up their minds to be."

The truth is that most of us get out of bed each morning in a state of suspended animation. At this point, your attitude is neither good nor bad: then the shower water turns cold before you have finished showering, the car has a flat on the freeway, and you get a ticket trying to make up for lost time. How's your attitude now?

Conversely, you get up, put on an outfit you haven't worn for a while and find $20 you'd forgotten about. In the mail is a much bigger refund check than you expected from the IRS and the first news you get upon reaching the office is that you have been promoted. Now how is your attitude?

As you can see, most of us start the day without attitude but quickly let the events of the day influence our attitude and our work accordingly.

Does Attitude Fix All? No, But It Sure Helps!

Having a positive attitude will not solve all your problems, but it can put you in a better frame of mind to make good decisions and take positive action. You may have no control over certain outside factors that affect your life, but you can have absolute control over whether you let these factors dictate your attitude. Follow Lincoln's lead and make up your mind to be positive. Don't let external factors push your attitude around.

Make up your mind to stay positive and you'll see a corresponding effect on sales!

CHAPTER 19

Conquering Your Fear of Money

Present fears are less than horrible imaginings.
—Shakespeare

Believe it or not, many salespeople are afraid to ask for money! I was giving a seminar to salespeople in South Carolina last year when I realized that my students were victims of this dreaded affliction. I devised a simple little exercise where they paired off, and each of them said to the other, "That will be just $3,000 please." I had trouble deciding if the results were tragic or hilarious! The first few times we did it, three of them actually couldn't get the words out of their mouths. We practiced for half an hour, going up and down in various increments until they could say "$10,000" just as easily as "ten bucks." By employing this exercise, and then explaining the reasons for their problem, we were able to conquer this long-held fear.

Why *are* salespeople afraid to ask for money?

It may be because they themselves never had enough money to buy the products they are selling. When this is true, the fact that they are selling a product they themselves cannot afford leads them to believe, at least subconsciously, that other people can't afford it either. This is very true with many people selling high-end products like club memberships or real estate.

In my work with the PGA, I have found that, despite the fact golf professionals are working with some of the most affluent individuals in the country, many of them are desperately afraid of asking for money. In this case, it's not because they don't make decent money themselves but because they don't want to be thought of as salespeople.

What golf professionals don't seem to appreciate is that 90% of the people they deal with are businessmen or former businessmen. They won't be offended by being asked for money. In fact, they expect it! According to the National Golf Foundation, 86% of the golfers in this country would spend more money on green fees, play more often, drink more beer in the clubhouse, and buy more clothes if ONLY they played better! The same report also points out that only 13% of the people surveyed actually took a lesson from a golf professional in the preceding year! If that's not a market waiting to happen, I don't know what is. But you have to ask for the sale in order to get it!

Never worry about what you can afford or what you would pay for a product or service; you are NOT your customer.

Don't let $ signs scare you; they are your friend!

CHAPTER 20

Frank's Story

We can communicate an idea around the world in 60 seconds, but it sometimes takes years for an idea to get through a quarter inch of human skull.
—Charles F. Kettering

Frank was a good friend of mine and ran a successful karate school in Southern California. He was located in a lower-income part of town, but he still had over 170 students, each of whom paid $60 a month for group tuition. In addition to this, at least 50 of these clients managed to find an extra $60 per month to pay for private lessons.

One day Frank called to invite me to his wedding. After congratulating him and chatting for a while, I asked him where he was going on his honeymoon. At this point he grew quiet and confided that he did not have enough money for a honeymoon.

I asked why he didn't just upgrade one of his students to the Black Belt course that usually sold for around $2,500. (This would allow the student to take lessons for some three to four years with no additional fees, thus saving a good deal of money for the student.) At the same time, Frank would have $2,500 in cash to use for his honeymoon. He responded that he had tried this approach, but people in his area simply could not afford the $2,500 fee for the course. I told him I could help him if he would dedicate an hour of his time to me.

The next day, the first thing I noticed as I walked across the parking lot and entered his school was a Mercedes coupe. In it sat a young boy wearing a karate uniform. Then I noticed that one of the parents waiting in the lobby was wearing a gold Rolex watch. When class ended a few minutes later, Frank and I sat down in his office and I pointed out that his poor students' parents could afford a Mercedes and a Rolex. He assured me these two people were exceptions to the general rule and that most of his students were indeed from lower-income families. I began to ask him some questions.

Don't Underestimate Your Customers or Yourself!

First, I asked Frank if he really believed karate lessons could help people improve their lives. He responded passionately that they could. Next I asked why one or two of the 50 or so students who paid him $60 a month for private lessons could not afford to pay $2,500 and never have to pay for a lesson again. He replied that it was just too expensive. I then asked if *he* thought it was too expensive. He thought briefly and then said that he could not have afforded that much money when he was paying for karate lessons.

I had unearthed problem number one: He was assuming by projection that his students shared his financial problems. Because *he* could not come up with $2,500 in cash, he automatically ascribed the same difficulty to his students. This of course was a false assumption! Then I asked how much he thought his time was worth. He replied that he charged $30 per half hour for a private lesson, and that he believed he was worth every penny. Then I inquired how long it took a private student to reach black belt. To this he replied, "About four years." I pointed out that $120 a month for four years came to almost $6,000, and that if he sold a student a prepaid black-belt program, he would save that student more than $2,500 over the course of study. This savings meant that if the student stayed with the program all the way to black-belt rank (only 1 in 50 does) he would be paying less than $15 per private lesson rather than the $30 he was currently paying. When I asked Frank if he thought that was a good deal, he replied that he thought it was a *great* deal! Maybe too cheap!

I reminded Frank that because only one in five completed the program, he stood a good chance of making considerably more per lesson. He glowed with delight at the improved prospect. Problem number two was solved. Frank had been focusing on the cost of the program instead of the actual savings and benefits his students would receive. As soon as he realized his error, he saw the whole matter in a different light. Now that he was focused on a program that saved his students a considerable sum, instead of worrying about the overall cost, he began to approach his students with new zeal and quickly sold the cash program to several students before his wedding day arrived.

This story is repeated a thousand times a day across the country by countless salespeople selling cars, shoes, paper, information, and other products and services. Salespeople too often place a mental barrier on themselves and, in doing so, thwart their own efforts to obtain the success they deserve.

The only real proof that prospects can't or won't buy is to ask them, ALL of them!

CHAPTER 21

Fear of Failure or Rejection

One of the reasons mature people stop learning is they become less and less willing to risk failure.
—John Gardner

Sometimes the problem is fear of failure or rejection. In this case, the salesperson apparently doesn't have faith in the product, or he or she would sympathize with the prospects for not being able to take advantage of the opportunity they are being offered.

A young up-and-coming executive with IBM approached the company president, Thomas Watson, Sr., and asked him the key to success. The older man turned to the younger and announced, "Fail twice as fast." The young man, perplexed, asked the question again. "But, Mr. Watson, I really, really want badly to make it. Please tell me what should I do?"

"In that case," replied Watson, "Fail three times as fast."

Sound advice, indeed, from one of the smartest salesmen who ever lived. Watson had learned that rather than fear failure, you must embrace it in order to become a top salesperson.

What the younger man failed to understand is that the quicker you get the inevitable failures behind you, whether they are of brief duration or last half a lifetime, the sooner you will reach success. If you double the amount of phone calls you make in a day, it will probably double your failures. However, it will almost certainly double your sales at the same time.

So you fail to keep the customer on the phone and he hangs up. Big deal! He's not the only prospect in the world. In fact, he's the one who lost out on that call because he didn't recognize the benefits of what you had to offer. Don't allow a hang-up on a telephone call, or the manager pointing coldly to a "No Soliciting" sign in the window as you walk through the door, or the no-show for an appointment to make you feel rejected or a failure. Confident salespeople go into every encounter ready to win. They have conquered their fear of failure. They know they will triumph in the end, although they may lose a few skirmishes along the way. There is no failure as long as you're still moving forward.

You are on the road to success when you
realize that failure is merely a detour.
—Anonymous

What's the Worst Thing That Can Happen?

When you make a phone call, knock on a door, enter an office, greet an appointment, or welcome a "walk-in," what is the worst thing that can occur? After you have introduced yourself, made a presentation, and asked for a sale, what's the absolute worst thing that can happen to you?

Ready? Here it is! The prospect can hang up, slam the door in your face, call your mother names, or say no. That's it! Those are the worst things that can possibly happen. Now that sounds logical, doesn't it? Great! Now let's move on. There is one small problem we forgot to deal with—**YOUR EGO!**

Our fragile human ego is such that when a person rejects our proposition, we take it as a personal affront. We feel humiliated, embarrassed, or belittled. Rejection attacks our self-confidence and self-esteem. Yet if we can let it go for what it is—a rejection of a sales proposition—we will have jumped a hurdle that many never cross.

Overcoming Fear of Failure

If you truly aspire to be a top salesperson, you must risk failure, but only in the short term. Notice the key words are "risk" and "short term." Concentrate on continuing with your plan to achieve your sales goals because you know the actual risk will be very small. It means asking for sales and then asking again and again. With every rejection you receive, you are getting closer to a sale. It is a fact that the more often we fail, the more often we succeed. Babe Ruth held the home run title for his era—but he also held the strikeout record!

As Henry Ford once remarked, "A failure is an opportunity to begin again more intelligently."

CHAPTER 22

Fear of Responsibility

Success at anything is no accident. Your success as a salesperson depends on one thing—and one thing alone—you. Consider for a moment: You are, without doubt, the person in control of your own destiny. Whatever path you take in life is your choice; it is your decision alone—for better or worse. If you are going to rise to the top and become the consummate confident salesperson, you must decide right now that you are in charge of your own destiny.

You Really Are the Boss

Perhaps one of the greatest mistakes you can make in life is to think you work for someone else—to think that other people control the outcome of your efforts and you are only a cog in some giant wheel. It makes no difference whether you work for IBM or for a "mom and pop" operation. It doesn't matter whether you own and operate your own business or are one of several thousand salesmen. *You ARE the company*. You are in charge of your own success or the lack of it.

You are the president, CEO, chief cook, and bottle washer of Your Personal Sales Corporation. If you work for a large company, let's pretend that they subcontract to you. You are in charge of five major divisions at Your Personal Sales Corp.: sales, marketing, operations, research and development, and accounting. Each of these divisions plays a key part in determining your income and your future. If you fail to attend properly to any of these five key areas, you will in some way inhibit your career growth. For example, imagine what would happen to IBM if they suddenly decided to spend no time or money on research and development. In today's marketplace they would very quickly fall behind and eventually fail. Suppose Nissan stopped their advertising and marketing efforts and tried instead to live on the quality of their products and their good name. That might work for a short while, but in the ever-competitive car market, they would have engineered their own doom! The same facts apply to you personally. Each one of these five areas is just as critical to your success as it is to a major company. You *are* your own company!

Being in charge of sales is straightforward enough. Your job, as vice president of sales at Your Personal Sales Corp., is to set sales goals that provide the company with the type of income and profit it needs to survive and prosper, and the type of income that will provide your family with the very best life has to offer. It is also your sole responsibility that these goals are met or exceeded. This means not only selling the products your client wants, but, also, since you are the most important product, selling yourself to the right partner company— the one that can provide you with the right products and opportunities to maximize your talents.

How about marketing? How can you be responsible for marketing if you sell for a large corporation? Well you are—to some degree at least. It is your job to generate leads, if not through advertising, at least through referrals, networking, trade shows, and so on. It is also your job stay in touch with existing clients by sending personal notes, thank-you cards, and so forth to ensure you retain them as happy customers.

Research and development are also in your hands. Even if your employer sponsors training programs, it's up to you to seek out new and better ways to sell your products. Read books like this one. Attend seminars, listen to audios, and watch videos. It's your job as vice president of R&D to keep up on the very latest in sales and motivational techniques, and to keep Your Personal Sales Corp. ahead of the competition.

As director of operations, you must see that everyday tasks, including reports, paperwork, and filing, are performed. Although it may not be the most interesting part of your job, a well-run operations department is essential to the smooth running of Your Personal Sales Corp.

Accounting is another essential area of your corporate responsibility. Are you selling enough product to live the way you want to live? Are you meeting and exceeding your financial goals? As chief financial officer, you will be the first to know how you are progressing each and every month—right after you deposit your paycheck.

You're the CEO of Your Life—Take Charge!

Now that you own and control your own company, you are free to do whatever it takes in order to succeed. Does that mean that you can't be a team player? Of course not. But it does mean that you have to rise above the level of dedication and effort that even a better-than-average member of the team puts in. As a confident salesperson, you should always be ready to constructively counsel, coach, and motivate other team members. Unlike other team members, however, you won't be waiting for the Glengarry leads to arrive, for the trade show to get here, or for the new ad to break. You will be too busy running your company and making things happen! The positive mental decision to run you own life like a company has been the turning point for almost all confident salespeople. Organize your personal company now!

Be aware that by assuming greater responsibility for your actions you will quickly experience greater success. The small investment you make in terms of increased time and effort will soon repay you with greater rewards. Confident salespeople realize they are in charge of their own destinies and never waste valuable sales time blaming other people, society, or life in general for their temporary setbacks. That's why they make more sales and enjoy bigger incomes!

"The buck stops here!"
—Plaque on President Harry S. Truman's desk

3

Building Rapport the Cunningly Clever Way

CHAPTER 23

Creating Instant Rapport with Your Prospects

Rapport is the ability to bond with another person as you would with a friend. For a cunningly clever salesperson, it is the most sought after of all conditions. The first step to any sales presentation is building rapport with your prospect. When good rapport exists, sales are easy; without rapport, making a sale is nearly impossible.

Good rapport puts other people at ease so they treat you as a person with whom they are truly comfortable, not as a salesperson.

One of the little "ice-breakers" I use at the start of my sales and marketing seminars is to ask everyone to write down their five favorite movies of all time. I go around and look at what they are writing and it tells me a lot about my audience. But that's not the main reason I do it. Once everyone has written their selections, I ask them to move about the room to try to find other people who have some of the same movies on their lists. (It's scary to think there really are people out there who think *Willie Wonka & the Chocolate Factory* was one of the best movies of all time!) The two people who have the most movies in common are declared the winners. The real objective, however, is not to find a winner, but to show a diverse group of people that there are others just like them in the room.

When people find someone who has listed one of their selections, they can't resist talking about the movie.

"What was your a favorite part?"

"The best line?"

"Do you remember the bit where...?"

Two people who have never met get together in a crowded room and find they both love the same movie and BANG, just like magic, you have achieved...what have you achieved?

Instant rapport!

When training membership directors or real estate agents how to sell high-end golf memberships or property, one of my favorite rapport-building questions is this.

> *Mr. Prospect, what's the best round of golf you ever shot?*

Instantly, they smile, they look up, they relax, and then they tell you where and when—as if it happened yesterday—even if it was 26 years ago!

What simple question or technique could you employ to get such instant and positive results?

The faster you can build rapport with your prospect, the sooner you can start selling!

CHAPTER 24

Conditioned to Resist Salespeople—Calming Your Prospect's Fears

A few years ago, a California auto dealership came up with clever advertisements to attract business. Three car salesmen for rival dealers were portrayed as a vulture, an alligator, and a jackal, all dressed in cheap suits. More recently, Johnston Automotive Group dealership had a series of badger ads where a surly badger sales manager badgers customers in various ways. The point of the ads is that while most car salespeople are like those in the commercials, theirs are different! I'm sure the ads got a chuckle and hit a nerve with consumers!

Unfortunately, salespeople are perceived by many as being on the lowest rung of the ladder as far as careers are concerned. The old stereotype of a fast-talking, hard-selling vulture still persists despite the fact that the average salesperson is honest and helpful. It only takes the occasional telemarketer calling at dinner time to keep the negative image of salespeople alive.

You start most sales relationships with one strike against you. People assume that you have *your* interests at heart, not *theirs!* Therefore, they naturally don't trust you until you can demonstrate that you are interested in *them* and can be helpful to *them*.

Because of this negative conditioning, it is essential that you go the extra mile to be courteous, friendly, and professional as you start building rapport.

When people explore buying something from you, it is very probable that they do so with some degree of trepidation. They are unsure about what to expect. Maybe you'll put a lot of pressure on them and it will be unpleasant. Maybe they won't be able to justify the purchases to a spouse. If it's a membership, maybe they won't feel that they could fit in.

Tell Your Prospect What's Going to Happen

One way to make most people more comfortable is to immediately tell them what will happen. For instance, when a prospect comes to my office, I'll say something like:

> *Here's what I was planning to do in our time together: ask you a few questions about your business, then tell you about our Marketing Commander product and how it will help you get better results. Then I will show you around the office, introduce you to some of the staff, and answer your questions. Does that sound reasonable? Is there anything you want to know before we get started?*

Put Your Prospect at Ease

Don't take the prospect's fears personally. Prospects walking into an auto dealership, electronics store, or computer supermarket are frequently apprehensive about making a mistake, being taken advantage of, or the salesperson being pushy.

Your foremost task in the initial sales contact is to make your prospect feel comfortable with you. Until this happens, it will be impossible for the prospect to make a buying decision. Use the first few minutes to remove the prospect's fear and help him or her to relax. While in some cases your sales presentation will be your main chance to sell, many sales require repeated contacts over time, so don't push. Remember that the person may come back again, or have a change in circumstances later. If you don't sell her immediately, you may have another chance—if you treat her well.

Tell prospects up front what is going to happen to put their fears to rest!

CHAPTER 25

Appearance May Not Be Everything — But It's Close

Men in general judge far more from appearances than from reality. All men have eyes, but few have the gift of penetration.
—Niccolo Machiavelli

If prospects do not like you, they will not buy from you! That's pretty straightforward, isn't it?

Consider for a moment: Do you buy products and services from people you don't like?

No!

Well, neither do I and neither does anyone else. Above all else, selling requires selling *yourself* to the prospect. If you don't do that, no sales technique in the world is going to save you.

The first few seconds of your contact with a prospect can determine your success in any sales interview. First impressions are lasting impressions and are usually the right impressions, at least as far as your prospect is concerned. Only a small percentage of all the information we absorb comes through our ears; that places a heavy emphasis on what we see!

People Are Very Judgmental About Clothes

The first thing that influences the prospect is your appearance. That doesn't necessarily mean spending $1,000 on an Armani suit. But imagine walking into a lawyer's office and finding him in a white 1970s-style polyester suit. Or going to the doctor and being treated by someone wearing cut-off jeans and a tie-dyed T-shirt. You would be turned off immediately. Although these are extreme examples, the basic rule holds true in every situation. People have a preconceived idea of how you should dress depending upon your function and industry, and you had better not stray too far from that perception if you want them to trust you.

Most successful corporate executives worry about how they look and believe in "dressing for success." Many salespeople don't.

Take care to dress professionally and appropriately. Remember that styles and colors come and go. Don't be caught sporting last decade's look! Keep up with fashion trends at least once a year.

People make all sorts of assumptions about you based on how you dress. For instance:

- If you wear the same suit to meet a prospect twice in a row, the prospect may think it's the only one you own. Of course, he may be right!
- If you wear the same color clothes all the time, people may conclude that you are dull.
- Loose-fitting clothes can make you look poor.
- If your suit is too tight, it can lead people to believe you are lazy.

- If you wear fake copies of expensive watches (and most people can tell), it tends to make people distrust you.
- If you dress flamboyantly, it can make people think you are not serious or responsible.

The old adage "you can't judge a book by its cover" is true. However, the cover, to a very large degree, determines whether or not the book will be picked up and read. If the book has an unappealing cover and few people pick it up and read it, it doesn't much matter what's inside.

The way you dress is very important in selling. Always be careful to strike a happy medium between overdressing and underdressing. Smartly attired people have an air of success about them. Without overpowering the audience you are selling to, make an effort to improve your image by improving the quality of your clothing and tailoring. In the words of Henry Ward Beecher, "Clothes and manner do not make the man; but, when he is made, they greatly improve his appearance."

"Things do not pass for what they are but for what they seem. Most things are judged by their jackets."
—Baltazar Gracian

CHAPTER 26

Dress & Drive to Suit Your Audience—Put Yourself in Your Prospect's Shoes

Last year a good friend joined me as a regular speaker at my seminars. He is good-looking, athletic, and razor sharp. He always takes meticulous care with his appearance, and is one of the best-dressed people you will ever meet. Two-hundred-dollar silk ties, handmade shoes, and very expensive tailored suits are the norm for him. He could easily be taken for a Wall Street tycoon or a real estate magnate.

At our first seminar together he delivered a dynamic, powerful, and motivating speech that was by far the finest of the three-day convention. Yet as we left the room, I could tell that something was not quite right.

I pulled aside a couple of people I know well and asked them for their opinions of the speech. They said that the speech was good, but added that they didn't like the way the speaker was dressed. I could hardly believe my ears. Then I took a look around. Out of a hundred or more people in the room, I was the only other person wearing a suit. My partner had scared the audience, made them feel inferior, and put them on the defensive—not by what he said, but by what he wore. As Raymond Chandler put it, "he looked as inconspicuous as a tarantula on a slice of angel food cake."

There is a fine line with any audience, and moving very far to either side of it can be bad.

Understand Your Prospect's Perspective

Victor Kiam, of Remington shavers fame, tells a similar story in his book, *Going for It!* In his early days as a salesman, Kiam had gone into a client's office hoping to sell him a line of expensive watches. The client wasn't happy with the price of the watches and brought the point home by pointing to Kiam's expensive loafers and saying that his clients wore sneakers, not Italian loafers.

Being a cunningly clever salesman, Kiam returned the following week with a less expensive line of watches more suited to his client's needs. To make *his* point that this was indeed what the client needed, he sat down at the desk and put his feet up on it. He was wearing sneakers. The account was won.

Two good friends of mine, one a stockbroker and the other an insurance salesman, both told me very similar stories about a key lesson learned when starting out. After some early success both had bought Porsches and showed up at a client's house to make a sale. The insurance salesman was calling on a union boss who could bring him a great deal of business. They hit it off at once but, as my friend was leaving, the union boss told him, "I don't care what you drive, but if you want to do business with any of my boys, don't show up in that!" My friend took the hint and bought a Ford Mustang, his first step in securing millions of dollars in union business!

My other friend had a similar story, although in his case the man told him that running around in a $100,000 car made it look like he was charging too much commission. He opted for an Acura, a nice, affluent, middle-of-the-road look for business. He drives his Porsche on weekends.

Choose your clothing, appearance, and style to suit your audience.

CHAPTER 27

Develop Winning Personal Traits

When asked what great secret he had found to influence people to his way of thinking, Abraham Lincoln replied, "If you would win a man over to your cause, first convince him that you are his sincere friend."

To a great extent, the way people react to you often depends on little things—like smiling. When you are introduced to someone, always respond with a warm and friendly smile.

Shake his or her hand firmly because there are few things that turn people off quicker than a limp handshake. Stand up straight with your shoulders back and chest forward. Make good eye contact and generally let the other person know by your body language that you are a successful, professional, and confident individual who is genuinely glad to meet them.

The Power of a Smile

It is amazing how few people actually smile or look even remotely happy that they are alive and healthy on this most interesting planet in the universe. There are a couple of reasons why a smile can do more to help you feel good, and gain a positive response from your prospect, than any other physical act.

First, it has been scientifically proven that when you stand up straight and smile, it is actually impossible to feel down and depressed. Just as when you scowl and hunch up, it is physically impossible to feel good. If you don't readily accept that as the truth, try it!

Second, when you smile, it makes you appear much less of a threat, and people will warm up to you much faster.

When my first child was born, an amazing thing happened. Whenever I was out with her in a stroller at the park, on the sidewalk, or in a supermarket, people I had never met before stopped and smiled. They were, of course, smiling at my beautiful daughter, not at me. So what did I do? Why, I naturally smiled back. This, in turn, often led to a greeting or conversation. Always remember, when you smile the world smiles with you, but when you cry, you cry alone.

How Do You Sound?

Next to your appearance, the tone of your voice and the way you deliver your words are the most important parts of making a good impression on the prospect. Make your conversation enthusiastic, friendly, and professional.

If the prospect talks in a loud voice, raise yours slightly above its normal level. If the prospect speaks quietly, lower your voice a couple of decibels. Mirror your prospect's speech patterns by speaking a little slower or a little faster as appropriate. Remember, people establish the highest levels of rapport with others who are just like them! Your voice can indicate to prospects that you are indeed like them.

Body Language

Just as you mirror qualities of your prospect's speech, you should mirror your prospect's basic body language. If the person you are dealing with has a military bearing and stands straight and tall rather than lounging or slumping, it will definitely pay you to do the same. In your office, if the prospect leans forward, so should you. In short, mirroring your prospect's largely unconscious physical demeanor is one of the most effective ways to rapidly establish rapport. Be sure to use this technique in conjunction with the others mentioned in this chapter.

Smile, use an upbeat tone, and use appropriate body language to increase your rapport and ultimately your sales!

CHAPTER 28

What's in a Name?

Why is it that at every convention there are hundreds of people walking around with their own names pinned to their chests? The obvious reason is that the organizers want the people at the convention to develop rapport, which leads to sound business relationships. They also know that one of the best ways to develop rapport is to remember a person's name. Since there are hundreds of people walking around the floor of the convention, that's impossible. By sticking name labels on everyone, they make it easy for conventioneers to greet one another by their first names.

In his classic book *How to Win Friends and Influence People*, Dale Carnegie stated, "The sound of a person's name said correctly is one of the nicest sounds in the world, at least to them." Using someone's name is indeed one of the sincerest compliments you can pay a person. It builds self-esteem, and shows that you think he or she is important.

If you have an appointment with a prospect, you have his or her name on your calendar. Instruct your receptionist to greet people by name when they arrive ("Mr. Jones…thank you for coming, Ms. Smith is waiting for you.") Then when they come in your office, greet them by name rather than asking their name. Enter the data from prospects' business cards into your database for follow-up if they haven't bought and for reference if they have. Make a positive effort to remember names, and people will be flattered that they have made an impression on you.

Remembering peoples' names is one of the sincerest compliments you can pay them!

CHAPTER 29

Elvis Solves a Major Sales Problem

A couple of years ago I hired a young man named Kemp. His unusual first name began to cause problems immediately.

He'd call a prospect and say "Hi, this is Kemp from Legendary Marketing."

The prospect would pause and then say, "Did you say Kent?"

"No," he'd say "it's Kemp."

The prospect, unused to the name, would invariably say "Ken?"

"No," he'd say with rising irritation "Kemp. K-E-M-P Kemp!"

By this point the prospect was either feeling stupid or Kemp was so frustrated and distracted from the sale process that he couldn't sell anything. It seemed as if every conversation he had started out as an argument!

One day I walked in and he was practically yelling at the person on the other end of the phone, trying to get the person to say his name right!

"That's the final straw," I said. "Every time I come in here you are arguing with someone about your name. Change it to something else—anything else!"

"Like what?" he said as I walked out the door.

"Like Elvis," I said. "No one will forget that!"

Despite his misgivings, the very next day he started introducing himself as Elvis Anderson. All of a sudden no one ever asked him to spell his name or asked him to repeat it!

And guess what?

People liked the name. They chatted with him, he built rapport, they put his calls through, people actually called him back, and sales went up!

Thank you. Thank you very much!

If your name is hard for people to pronounce, use a nickname or your initials.

If you have a difficult or unusual name that will inhibit your sales, change it!

CHAPTER 30

How to Open a Rapport-Building Conversation

I walked into the office one day to find a salesman casually reading the paper while he waited for me. Before I could say a word, he turned the front page of the paper towards me, pointed at the headline and said, "What do you think about this?" I looked at the headline and was immediately drawn into conversation with him. For a few minutes we discussed a couple of issues relating to the headline and he agreed with my position on the subject. Then he said, "I'm sorry. I didn't introduce myself. I'm John Steventon. I work for XYZ. Have you seen our new line of..."

This was one of the most innovative openers I have ever encountered. The salesperson developed a strong rapport with me merely by seeking my opinion of a newspaper headline. I watched through the window as he visited three neighboring businesses, paper in hand, instantly engaging each person he met in conversation.

In order to build rapport beyond the superficial stages, you have to get the prospect to talk to you. The best way to accomplish this is to ask open-ended questions. By open-ended questions, I mean ones that can't be answered with a simple yes or no. They demand a more detailed response. Not only does this method build rapport since you allow the customer to respond without interruption or contradiction, but it also provides you with valuable data for use in the sales presentation. After you swap names, it's time to start questioning. This time, however, we will be using the responses not just for data, but also to develop future questions.

"Where are you from, Jack?" (In states with rapidly expanding populations like California, Florida, Arizona and Nevada, this is a good question, since the majority of people were born elsewhere.)

"How long have you been with the company?"

Move smoothly from basic questions to more specific lines of inquiry:

"How long have you been in this position?" or, "How did you start with the company?"

The more people talk about themselves, the more rapport you will be building, especially if you use active listening techniques.

Seek people's opinions to build rapport!

CHAPTER 31

Developing Your Active Listening Techniques to Increase Rapport

Listening is one of the most important skills any salesperson can have. How well you listen has a major impact on your effectiveness. Given all the listening most salespeople do, you would think they'd be good at it! In fact they are not. Depending on the study being quoted, we remember a dismal 25–50% of what we hear. What are you missing that is important to your prospect or client?

Turn it around and it reveals that when you are presenting, your prospects aren't hearing the whole message either. You hope the important parts are captured in their 25–50%—but what if they're not?

By becoming a better listener, you will improve your productivity, as well as your ability to influence, persuade, negotiate, and sell. The way to become a better listener is to practice active listening. This is where you make a conscious effort to hear not only the words that another person is saying but, more importantly, try and understand the total message being sent.

In order to do this you must pay careful attention to the other person. You cannot allow yourself to become distracted by what else may be going on around you, or by forming counterarguments that you'll make when the other person stops speaking. Nor can you allow yourself to lose focus on what the other person is saying.

Active listening also means showing prospects that you are not only listening to what they have to say but you are interested in what they are saying.

Here are some of the ways you can do this:

- By holding eye contact and not looking around at anything else.
- By nodding or shaking your head at appropriate points.
- By raising an eyebrow (like Mr. Spock in *Star Trek*) to express surprise.
- By laughing or smiling and using open and positive body language.
- By making occasional comments like, "Yes," "Interesting," or "I see," to show you are an active participant in the conversation, even though you aren't doing the talking. You aren't necessarily agreeing with the person, you are simply indicating that you are listening. This encourages the prospect to keep on talking.
- By occasionally repeating back the essence of what the talker has said to make sure you understand or to ask an occasional clarifying question when you're not sure what the speaker means.

Active listening draws people out and generally makes them consider *you* a more interesting person.

CHAPTER 32

Make the Prospect Feel Great!

Giving genuine compliments to your prospect will almost certainly bring a favorable response. However, use caution in this area. Prospects easily detect insincerity. If you are not sincere, you will lose their confidence, never to regain it. There are ways to make sure this never happens to you. Don't give a compliment you do not mean. And, to give your compliments increased weight, add a qualifying statement.

Your compliment is made more meaningful if you add a brief remark to prove you mean what you say. For example, you might say to a women who walks into your place of business, "That's a beautiful sweater." Then immediately add a qualifier: "I gave one just like that to my wife last Christmas." You have demonstrated your sincerity. Why would you buy a sweater for your wife if you didn't find it attractive?

Similarly, a client arrives in a 1973 Cadillac Eldorado convertible. You say, "That's a lovely car and you've kept it in such beautiful shape." It is a sincere compliment and will almost certainly be taken as such, but let's add a qualifier to give it even greater effect: "My father always wanted one of those. He said it was one of the finest cars ever made." Now, if your father always wanted one, and you so obviously respected his opinion, how do you think the prospect is going to be disposed toward you? The chances are, he's going to take an instant liking to you!

You make a sales call at a client's house and see a swing in the back yard. You turn to the prospect and say, "You have a wonderful home." It's a believable but weak compliment on it's own, but with a quick qualifier you can boost its effect. "The swing out back and that brick fireplace in the family room remind me of my uncle's place. I have fond memories of the happy times I spent there as a child."

Qualify your compliments and praise to maximize rapport.

CHAPTER 33

How People Process Information Affects Rapport

Essentially, people process information in one of three main ways—visually, aurally, or kinesthetically. Knowing which of these applies to a particular person can give you a much better chance of getting your point across.

To illustrate, suppose someone is describing his trip to the Super Bowl. You might hear one of these three statements:

1. "It was great. The grass was vivid green. I could see the Goodyear blimp above the stadium as clearly as I can see that car over there. As far as the eye could see, people were wearing blue or red. You should have seen it—it was really something."
2. "The sound of 80,000 people all yelling at once was incredible. You should have heard it. And wait until you hear about how we met the Cowboys' quarter-back."
3. "The smell of hot dogs and popcorn was everywhere. It was wonderful. Before the game you could just feel the electricity in the air. You should have been there."

Okay, you've read three descriptions of the Super Bowl. Is the first person visual, aural or kinesthetic? The second? What about the third?

If you said *visual, aural* and *kinesthetic*, in that order, you have the idea. So, does this make a difference to your sales figures? It makes a big difference in terms of building rapport.

If a prospect asks to *see* something, or comments on the view, he is almost certainly visual (and the majority of people fall into this category.) If he asks you to tell him about your offering, or explain your benefits, then he is probably auditory. If he wants to try it for himself or comments on the smell of the trees, he is probably kinesthetic. In cases where someone displays a combination of two, or even all three of these forms, you can use multiple approaches but one of them will usually be dominant. Understanding this human characteristic can be invaluable to your presentation by helping you to communicate better and faster with your prospect.

Asking a kinesthetic prospect to look at something is not nearly as valuable as having him do it himself. If you prevent a kinesthetic person from "feeling" things, you risk losing the sale. Similarly, if you simply talk to a visually oriented person, you will soon lose his interest.

If you can't tell which method your prospect uses to process information, try to use all three in your speech patterns. (It takes a little practice!) You will either find out what you need to know, or at least be sure that you have covered all the bases.

How Visual People Respond

Many people who are in what we call the visual group can watch something happening and can then recall and repeat that action with few errors. They learn by watching. When they recall data from their minds, they see pictures and use these pictures to process that data. When asked to recall something, they are likely to close their eyes to aid them in visualizing the matter.

How Aural People Respond

Aural, in this context, describes people who process mental data most efficiently by hearing or listening to what other people say. This group will listen to what you have to say, so long as it is of interest to them. They are then able to process this information and store it in their minds. When they read, most of them can clearly hear the words in their heads.

How Kinesthetic People Respond

People in this category learn by touching or by a sense of feel. In contrast to visuals, they process information by developing a sense of rhythm, flow, and feel. They learn best by touching and by using and it would be a mistake to discourage them from doing so. Get your product in their hands as soon as possible. They tend to describe themselves as "hands on" people.

If you can tell which method your prospect uses to process information, you can easily get on the same wavelength by speaking in the same terms.

CHAPTER 34

More On Learning Styles

Now let's have a little fun. Write down the names of five people who are important in your life and with whom you communicate often: perhaps your spouse, your boss, a couple of close friends, and a good customer.

1. ____________________
2. ____________________
3. ____________________
4. ____________________
5. ____________________

Listen very carefully to each of these people next time you converse with them and try and discover the way in which each of them prefers to absorb and process information.

Playing this little game with everyone you meet can be most entertaining and the information it provides can do a great deal to quickly improve your communication skills. Once you have decided into which group each person falls, start to use appropriate key words and phrases to build rapport with them.

Key Words for Each Style

Here are some key words and clues that will help you classify people:

VISUAL

- Let me see
- I've been looking at
- Picture this
- Can you see my point?
- Let me show you
- Imagine that
- Look at it this way
- It's plain to see

AURAL

- Tell me about it
- I've heard a lot about
- Listen
- Do you hear what I'm saying?
- Please explain
- Is he in tune?

KINESTHETIC

- It doesn't feel right
- Can you grasp this situation?

- I feel I should tell you
- Are you catching on now?
- Contact
- I have a feeling
- I can handle that

Applying Learning Traits to Build Rapport

Some people like to be shown things, others prefer to hear information, while still others like to experience and feel things before they are convinced. By paying careful attention to which approach appears to draw the best response, you can modify your sales approach to suit. If you are a visual person and you are talking to someone who appears to be kinesthetically inclined, avoid the temptation to talk in the visual terms that appeal to you. Don't say, "Hank, can you picture yourself using this," because Hank is not going to picture this in his mind as you would. Say instead, "Hank, when you use this you are going to feel great!" For the aurally inclined, you might say, "Hank, how does using this sound to you?"

If you are not sure how someone processes information, use all three approaches in your conversation to insure you connect with the one your prospect uses.

CHAPTER 35

Talking the Same Language as Your Prospect

You can gain a great deal of insight into a person from their choice of words, above and beyond their basic learning modality (visual, aural, kinesthetic). Do they talk in terms of "strikeouts" and "home runs" when describing events, indicating a strong interest in baseball, or do they use words like "playbook" and "touchdown?"

Do they talk in military terms such as "campaign" or "rallying the troops?" These are, of course, very obvious examples but if you prick your ears up a little, you will be surprised how quickly you can zone in on somebody's interests and therefore develop rapport.

In addition to phrases that give an indication of a person's interests, there are other phrases that are generally known as "pet" sayings. These are phrases that a particular prospect tends to use habitually in speech—like "I didn't get where I am today without..." or "You can't be serious!"

Most people have pet phrases they use often in normal conversation. If you can pick out these phrases and employ one or two of them casually in the conversation, it will go a long way toward establishing good rapport with your prospect.

For example, your prospect might make several references to his previous employer such as "Back when I was with IBM they did this..." "At IBM we used to…" This gives you a perfect opening to play back this obviously influential experience to your prospect:

> *I bet it must have been exciting working for IBM at that time.*

Or an even more sales-like approach:

> *When you were with IBM what criteria did they use for choosing a new vendor?* (Assuming, of course, that you think the answer will play into your hand.)

Make sure you keep good notes in your customer relationship management system for future use. Remembering a couple of key phrases six months from now could make a huge difference to your sales effort the next time you talk with the prospect.

Notice and use your prospects' pet phrases to build rapport.

CHAPTER 36

Is Your Office Sabotaging Your Chance to Develop Rapport?

If you are selling on the road, this may not apply to you; but if you are selling from your own office or sales area, take heed. The way your office looks and feels can cost you sales. In the last few years, I have bought two cars for my wife. Both times, I went through the usual back-and-forth negotiations that often accompany the process of trying to get the best possible deal.

Both of the salespeople I dealt with were professionals. Each of them had decorated their small offices with their respective sales awards—salesperson of the year, highest volume salesperson, and the like. Now these are awards of which they should indeed be proud. But, as a consumer, I don't want to see them when I am trying to *buy* a car.

It always amazes me that salespeople choose to put awards for sales up in their offices for the whole world to see! The prospect is not going to feel any more comfortable with you when he knows what a great salesperson you are. He wants to talk himself into buying—not be bamboozled into buying by a slick-talking salesperson looking for another plaque.

Although I am a salesperson myself, seeing these awards could not help but trigger my defense mechanisms. When you win awards, that's terrific. But keep them away from your customers' eyes. Take them home! Put them in your den. Your friends and family will appreciate them.

Look at Your Office from Your Prospect's Point of View

No matter what we are selling, we often forget to think like our customers and see things from their point of view. Picture this scenario. You have decided you want to take ballroom dancing lessons. You have never been in a dance studio before and you know nothing about ballroom dancing except that it sure looks like a lot of fun on the television show *Dancing with the Stars*.

You walk in the studio and a class is in progress. You stand there uncomfortably, wondering if you are going to be noticed or if you should leave and come back later. Just as you are about to go, a young instructor comes up and asks if he can help.

You tell him you want more information about how the dance instruction works. He motions for another instructor to take his place and leads you to the back. There are three offices, and he ushers you right through a door that is clearly labeled *Membership Office*. You sit down across from a desk and the first thing that catches your attention is a six-inch square sign set under the glass covering the desk top. It reads *ABSOLUTELY NO REFUNDS*. To the right of that, also under the glass, are two large *Visa* and *Master Card Accepted Here* stickers. On the wall behind the desk hangs a sign that instructs you to *Make Checks Payable to Walking on Air Ballroom Dancing*.

As you glance casually at the bookcase, you notice it is filled with DVDs and books with titles like *How to Close Every Sale, The Secrets of Selling,* and *The Psychology of Selling;* it looks as if just about every published work on making a deal that exists is on those shelves. You are impressed with the instructor's quest for knowledge BUT...! The instructor hasn't even opened his mouth yet, and you already have a wall around your brain that makes the Great Wall of China look like a garden fence! He obviously intends to talk you into signing something you're not sure you want to sign. You politely smile at the instructor as he starts to speak, but you don't hear a single word. You thank him for his time and tell him you will have to think about it.

Let's Try That Again

What if instead of the sign on the wall saying *Make Checks Payable to Walking on Air Ballroom Dancing*, there are several letters from satisfied clients that speak to concerns prospects tend to have:

> *I had always thought of myself as a complete klutz. I was afraid I'd make a complete fool of myself taking lessons. But you and your staff made me feel comfortable every step of the way. It's fun learning and I no longer hesitate asking someone to dance. I look forward to improving and learning a couple of new dances.*

* * *

> *Thank you! Thank you! Thank you! I dragged my husband here kicking and screaming. He only came to please me, but when we went on our anniversary cruise, we danced every night—several people commented on how good we were. My husband sure enjoyed the compliments from all the women!*

* * *

What if instead of the bookcase filled with how-to-sell books, the shelves held photos of your clients dancing? Some photos of classes. A photo of young children dancing. Photos of a boy dancing at his bar mitzvah. A photo of "twenty-somethings" during a salsa lesson. A photo of an elderly couple. Now, no matter who comes into your office, they'll see that people like themselves take dancing lessons.

The ultimate sales skill is to create in your prospect a powerful mental image of enjoying the benefits you offer. Be sure to avoid displaying anything that could create a negative response in a prospect. The power of one negative image is almost ten times stronger than the power of one positive image.

Avoid displaying anything in your office that might cause alarm bells in your prospect's head!

CHAPTER 37

How Your Elvis Calendar, Your Kids, and Your Dream Car All Conspire to Cost You Sales!

I had a large wooden model of a Chinese junk (boat) on my desk in my karate school office. As a parent was listening to my pitch, the child would invariably touch it. The child would be quickly rebuked by the parent. A few minutes later, the kid would be back at it again. The parent would be completely distracted during the presentation. Worse still, the parent would often use the child's misbehavior as an excuse to leave!

Another karate school owner hired me to give him advice on improving the business side of his school. I showed up at his office one day as a prospective customer. He did not see me. His manager, who did not know me, led me into the office to make a sales presentation. The only thing on the office wall was an Elvis calendar. I commented on the calendar and asked if Elvis ever took karate. (Of course, I already knew that he did.)

The salesman enthusiastically started talking about Elvis and his instructor, Ed Parker. This had gone on for at least seven or eight minutes when I turned my attention to the Porsche Turbo model on his desk. Once again he was only too glad to talk—this time about cars. Five minutes later I announced to the stunned salesman that I had to go to an appointment but would be back another time!

While sometimes personal items can aid in building rapport, even pictures of family members can cause needless distractions to the sales process as people make polite inquiries about your children or grandchildren! I see this a lot when I visit with membership directors at country clubs. To illustrate my point, I used to make a game of how long I could talk to a salesperson about something trivial on their desk or wall without talking about the product or service I was supposed to be interested in. Normally the length of time they were prepared to spend was WAY TOO LONG. In fact, I was almost always the one who had to bring the conversation back to the sale!

Make your office the image of what you want to accomplish. If you want to sell cars, decorate the office to inspire the prospect to want to buy one of the cars you sell. Try hanging pictures of top-of-the-line models and perhaps some promotional photographs of factory scenes. Impress them with the quality of your product and create in them the desire to consider upgrading their original choice.

Display before-and-after pictures showing weight loss, white teeth, cosmetic surgery, or body work—anything that supports your sales message or helps to allay prospects' fears. And whatever you sell, framed letters of thanks from happy customers are never out of place!

Everything in your office should facilitate the sale; everything else should go!

4

Maximize Your Sales Opportunities

CHAPTER 38

An Italian Boy's Confession

An Italian youth goes to confession.

"Bless me Father, for I have sinned. I have been with a loose girl."

The priest asks, "Is that you, Joey Pagano?"

"Yes, Father, it is."

"And who was the girl you were with?"

"I can't tell you, Father. I don't want to ruin her reputation."

"Well, Joey, I'm sure to find out her name sooner or later so you may as well tell me now. Was it Tina Minetti?"

"I cannot say."

"Was it Teresa Mazzarelli?"

"I'll never tell."

"Was it Nina Capelli?"

"I'm sorry, but I cannot name her."

"Was it Cathy Piriano?"

"My lips are sealed."

"Was it Rosa DiAngelo, then?"

"Please, Father, I cannot tell you."

The priest sighs in frustration. "You're very tight lipped, Joey, and I admire that. But you've sinned and must atone. You cannot be an altar boy for the next four months. Now, go home and behave yourself."

Joey walks back to his pew, and his friend Franco slides over and whispers, "What'd you get?"

"Four months vacation and five good leads!"

Nuff said!

Opportunities can come when least expected.

CHAPTER 39

The Fine and Profitable Art of Spotting the Difference Between a Flake and a Genuine Prospect!

There is an old Cuban proverb that says, "When the sun rises, it rises for everyone." Nowhere is this a truer statement than in the world of selling!

Back in my karate school days, at the beginning of each week I would meet with the instructors who ran my schools, and we would discuss three key statistics.

1. How many people called for information?
2. How many people came in to take a trial lesson?
3. And, most important of all, how many signed up?

Once we had established these figures, it was pretty easy to see who was doing well and who was in need of help. A school that had twenty calls and signed up only five students needed help. When this was pointed out, even in the most diplomatic way, the instructor would immediately tell me that most of the people who called were just flakes—not real prospects.

Why? It is much easier to blame your sales failures on your

prospects than on yourself. This holds true whether you sell cars, your services, real estate, factory machinery, or anything else.

On one occasion, I watched a real estate salesperson pitch a young man on a new condominium development. After a short discussion, during which the prospect seemed to be enthusiastic and excited, the prospect left without buying or even looking at a unit. I asked the professional what happened and she replied, "He was a flake; he has no money!"

The prospect had been wearing top-of-the-line sneakers, an expensive wristwatch, and a designer sweater. I walked over to the window, just in time to see the prospect leave the parking lot in a brand new truck. Now tell me again that the young man who just left had no money!

Someone paid for all that stuff!

The truth of the matter is that the salesperson both made an assumption based on the prospect's age and didn't convince the prospect to buy. The young man had the money, or access to it. He just wasn't given reasons compelling enough to spend it! The salesperson insulated herself against failure—as many salespeople do—by dismissing a perfectly good prospect as a flake.

Very often the difference between worthless flakes and profitable buyers is only in your head!

CHAPTER 40

How Often Do You Deliberately Waste Someone's Time?

Let me pose a serious question. How often do you go to the Yellow Pages or the Internet, look up the number of a specific business, and THEN call them to make an appointment or go down for a demonstration, while having *absolutely no intention whatsoever of buying their product or service?*

I certainly do not have that kind of time to waste in life. I'm not about to drive miles to look at products or services in which I have absolutely no interest! How about you? No? Well, 99.9% of people will give the same answer.

Now, with an expensive product like a house or car, it's possible that some people may get a little ahead of themselves in making the first inquiries, but the desire to buy is still there. Whether the person has the desire to buy is the important factor in determining who is a likely candidate for a sale.

Rather than let my staff dismiss people as flakes, I train them to treat every person as a possible client. If you treat everyone as an important potential prospect and talk to them as if you expect them to accept your proposal, you will be pleasantly surprised by the number of "flakes" who become buyers—or who recommend you to friends, family, or colleagues.

The key is you have to treat them like real prospects. Often when salespeople don't think a person will buy, they give subtle hints with their tonality, body language, or choice of words that subconsciously sends a negative message to the prospect!

A prospect is ALWAYS a prospect until you disqualify them through the natural, orchestrated progression of questions and information gathering.

CHAPTER 41

"It's Your Lucky Day!"

One afternoon I was sitting in my office, feet up on my desk, playing with my computer and waiting for the world to discover me when the phone rang. I picked it up on the third ring and answered in my standard fashion. "Martial Arts America, how can I help you?"

The caller did not respond immediately. Then a woman's voice said in a confused way, "Er-r-r, is this the pet shop?"

Realizing that not much had happened so far that day, I decided to give it a shot. "Well you're close. This is Martial Arts America. Let me ask you something. Are you always this lucky?"

"What do you mean? I think I have the wrong number," she replied.

"No," I insisted. "You have the right number, and you are our 13th caller. You've just won our grand prize!"

"I did? Really?" she exclaimed. "I never win anything! What did I win?"

"A free week of karate lessons!" I replied with enthusiasm.

"Karate lessons? You're kidding...really?"

"You bet. When would you like to start? Tonight or Friday?" I said.

"Just a minute." She hesitated for a moment. "Can I let my boys have the lessons instead?"

"Of course. In fact, you can bring the whole family if you like."

"What time on Friday?" She was beginning to sound interested.

"How about 4 p.m.?" I replied.

"Yes, that's great. Brett and John will be so excited! Thanks. Where exactly are you located?" she asked.

"You know where the pet shop is? We're four doors down to the left as you face the front of the building. I look forward to meeting you and your boys on Friday at 4."

I hung up knowing I had a new idea for rainy days.

The caller was probably in her early thirties by the sound of her voice, so I thought the chances were good that either she or her children might be interested. Now, if you try this, I am not trying to suggest that sales will jump, but over the course of a year, depending on your product, you might make sales to three or four people who would not otherwise have become clients. Look at it as an entertaining challenge to your enthusiasm and sales skills.

By the way, the lady brought her boys to the school and, after the free week of lessons, enrolled both of them for a year. She even took a few lessons herself!

The first time I did this, I have to admit that I did it as a joke, but after that I came to look upon it as a challenge. Unless I was busy, I would always try to persuade the person on the other end of the phone to come down to the school. If I could not do that, I at least tried to make them feel good about calling me. I am sure they told all their friends about their lucky phone call.

Making It Big by Making an Effort!

One year I sold three sets of my audio program, *Making it Big In America, How to Get Ahead in Business and in Life,* at $60 a set, to wrong numbers.

One was a man from North Carolina looking for an auto parts store.

Another was a local mortgage broker looking for a Mr. Dillard, and the third set went to a 72-year-old man looking for house paint!

I told him that it was his lucky day, because he had reached Personal Quest and we teach success. He said he was 72 years old, retired for seven years, and that he didn't need to worry about success any more. I quickly asked if he had any sons. He replied, "Yes, and they're all bums." After I explained exactly how my audiotapes might help them get their act together, the sale was made, closed by offering our special wrong number discount of 20% off the retail price!

Remember the great majority of sales are lost, not because of poor sales technique, but simply because the prospect is not directly asked to buy!

CHAPTER 42

Selling to the Salesperson

I am always amused when I see a business with a sign on the door that says, "No Soliciting." If they don't want to meet people, why are they in business in the first place? I was sitting in a karate school office talking with the owner when the door opened to admit a young, well-dressed guy with a big smile on his face. He greeted us enthusiastically and then rolled up his sleeves to reveal about a dozen gold chains on each arm. My friend told him that we were not interested, but I told him to hold on and give the guy a chance to make his pitch.

Whenever possible, I always like to hear the sales pitch—no matter what the product. None of us is ever so good that we can't benefit from a new line or new technique. Some of the people who go door to door on the street can be the best salespeople. If they are not, they don't eat. In fact, I have often asked people who walked in off the street to come and work for me because they were so good at what they do. On top of that, *everyone is a prospect.*

We listened to his sales pitch as he showed us each of the gold chains, described the style in detail, and told us just why we had to have one at his ridiculously low prices. In short, he was pretty good.

When I asked him if his merchandise was real gold, he replied, quite indignantly "Of course, it's real gold." Then I asked the price, and he told me each chain had a different value, but they started at just $99. I asked if he carried a gun when he was selling the chains, and he said no.

I asked if he carried a knife or some other type of weapon, and he shook his head. Incredulously I asked, "You walk around this city unarmed, with $3,000 worth of gold on your arm? Do you know how many people get mugged every day? You must have taken martial arts lessons. Right?" Again, he hesitated and said, "No," then qualified it with, "but I've thought about it."

I asked him to come into the workout area for a moment, so I could demonstrate a few grab techniques. After a few minutes he was bubbling with enthusiasm. "Hey, that stuff's good. How much are lessons?" he asked. Now it was my turn. I went into my normal sales pitch, after which he responded, "Man, I'd like to do this, but I haven't sold anything yet today and I don't have any money."

Guess what we took as payment for his first month of lessons, registration, and uniform? You've got it—two gold chains. My buddy could hardly believe what had happened, and it was fun for me. After that he never threw out a salesperson again.

Make a game of getting the most unlikely person you can find to buy from you. Even if nothing else happens, your performance will improve in the vital area of creativity. After all, have you ever met anyone who could not benefit in some way from your wonderful product or service? Get yourself and your staff into the habit of believing that everyone is a prospect until they prove they are not

"One cannot afford to neglect opportunity."
—Sun Tsu

CHAPTER 43

The Danger of Prejudging Prospects

Prejudging prospects is just human nature. We all judge looks, clothes, cars, hairstyles, watches, and a million other little things that slant our personal perceptions. The problem with prejudging a prospect's ability to buy is that, no matter how good a judge you are, you will often be wrong, and that results in lost sales.

As you already know, everyone wants to feel important.

When you prejudge a prospect as being unable to buy, it is often revealed in your voice, body language, and actions. The prospect is quickly turned off, and you can lose a sale. People do business with people they like! Prospects like people who make them feel important.

Unemployed, Unloved, and Ready to Buy

In the karate business, I found out several times at first hand that prejudging prospects is dangerous to sales performance. Jack, an auto mechanic, wandered into my studio one evening at about five p.m. My questions elicited the information that he had taken karate lessons "back east." Then he told me his wife had just walked out on him, leaving their two small children. On top of all that, he confided that he had lost his job three hours previously. Now, he was not exactly the type of A-1 prospect for whom I was looking. Still, I made my sales pitch with all the enthusiasm I could muster. The only question he asked was how much it would cost for a program for him and his kids to reach black belt status—a three-year program. I told him and he left. I figured I'd probably never see him again. The next day, he walked in with $2,000 in cash as a down payment.

Sally? I Don't Think So!

About the same time, we had a student named Sally, who was nineteen and a little overweight. She was attending college and working nights at McDonald's. She lived with an elderly grandmother because her parents had died in an accident. Over the course of a year, we would give our sales pitch for a long-term program to just about every student. Finally her name came up. I nearly passed her by because I thought it would be a waste of time, but I went ahead anyway and approached her as if she were a strong prospect.

The next day, she walked in with a check for over $2,500: payment in full for three years of lessons in advance. Her grandmother thought that karate was the best thing that had ever happened to her, and was glad to give her the money she needed for the long-term program.

Never allow yourself to prejudge who is able to buy based on what you THINK a person's circumstances are!

CHAPTER 44

Riding into the Sunset

A number of my clients own auto dealerships and all have one kind of similar story. For example, one day a very large man with a big belly, black T-shirt with the picture worn beyond recognition, and a scruffy beard, pulled into the dealership on a Harley-Davidson. The salesman showed him two brand new compacts, one red and one blue. The prospect seemed to be interested but unsure which color to pick. Meanwhile my friend held out little hope that he could get this man financed. However, having learned from experience not to prejudge, he treated him with courtesy and respect.

Twenty minutes later, he was rewarded for his behavior. The man walked wordlessly over to his bike, reached into the leather saddlebag on the back of the Harley, and pulled out a giant wad of cash. With it he put down $5,000 on each car and bought both cars as graduation presents for his twin daughters. The transaction was completed with hardly a word more being spoken, and the man climbed back on his bike and rode off into the sunset. Never prejudge who is able to buy. It will cause you to lose business.

All kinds of people buy:

$ Poor people buy.

$ Rich people buy.

$ Ugly people buy.

$ Pretty people buy.

$ Scruffy people buy.

$ Smart people buy.

$ Dumb people buy.

$ Intelligent people buy.

Everybody buys something sometime. It's just a question of what, when, and—most important from your point of view—from whom? Increase your chances by being open-minded about people until they prove beyond a doubt that they are not prospects!

Never allow yourself to prejudge who is able to buy based on looks, cars, or clothing!

CHAPTER 45

Double Your Income in Sixty Seconds!

Back in the late 1980s on my way to work on Saturday mornings, I used to stop at a donut shop to get a cup of fresh coffee. Every Saturday, the person serving me a medium-sized coffee would ask, "Do you want a donut?" Each Saturday I would reply no, and each Saturday as I walked out of that shop I wondered what the owner would pay me to double his donut sales—which I could have easily have done in a 30-second meeting.

The counter employees had the wrong approach. Rather than asking if the customer wanted a donut, they needed to change the question to, "What kind of donut would you like today?" Sales would have doubled. If they had assumed that customers wanted a donut to go with their coffee, most replies would have been positive. The difference is just a few words, but a few words can make a huge impact when it comes to being a cunningly clever salesperson.

Let me give you another example, only this time it isn't some kid working for seven dollars an hour, but a golf professional. I recently took lessons from two different PGA golf pros.

When I booked a lesson at my own country club, I was asked, "Would you like to pay for one lesson or take a series of five?"

At the local driving range, I was given the very same option, although this time the pro did stress the discount if I chose five lessons instead of one.

For the record, the situation is more or less identical in Florida, New York, California, and around the world. It's as if someone appeared from the heavens at some point in time and decreed that golf pros could only offer lessons in increments of one or five. While there may well be a handful of pros who use other numerical combinations, the self-limiting principles are the same. Not one of the golf pros I visited ever asked me how good I wanted to be. Never did it cross their collective minds to ask me how much I was willing to pay. Even worse, some actually seemed embarrassed to ask me for money at all.

Finally I sat down with one of them and told him how much I was prepared to invest if he could reduce my handicap by four shots and return my game to where it was seven years ago. He sat and stared at me in amazement. In all his dreams he never thought that anyone would pay him that much money for lessons. Of course he had never asked.

Don't Be Afraid to Ask for More

Before I left, I persuaded him to try an experiment upon returning to the range where he worked. I challenged him to offer the next new student either ten lessons or twenty instead of one or five. In spite of his protests that people would not pay for that many lessons, he did as I asked.

To his utter astonishment the very next student choose ten. So did the next and the next. By the end of the second week, three students had chosen the twenty-lesson option. Suddenly he was busier than he had ever been in his life. Students who might normally have taken one lesson, never to be seen again, were now booking ten or more lessons, simply because that's what they were offered. Not only is this a far better situation for the golf professional, it's a far better situation for the student as well. After all, whoever heard of anyone significantly improving one's golf game in a handful of lessons? It just doesn't happen!

By structuring your sales presentation to encourage a longer commitment and a bigger sale, both parties win!

But you have to actually ask!

CHAPTER 46

Butch Cassidy on Sales

There is a wonderful scene in the movie *Butch Cassidy and the Sundance Kid* that perfectly demonstrates one of the key attributes of a cunningly clever salesperson. In this scene, Butch's Hole in the Wall Gang has just robbed the Union Pacific Flyer. The sheriff is standing on the porch outside his office talking to a crowd of indifferent townsfolk. He is trying desperately to raise a posse to go after the gang, while Butch and Sundance watch from the balcony of a hotel across the street.

After the sheriff has failed to arouse any interest in joining a posse, a man wheeling a bicycle steps to the front of the crowd and joins him. Turning to the crowd he announces that it's time for them to meet the future mode of transportation. The sheriff demands to know what the man thinks he is doing, to which he replies, "Well, sheriff, since you got such a nice crowd together, I just thought I'd do a little selling."

Now that's the cunningly clever salesperson at his finest, seizing each and every opportunity to share his product or service with the world.

Motto for the Cunningly Clever Salesperson

In the movie *The Dead Poets Society,* the teacher, played by Robin Williams, offers the boys he teaches a wonderful motto to live by. The words could well have been written for the consummate salesperson. The motto was *Carpe Diem,* (pronounced *car-pay dee-em.*)

It is Latin for "Seize the Day!"

"A wise man will make more opportunities than he finds."
—Francis Bacon

CHAPTER 47

Who Wants to Sell Me a Porsche or a Maserati—or How about Just a Truck?

Carl Sewall, president of the most successful Cadillac dealership in the world, Sewall Village Cadillac in Dallas, Texas, makes an interesting observation in his book *Customers for Life*. He estimates that a customer is worth more than $300,000 to him over a lifetime. (That was in the late 1980s.) Apparently no one ever conveyed this information to the Southern California Porsche dealers.

Two decades ago, I decided to buy a late model Porsche. The first place I called was the Porsche/Audi dealership where I had bought a brand new Audi GT three years before. I had been very happy with the car and I had recommended the dealership to two friends, both of whom bought new Porsches through the salesman from whom I had purchased the Audi. I still remember his name—Dante J. Andre. He was a young, good-looking man and a snappy dresser. When I called, I asked for him by name, even though we had had no contact in three years. He was no longer at the dealership, so they turned my call over to another salesman. I told him that I was looking for a late model Porsche.

He told me they did not have any and hung up.

Quite frankly, I was more than a little surprised that he did not take my name or offer to call around and find one. I called five more Porsche dealerships in Southern California before a salesman at Downtown LA Porsche offered to take my name, call around, and call me back. Unfortunately, he apparently didn't trouble himself calling any other dealers. If he had, he would have found the car I wanted at Pioneer Porsche in San Diego, and I would undoubtedly have called him the next time I wanted a car. Because he did not call back, I made a few more calls the next day, and eventually bought the car (over the phone) from Pioneer.

When Someone Wants to Give You Money, Let Them!

A couple of years later, I was in the market for a newer Porsche, and not much had changed. Because the salesman who had sold me the previous car did so over the phone and never followed up, I couldn't remember his name. It apparently required too much effort to actually call a past customer and thank him personally for his business.

The first couple of places I called said they did not have what I wanted and hung up. Two salesmen took my name and number. I decided to give them a couple of weeks to see if they could locate what I wanted.

Three weeks passed and—surprise, surprise—they didn't call! Why not? Certainly it can't be because it's such a rare automobile or because they wouldn't make a worthwhile commission selling it. Even if the profit margin on a used Porsche is small (ho, ho) they might be able to sell me a new one in the future. They might even sell my wife a car, and I would certainly tell my friends where I got the car. Why didn't they do it? Obviously, it would have taken too much effort! Too much effort to pick up the phone and call a few fellow dealers; too much effort to follow up with a few cards to me (other than those offering an oil change and filter at reduced cost.) I soon tired of waiting for one of the Porsche salesman to suddenly become energetic and call me back.

I bought a Ferrari instead!

Fast forward twenty years to a couple of months ago when I called the local Maserati dealer where I had previous bought a Porsche Turbo. They had one car in black but I wanted red; the salesman said he'd find me one.

He never called back!

So I called the next dealer south, Naples, 300 miles away from my home. They had lots of cars including a red one, I agreed to go look at it in two days time. That morning I called to make sure the salesman was there as well as the car. "Oh, I'm glad you called, I'm sorry," he said, "I sold the car last night, but I've got some others. How about a blue one—I know we can make a deal on that one."

"Okay," I said "Blue's, fine call me back with a number!"

"No problem!" he said. That was three months ago and I'm still waiting for the call, so I bought another Ferrari instead!

Maybe you think that this type of incompetence only happens with exotic cars but I assure you it does not. I had a similar experience when buying my wife a truck!

Any one of these "salespersons" could have been my go-to car guy for the next twenty years, but none of them will be!

Yes, it really is easier to make it to the top in sales than to fail. All it takes is a little extra effort to separate yourself from the pack!

CHAPTER 48

Speed Is a Sales Strategy

In today's world where everything happens at blinding speed, many salespeople overlook the power of speed as a sales strategy, especially if they have been in sales for a long time. In today's world of overnight letters, email, cell phones, tweeting, and texting, tomorrow is often no longer good enough.

All things being equal:

- The faster you respond to inquirers, the more chance you will have of making the sale.
- The faster you get out the proposal or response to the RFP (request for proposal), the more chance you will have of making the sale.
- The faster you respond to an email question or objection, the more chance you will have of making the sale.
- The faster you respond to a phone call, the more chance you will have of making the sale.
- The faster you can deliver the product or service, the more chance you will have of making the sale.
- The faster you follow up after the sale and ask for referrals, the more chance you will have of making future sales!

Make speed one of your key strategies for sales success.

CHAPTER 49

The Amazing, Cunningly-Clever Power of the Rule of Three

One day I called one of my karate schools in San Diego to see how we were doing for the week. My instructor, a pleasant and bright guy named Victor, answered the phone. It was about 11 a.m. before classes would usually start, but an hour or so after he started work.

"What are you doing?" I asked.

"Oh, nothing," he said.

"In that case can you do me a favor?" I said.

"Sure!"

"Do you have a San Diego phone book there?"

"I think so," he said as he fumbled around in the bottom drawer.

"YES!" he replied triumphantly.

"Good, see if you can find a guy called Smith," I said.

"What's his first name?" he asked innocently.

"You know, I'm not sure but the Smith I'm looking for is the one who has been thinking about taking karate lessons. Start with the first one and call until you find him. Oh, and Victor—the next time I call, don't tell me you are doing nothing!"

If you can think of nothing better to do in the name of marketing remember the rule of three. Every day you need to make:

- three contacts with existing customers
- three contacts with previous customers
- three contacts with new prospects

Every day!

It could be a call, an email, a postcard, a magazine clipping, a sales letter, perhaps even a personal note, but it must be interesting to that person.

If you do this and only this you will out market and out sell 99% of your competitors.

"Above all, try something!"
—Franklin D. Roosevelt

5

Qualifying Prospects

CHAPTER 50

Why Cunningly Clever Salespeople Always Qualify Their Prospects, Saving Wasted Years in the Process

In order to make a sale, you need a pool of REAL prospects. Prospects are defined as having a need and the means to pay for a product or service. That is to say, they want the results your product or service provide and can afford to buy it. A great many of the people you come into contact with may not have the means or, if they do, the desire to act. Having a professional and systematic qualifying process will maximize your time and effort.

Spending a little time up front qualifying prospects will save you hundreds of hours of chasing dead-end leads, not to mention the printing and mailing costs you will save by reducing the number of follow-up mailings sent to uninterested parties. That said, many salespeople resist the qualifying process.

Some will argue that everyone is a prospect. That, of course, depends to a large degree on what you are selling, but until evidence is acquired to the contrary, it's the premise you should use. Some might argue that some prospects give false information that puts them into the unqualified category because they don't want you bothering them. Others might argue that you may scare off legitimate prospects with unwanted questions, but the few you lose will be more than made up for by the vast number of unqualified prospects you can dismiss in favor of spending time on real prospects.

By far, the biggest reason many salespeople resist qualifying and labeling their leads is to create a greater feeling of success and security. After all, if you have 50 prospects in your lead pipeline or database (unqualified though they may be), it sounds a whole lot better than having just five well-qualified prospects even if 49 out of the 50 are totally unsuited for your product.

Over and over during the last twenty years, I have seen salespeople essentially conning themselves by refusing to qualify their leads! You will find the time and energy spent on qualifying your prospects up front is ultimately a far better use of your efforts than not qualifying and trying to follow-up every lead. As with most things in life, the 80/20 rule applies!

The faster and more thoroughly you qualify a prospect, the more effective a salesperson you will be!

CHAPTER 51

Categorizing Your Prospects

Prospects are categorized somewhat differently in various sales systems. We'll use the terms *suspects*, *prospects*, and *qualified prospects*. Most sales systems stop here, leaving out the most important category—*motivated prospects*.

Suspects

A suspect is someone whom *you* think might be a prospect.

Prospects

Prospects may already buy a similar product or service. They move from your suspect list to your prospect category when they acknowledge their interest by making a call, filling in a contact point on your website, or requesting product information.

Qualified Prospects

To have success in sales, basic prospects are not enough. Prospects must have the means to pay for your product. This makes them *qualified* prospects. Many people might have the potential means to purchase your product or service, but operating budgets do not give them the financial strength to actually purchase.

Motivated Prospects

Many people who can afford your product and are interested will not seriously consider buying from you. They are qualified prospects but not *motivated* prospects. They may like the idea of your product's features but there is no *urgency* to purchase. They may already have whatever it is you sell, or maybe they are not currently experiencing any specific challenges in your area of expertise. One of the objections you'll hear from this group is that it's easier to continue on with the vendor they have used in the past as there won't be any surprises. (See the Objections section for coverage of similar objections.)

Motivated prospects are qualified and *want* to take action. Often this motivation comes from a release of funds from the company or organization that they are associated with, or their existing vendor may have failed or annoyed them. Other times it can be an accumulation of desires over time, or something happens that intensifies their pain dramatically.

A big part of your job in sales is to find people ready to act, or to increase qualified prospects' motivation levels so they will want to act now!

Categorize each of your prospects in your CRM (database) and focus your attention between closing the motivated prospects and moving the qualified ones up another rung on the ladder.

CHAPTER 52

Will the Real Prospect Please Stand Up?

One of the biggest complaints by salespeople the world over is that they are receiving unqualified leads. The corresponding complaint from sales managers is that their salespeople can't close sales from the "great leads" they are given.

But What IS a Qualified Prospect?

How qualified a person must be to buy depends a great deal on what you are selling: if it's candy, not very; if it's million-dollar homes, they must be very qualified. For most products or services, a handful of questions is all that is needed to find out if prospects are qualified. As Francis Bacon said, "Knowledge is power," and there is no more powerful information that a salesperson can learn from a prospect than the answers to the five key questions that tell him:

1. The prospect's reasons for buying, along with supporting "hot buttons" if possible.
2. The prospect's financial ability to buy. Does he have the money or will he qualify for financing?
3. Whether the prospect has final authority to make a purchase. Or does he have to ask a manager, business partner, board, or spouse?

4. The prospect's timetable for making a purchase—this week? this month? this year?
5. What other companies, if any, the prospect is considering.

Getting a positive answer to the first four questions makes the prospect highly qualified; if you get the fifth, it's a bonus!

Get the answers to the five questions above and you will have a big head start in the sales process!

CHAPTER 53

Using Cunningly Clever Marketing to Generate Higher-Quality Leads

Before we get into the business of your personally qualifying prospects, let's take a quick look at what part marketing can play in delivering higher-quality leads to you. Many people waste a great deal of time and money by engaging in marketing that produces a good number of unqualified leads. This wastes salespeople's time and energy while serving to demotivate them in the process. It is far better to generate a small number of high-quality sales leads than a large number of dubious ones. While this book focuses on the sales aspects, there are some basic, simple steps you can take to improve your results and generate higher quality leads. (See *Cunningly Clever Marketing* for much more information on producing high-quality leads.)

Set a Written Criteria for Prospect Qualification

First, decide on the criteria you are going to use to judge a prospect's worth. This is critical so you can weed out the suspects early on and focus your time, money, and effort only on qualified prospects.

For example, I use the following criteria for qualifying prospects when selling our Marketing Commander technology to golf clubs:

- clubs that are not run by large management companies (management companies are too hard to deal with)
- not run by committee (committees are also hard to deal with)
- have at least 18 holes
- green fee is over $50 (club is therefore likely to have a reasonable marketing budget)
- playing season is longer than 5 months
- can make a buying decision
- existing technology is weak

We have sold our technology to clubs that don't meet all of the above criteria, but as a rule those criteria indentify clubs that are likely to buy from us. If they fit the above criteria, they are an "A" prospect: Anything else for us is not!

Having clear and specific qualifying guidelines makes decisions about where to spend your efforts easy.

Look at your best clients, then list the criteria for qualifying others just like them!

CHAPTER 54

Make Clear Qualifying Statements in Your Sales Copy So the Majority of Your Leads Are Qualified!

One of the least used and most powerful ways to qualify prospects is by correctly wording your lead-generation copy. In your letters, ads, websites, and brochures, make qualifying statements that both attract the right type of prospects and discourage the wrong or unqualified types. The wrong type of leads eat up your time, money, and effort!

The easy way to qualify REAL prospects is to state your prices since that alone will instantly discourage a good many people. Do you want to discourage people? Yes, you want to discourage the time wasters and tire kickers as much as possible!

For example, consider a headline like "If you are willing to invest as little as $10,000 then this could be the right opportunity for you!" You won't get people who can only invest $5,000 responding—your ad has qualified your prospects.

"Home sites from $150,000 to $500,000." This simple statement clearly tells a prospect whether or not he is qualified financially to buy. You are not going to get many calls from people making $30,000 a year! While this is a common practice in real estate advertising, it is far less common in many other fields.

A more subtle way to do it is by clever wording:

> *Membership at Legendary Country Club is not for everyone, it's for those few individuals who appreciate a classic course layout along with the ambience, camaraderie, and benefits you'd expect of a fine club!*

Now here you are not directly talking price, but you are setting the stage—it doesn't sound cheap!

Here's another example:

> *Marketing Commander is not the cheapest product in the market by any means, BUT, and it's a big "but," it will produce a greater return on investment than any other website or marketing software you have ever considered for your company.*

Once again you are telling bottom feeders that your product may not be for them without actually divulging the price prior to explaining the product's value.

Using qualifying statements in all of your marketing efforts will result in higher-quality leads!

CHAPTER 55

Your Wesbsite—the Easiest Way to Qualify Leads

The very best way to initially qualify leads is to ask your website visitors to fill in a short survey in order to receive information or to download a brochure or "white paper." You'd be astonished by the amount of information people are willing to part with when interacting with a website. This includes how much their budget is and a host of other details that not only qualify them but also provide "hot buttons" for the actual presentation.

This is such a potent strategy that I could devote a great deal more space to it. For now, let me just say that if "Free Special Reports" are the quickest and most effective way of generating leads, "Free Audio Seminars" about your products or services are by far the most potent.

Set up a contact point on your website and simply ask the five or more most important questions you need to qualify and sell a prospect. Ship all who answer a free CD or allow them to download more information.

For example, in exchange for a free report, ask website visitors to fill in a form where they give the following information:

Company

Name

Address

City State Zip

Phone Email

Website Address

How large is your marketing budget?

Who makes the marketing decisions at your company?

Who designed your current website?

Which of the following are you interested in?
Websites, Advertising, Sales Training, Direct Mail, List Rental

What are your three biggest challenges?

1

2

3

The questions above provide more than enough information to determine whether the person downloading the info is a prospect or a suspect. Based on which of the last options they choose, they also zone me in on their specific area of interest. (For more on lead generation techniques, read *Cunningly Clever Marketing.)*

Always ask your prospects qualifying questions in your website's contact points. There is no easier way to get great information!

CHAPTER 56

Qualifying Referral Leads

Asking those who refer prospects to provide a little basic information is another way to help prequalify prospects, although referrals are typically the most qualified prospects of all.

This might be done through a referral page on your website where you ask specific questions or on a referral card that you hand out to a professional service provider. Or call the referrer and ask for specific information on the prospect. Having this information will double, if not triple, your chances of qualifying and bonding with the prospect.

Make every effort possible to get a little background on the person you will be dealing with.

Ask how the referrer knows the prospect. Ask what line of work the prospect is in. The more information you have about the referral, and the clearer you are about the referrer's relationship with the prospect, the easier it will be to qualify the prospect. For example:

Ring, ring, ring...

Salesperson: *Hello, Mr. Smith! I called to thank you for referring Don Hines to me; I will be following up with him today. Do you mind if I ask what Don does over at the country club? How do you know him? How do you think I can help him?*

Mr. Smith: *Actually, Don is the general manager of the club. He and I went to college together. He's a great guy and a fine player. He's been telling me lately that his owners are pressuring him to produce more play.*

In a few words you have qualified your prospect and targeted his needs. Don is a GM, a longtime friend, and Mr. Smith has given you some insight into his motivation for buying. (Also see the Referrals section.)

Always try to prequalify any referral with the person who referred them.

CHAPTER 57

Qualifying in Person With a Questionnaire, Application, Survey, or Needs-Analysis Form

A good many of the people with whom you have appointments will already have provided a great deal of information over the phone or through your website. For those who have not, or for those who show up unannounced, a questionnaire, survey, or needs analysis is an excellent way to get detailed information on a prospect.

I have used a basic questionnaire as a way of quickly qualifying walk-ins ever since my days in the karate business. We also use this technique at many of the clubs, meeting venues, and professional services that we represent.

As soon as the greeting is over, you should immediately hand the prospect a pen and a questionnaire and ask him if he would please fill it out while you excuse yourself to go and fetch a detailed brochure, a cup of coffee, or make a brief visit to the restroom (say, for example, "Mrs. Smith, if you wouldn't mind filling in this short survey, I'll go and get you a complete information kit."). By leaving the room for a few minutes, you direct the prospect's full attention to the application and away from asking too many questions that are unrelated to making the sale. Most people will put more effort into filling out a survey when you are out of the room.

The questionnaire asks all the obvious questions along with detailed questions about your prospect's particular business or personal challenges. I can't remember a single instance where someone refused to fill it in or wrote nothing while I was gone.

When you walk back in, you can glance at the key answers and make an instant decision on how qualified your prospect is. If nothing else, you now have all his contact information for later follow up.

Handing your prospect an application or questionnaire and leaving the room is a proven and painless way to qualify prospects quickly!

CHAPTER 58

Qualifying Your Prospect's Interest (Pain) in What You Have to Offer!

When you are qualifying prospects, it is wise to focus on their pain—not pleasure, love, desire, or greed! None of the positive emotions are as strong, so always start with pain. Cut below the surface to uncover prospects' real motivations and expose the pain. Pain is such a strong emotion that prospects will do anything to avoid it. When you get your prospects to feel pain, especially pain in the present, demonstrate that you can end their suffering, and you'll be a step closer to the sale.

Here are some questions with which you can uncover your prospects' pain:

- What was it about the brochure (or letter, advertisement, website, etc.) that caught your attention? Why did you invite me to call?
- How serious would you say the problem is today?
- How do you feel about that?
- What were you hoping I could do for you?
- Is there anything about your present situation you don't like?
- What do you like about what you are currently using, and what would you like to change or improve, if anything?

- How do you see that working for you?
- Sounds like no matter what I say or what our system can do, it wouldn't make any difference. Isn't what you already have doing the job?
- How long has this been a problem?
- Have you tried to fix it in the past? Did it work?
- In the industry, we've noticed a problem with... Have you experienced anything similar?
- If you were to change today, what would you do differently?
- Does that mean that you're not open to new ideas?
- If you were to pick one thing you didn't like about that, what would it be?
- Do you have any problems in relation to...?
- Where do you see a need for improvement?
- When did you first decide you should look into...?
- Why am I here? Why did you agree to see me?
- Good. So what I hear you saying is that finding a better way of helping the _____ isn't that critical. Am I right or wrong about that?
- How long have you been thinking about this?
- And you never had a problem with...?
- That probably means that you are happy with...?
- How much is the problem costing you?

- What impact does this problem have on you, specifically?
- If you could wave a magic wand, how would you solve this?

Rule of Thumb: You'll need to ask at least three questions to get to pain. The first two will result in smokescreen answers. They're pain indicators, but not real pain. Keep asking questions!

When the prospect starts using words like worried, concerned, frustrated, wasted effort, angry, upset, afraid, lost all hope, terrible situation, disappointed, and so on, *that's pain*! Pay careful attention to their body language if meeting in person. This too can indicate pain such as slumping down in their chair.

Once you've identified three to five pains, it's time to move on to the fulfillment step in which you give your presentation.

Ask open-ended questions that quickly qualify your prospect's level of pain!

CHAPTER 59

Qualifying Your Prospect's Budget

If you've done the pain-qualifying step successfully, then you've already conditioned your prospect for the next step: determining if he has the money. The more pain the prospect experiences, the more money the prospect will be willing to pay for your product or service. Prospects who are in real pain will pay whatever it takes to get rid of the pain.

Begin this step by reviewing the pains and confirming the prospect's agreement that those are in fact the pains he's trying to get rid of, then ask:

> *Do you have a budget set aside for a new website (new fleet of trucks, meeting space, or whatever)?*

If no:

> *That's not unusual. How do you plan to make this investment?*

If yes:

> *Would you mind sharing with me what you had in mind?*

If yes, but I can't (or won't) share it with you:

> *That makes sense. As you can probably imagine, we have many different service levels that might be able to solve your problem. Some of our solutions range in*

price from $2,000 to $5,000, and others from $5,000 to $12,000. Now, I understand this is confidential information. But, off the record, should we address the two to five range or should we go for the five to twelve range?

Alternatively, you can ask:

Assuming that we have a fit between your problem and what I'm offering, the investment in our product is going to run between $5,000 and $10,000 depending on just what you will need. Is that going to be a problem?

If that could be a problem, ask:

What are you planning to do to solve your problem if the investment needs to be higher than you had budgeted?

Highlight the pain of inaction.

If you are not in the budget ballpark, you are very unlikely to make the sale. Don't waste your valuable time.

Establish budget ranges early!

CHAPTER 60

Qualifying Your Prospect's Decision-Making Ability

Traditionally, salespeople have been taught to make the presentation first, and ask for the decision last. It's far better to qualify the prospect's decision-making abilities *prior* to making the presentation, saving you vast amounts of time, money, and personal frustration!

If the prospect doesn't qualify, you can decide not to deliver the presentation and spare yourself the aggravation. This takes discipline because most salespeople don't want to let any lead get away. But I assure you that after years of testing in multiple industries, this is one of the very best actions you can take to increase the productivity of your salespeople and help avoid burnout! (When salespeople turn down a suspect, it makes up for a lot of rejection.)

If the decision maker is not going to make a decision, or has not had time to read our literature or listen to our 45-minute CD, we just say NO!

> *Mr. Prospect, I don't want to waste your valuable time or mine. Prior to our meeting, it's very important that you and your boss listen to "The 12 Laws of Marketing" CD to make sure we are all operating out of the same playbook. Would you like to reschedule*

for the same time Friday or would the same time next week be better for you?

If the prospect does qualify, you may never have to deliver the full presentation anyway because really qualified prospects tend to close the sale themselves.

Before moving full-steam ahead in the decision step, it's important to review the Pain and Money steps before you proceed.

Ask your prospect:

What you are hoping that I can do for you to get rid of Pain 1? Pain 2?

Explain the desired outcome your product or service will specifically produce for the prospect:

Is that a fair statement?

If yes, then review the money step:

And you said that assuming I can do this for you, you've got a budget of somewhere between $5,000 and $10,000 to get rid of the pain. That's also a fair statement, isn't it?

We are now ready to tackle the decision step using questions like:

- What decision making process do you (your company, you and your wife) go through when deciding on a purchase such as this?
- When do you see yourself moving forward with this project?
- Assuming that you want to move forward, how is it

going to happen? Do I get a purchase order? A check? How exactly will it happen?

- Who besides yourself will be involved in the decision-making process?
- You mean you don't get help from an owner, a president, or a committee (spouse, partner, or other individual)?

The Intermediate Decision-Making Technique

If the prospect is *not* the final decision maker, you have some options. You can try to arrange another meeting date to include the others. This is by far your best option, no matter how frustrating it may be or how impatient you may be.

If you can't involve the others, then this intermediate decision-making technique will help.

1. Acknowledge that the prospect will gather information from you and then report to "the committee" of decision makers. Be willing to oblige the prospect, but first say something like:

> *I understand that you won't be making the decision on your own, and you would like me to give you the presentation, which I'm happy to do. But let me ask you this: After I give you my presentation, would you be nice enough to tell me if you would buy my product if the decision were up to you?*

2. Following the presentation, ask for a preliminary answer. You can say:

> *We've covered a lot of ground today, but based on what you've seen, would you buy my product or service if it were up to you?*

If no, turn out the lights, the party's over.

3. If your prospect wants to buy, ask for his or her help. You'll need to coach him on how to best relay your sales points to the committee. So after he agrees that he would buy your product, you say:

> *I appreciate that, Mr. Prospect. The committee is going to ask you some questions about my product. Based on what you know about the committee, what type of questions do you think you will be asked?*

Having GREAT audio, video, and written take-home sales materials is essential to help someone else make YOUR sales presentation!

If you are certain that your prospect is, in fact, the sole decision maker, ask for a decision. Your final question should sound like this:

> *There are three things you can say to me today. You could say no, of course. What that means is you have no interest in my product. I appreciate your seeing me, and I'll be out of here in just a few minutes.*
>
> *On the other hand, you could say yes, and what that means is that you have some interest in my product and you would like to see a presentation to make sure my product will solve your problem.*
>
> *Or you could say some form of "I want to think it over." What I suggest is that a no is okay, a yes is okay, but what shouldn't happen is for you to tell me you want to think it over. Is that something you can handle without feeling any pressure?*

Force the decision step before you proceed.

If the prospect is not the final decision maker, you need to insist the prospect be in on the presentation or resign yourself to presenting multiple times without making a sale.

The first option is always better!

CHAPTER 61

Destroying the "I'll Think About It" Stall with the Pre-Pitch Agreement

Perhaps more sales time is lost from following up on people who say they will "think about it" than for any other reason. Eighty percent of these people are—surprise, surprise—NOT actually thinking about "IT" at all—not for a week, a month, or forever—they just don't have the nerve to say no!

Your key to a massive increase in productivity and sales is the establishment of an agreement before you make your presentation, thus eliminating the most destructive of all responses once and for all.

Establishing a Pre-Pitch Agreement

Start your presentation by saying something like:

Mr. Prospect, I know your time is valuable, so I'd like to outline how I see our meeting progressing today. First I'd like to ask you some additional questions to make sure I understand your business or your problem. You probably want to ask me some questions to see if we're the right kind of company for you.

As we ask and answer each other's questions, two things can happen. One, you might say, "Your answers don't help my problem." If that happens, so that we don't waste each other's time, are you okay telling me no? You can say, "Hey stop! I don't think there's anything we can do together," anytime you want and I'll be just fine with it.

On the other hand, it's possible that we might see eye to eye on what we are discussing and, in that case, I would expect you to say yes.

What I hope you won't say is, "I want to think it over." If you feel like you have to think it over, I'd rather you say no. Are you okay with that?

Validate the Pre-Pitch Agreement

Go over it again:

Are you sure you're okay telling me no?

Or, if I can fill your needs, are you okay with telling me yes? It's not unusual for me to talk to people who say they're sure they're okay with this, but when it comes time to say no, most people don't like to do it. So I just want to be sure—do we have an understanding on this?

Not everyone you talk to will agree to meet your terms, in which case you must evaluate your chances of closing that particular sale. With practice and a little tweaking of the script for your industry, the majority of people will agree.

Getting your prospects to verbally agree to a pre-pitch agreement will massively increase your closing ratio.

CHAPTER 62

Short- versus Long-Term Qualifying

There is another important aspect of qualifying that most systems overlook. In the overall sales process, you know that many people are not ready to buy now. In some research, as many as 75% of prospects bought within a year but few of these bought within three months.

You need to set up a system of qualifying that produces short-term sales *and* sets the stage for later sales. Most systems essentially write off "delayed" sales. But they can be your bread and butter in a well-designed sales system.

When you can sincerely convey to people that you are not focusing on the hard sell now, they will often talk to you further. In contrast, when you are "selling," they will resist. Your conversation possibilities become limited and your prospects are defensive. In a good conversation between two people, your prospect will often relax and tell you how they really feel. And if they've agreed to have you call them later, they have opened the door to future contact and your "role" in their lives.

It is your follow-up that creates the majority of sales down the road. This may be as simple as recording prospects' birthdays and sending them cards or keeping them on your newsletter distribution list. You need information that provides reasons for keeping in touch with them. You need to develop your contact tools. Perhaps it's an email or a clipping that relates to planning the perfect marketing campaign. You need a system to keep in touch on a regular schedule and you need to make your communications worth the prospect's time.

Design your system for both short- and long-term sales. While you harvest the "low hanging fruit" you will be building relationships for long-term sales. Even prospects who never buy may become sources of referrals and positive word-of-mouth when they are treated professionally and respectfully.

Design your qualifying system for both short- and long-term sales!

CHAPTER 63

When Qualifying a Prospect, Do Not Let Personal Feelings or Prejudices Cloud Your Judgment

We all have our own prejudices, whether or not we are willing to admit them. It is critically important that you do not dismiss anyone simply because they are fat, young, old, a smoker, a poor dresser, arrive for an appointment late, or drive an older model car. Qualifying people superficially is rarely a good idea and is certainly not part of a professional sales system.

While it's easy after the fact to say, "I knew he wasn't a real prospect because the guy wore a cheap watch" or "the woman wore a cheap perfume," it pays to remember that very few people fit into standard stereotypes. Smart people buy, dumb people buy, pretty people buy, and ugly people buy. People with a taste for the flamboyant buy and people who value functionality buy.

Always take your prospect through a professional qualifying process before allowing yourself to make ANY PERSONAL judgments and even then do everything in your power to keep prejudicial judgments to yourself.

I myself have been dismissed as a lousy prospect. When I walked into a high-end golf club in California many years ago as a successful 27-year-old entrepreneur and told the head professional that I wanted to join the club, he actually laughed at me and said, "REALLY?!"

Even after I handed him the membership agreement and the check he continued to shake his head in disbelief. I wonder how many people he "blew off" over the years.

I have all too often witnessed poor tonality and body language from salespeople based solely on the fact that the prospect was driving a truck rather than a BMW!

Check yourself for this; very often you will not be conscious of any change in your tone or manner when dealing with people you instinctively don't think will buy or who have personal habits you consider in poor taste (tobacco, spitting, whatever). Simply being aware of the possibility that it can happen, even to you, will improve your results. (There's more on this topic in the Maximizing Your Sales section.)

Don't prejudge prospects. Let your professional qualifying system take its course and decide for you!

CHAPTER 64

Categorizing Your Prospects for Consistent Follow Up

You should have already set up your own written criteria for each type of prospect that you are likely to encounter, and described each in detail, so you are consistent in the way you qualify each lead. This is important so you can judge your own performance in rating leads and closing sales. It's also important so that each lead is followed up in a systematic way, the same way every time, based on their prospect status.

For example we qualify and follow up prospects in the following way:

"A" prospects are those who want to buy in the next three months and have the money and desire. These would include most referrals, people who are in planning and budgeting season, and those who are in desperate need to turn their businesses around and produce results. "A" prospects are also people who are very dissatisfied with another provider and people with a recent change in position within their company or organization. *Follow up:* Immediate.

"B" prospects want to buy and have the money but are in no rush to make a decision. They will decide in the next 6–12 months. These include prospects who are happy with their current provider, those gathering advance information in preparation for a change next season, and those who don't have any organizational pressure to produce results right away. *Follow up:* Consistent contact over the next 12 months by phone, and ongoing email.

"C" prospects would like to buy but are unsure about the budget and currently may not have the money or they are actively looking at other providers as their first choice. *Follow up:* Occasional contact over the next 12 months by phone and ongoing email.

"D" prospects do not seem to have the money or motivation to buy; more likely, they are looking for free information and ideas. *Follow Up:* Yearly contact to see if either the financial situation or motivation have changed.

"E" prospects are essentially NON-prospects until current management changes. *Follow Up:* Yearly contact to see if interest levels or management have changed, plus ongoing email contact.

"F" prospects are people we simply do not want to do business with. *Follow Up:* None.

You may want to add additional categories (for example, seasonal prospects), but, in any case, all leads should be logged into your customer relationship management system so accurate records of the number and quality of leads generated through your marketing efforts can be tracked. Once all leads are logged, you should follow-up in the predetermined manner based on priority.

Following up each prospect in a predetermined and systematic way based on their level of qualifications will always produce more sales.

6

Cunningly Clever Phone Techniques

CHAPTER 65

Secrets of Successful Inbound Telephone Sales

It is well known that first impressions are vitally important and that they are formed during the first two or three minutes of the initial contact. Many prospects make their initial contact with you and your business by telephone. The busier you are, the more important the telephone becomes in building a successful business. There is no doubt that the success or failure of your business or career may be directly proportionate to how well you present yourself on the telephone.

Do not let anyone answer the sales phone line unless they are completely trained and scripted to handle sales inquiries. By trained and scripted, I mean that they know exactly what to say in every situation that can be reasonably anticipated. In a small business, probably no one is better qualified than the owner to answer the telephone. For the owner, the telephone is a matter of customers and orders won or lost. Employees manning the telephone often lack the necessary skills, presence of mind, or motivation to handle sales calls effectively. Their lack of personal involvement may lead them to handle sale inquiries in a cold, mechanical fashion.

If you work in a larger organization, pay particular attention to the people in your office who handle and process your calls. They can quickly and easily affect the way your prospects feel, positively or negatively. Make sure you go the extra mile to develop rapport with the employees who answer the phone, so they quickly, cheerfully, and professionally pass calls on to you!

Make it a point to randomly call your own office to check on how the phone is being answered, or have a friend call while you listen in. The information you gather will be invaluable in fine tuning the all-important first impression that is being made by your employees or subordinates.

You are likely to hear, "Sorry, he's not here right now. Why don't you call back in an hour." Or, "Mr. Smith is with a customer right now and can't be disturbed." Neither of these statements is in your best interest. Remember, one chance is often all you get to make contact with a potential customer. Make sure you have scripted answers to all common questions and train your people to use only those answers, not ones they make up on their own!

Do not let untrained people answer your phone—it can literally make or break your business!

CHAPTER 66

Your Phone Voice

The first and most important skill to master on the telephone is the way you use your voice. Your prospective customers can't see you, but they will build a mental image of who you are and what you look like from the tone and power of your voice, starting from the moment you pick up the receiver and say hello.

You do it yourself, don't you? Think back to the last person you talked to on the telephone whom you have never seen. How about when you called another company to order something by mail? How did you picture the person on the other end of the line?

- Was the person you spoke to a man or a woman?
- Was the person you spoke to attractive? Tall, short, fat, blonde, or dark?
- Was the person young or old? How old?
- What part of the country did he or she come from?
- Was the person you spoke to having a good day or a bad day?

Chances are, although you have never met this person, you have a pretty clear idea in your mind about his or her appearance and attitude based solely on the voice you listened to for just a few minutes.

Now ask yourself what kind of impression others form of you after a brief conversation. It's powerful stuff if you can get people to paint a glowing picture of you in their minds after merely listening to you for a few moments.

Your voice paints a picture of you to the person on the other end of the phone; make it a good one!

CHAPTER 67

Stand Up and Be "Up" — It's Showtime

Your voice *must* convey a feeling of confidence, enthusiasm, professionalism, and sincerity to prospects. This puts callers at ease and signals that you are a solid, reliable person with information that he or she can trust. Your voice should be neither too loud nor too soft—not too slow and not too fast. If your voice does not have it already, put some character into your voice by using a variety of tones. Watch the ways in which movie actors use words and modulate tones. Incorporate some of these different techniques into your speech so your voice is never drab and monotone. In short, get into the conversation and get excited. Practice getting excited, and record yourself as you do.

People who talk to me on the phone often comment that I sound "up" or excited; one reason for this is that I *am* up! Whenever I take a phone call or make one, I do so on a wireless or on my cell phone so I can move about. The very fact that I am standing up, and often walking about, goes a long way to creating and conveying a sense of action and excitement in my voice. When the phone rings, it's SHOWTIME. Stand up and be up. You'll be surprised just how much this simple act can improve your attitude and the sound of your voice, not to mention your overall health and well being. About the only downside is that you'll wear out the carpets quicker from continued pacing, but that's a small price to pay.

If you do not move about physically, at least smile when answering a phone. It changes your voice for the better.

In addition to the correct tones, your choice and usage of words is also very important. In general, people judge you by your command of the English language, particularly if they don't know you personally. Eliminate slang and other poor speech habits (unless that's exactly the type of speech expected from the market to which you are selling). Poor English can create doubts about your intelligence and education. Do not swear or use other types of questionable language, even jokingly. Although your speech pattern may be part of your unique personality, it can hinder a sale if the caller focuses on how you speak instead of what you have to say; your personal style can be self-defeating for your business.

If you feel your command of the English language may be lacking, get someone to help you. Buy vocabulary and grammar tapes. Take a class or hire a private tutor. Your voice is your sales tool—so make it a good one. Waste no time acquiring the phone qualities you need. If your phone presence lacks any of the properties I have mentioned, your ability to create the image you need is diminished, and you will find it harder to get a potential customer motivated enough to seek you out personally.

Always convey, in clear speech, your enthusiasm, professionalism, and excitement on the phone!

CHAPTER 68

Maintain Control of the Phone Conversation

We have already determined that when someone calls for information you probably have only that one chance to persuade them to do business with you. If you stay in control of the conversation, you will enjoy greater success at taking advantage of that opportunity.

The person asking questions is always in control. When you ask repeated questions, you do so not only to qualify the caller and create a bond, but also to lead her in the direction you wish to go. If the caller takes command and stops the flow of your sales presentation by asking questions every few seconds, your chances of making the sale are lessened substantially.

Maintain control of the conversation. You can do this by politely and professionally asking relevant questions. Once you have established control, suggest that it would be best to meet in person. In this way the prospect can see your product or service, perhaps take a look around, and receive in-depth answers to questions. You probably need to be face to face to make your sale, especially the initial one, and prospects certainly can't sign contracts over the telephone!

Even if callers insist, don't agree to mail information without first exhausting every available means of motivating the caller to come to your place of business or make an appointment with you.

Scheduling Appointments

Suggest it is in the prospect's best interest to schedule an appointment and come to see you in person, or for you to go and see her. In this way, you can set aside an adequate amount of time to show her everything she needs to know about your business or the service you sell.

Without firm appointments, potential customers often have no reason to come to your business. Committing them to an appointment is the first key to ensuring their appearance. Even the innocent question, "Will you be stopping by today?" increases the chances that they will do so. The prime objective of all telephone conversations related to business is to persuade potential customers to come and see you in person or to set firm appointments to meet them.

Give Accurate Directions to Your Location

We have all experienced the phenomenon of potential customers who say, "Yes, I know where you are," only to end up at another competing business in your area, thinking it was yours! One otherwise successful business owner complained to me that this happens to him three or four times a month.

Give clear directions that include cross streets and landmarks. Why sabotage your own sales effort by sending prospects to a competitor after working hard to motivate them to visit? (You can even fax or email them a map if necessary.)

Before You Hang Up the Phone

Always finish your conversations by telling prospective customers how much you look forward to meeting them. Make sure your voice conveys excitement and eagerness to meet and know them.

You must maintain control of the conversation to maximize your sales.

CHAPTER 69

A Basic Phone Script to Close for an Appointment

Here is a basic script that is typical of the kind of conversation I have had hundreds of times with prospective customers. It can easily be adapted to any type of retail situation. It illustrates some of the points I have already mentioned and it will be a simple matter for you to substitute words and phrases more suited to your own field.

Instructor: *Good afternoon; this is Martial Arts America. How may I help you?*

Prospect: *I want some information about your martial arts classes. How much do they cost?*

Instructor: *My name's Andrew. What's yours?*

Prospect: *Pete.*

Instructor: *Pete, we have several different programs, each tailored to meet individual needs. Will these classes be for you or for someone else?*

Prospect: *For me.*

Instructor: *Have you ever studied the martial arts, Pete?*

Prospect: *No. I wrestled in high school, though. Is that considered martial arts?*

Instructor: *Yes, it is. The best thing for you to do is stop by the studio and pick up our free 8-page information kit that will answer all of your questions. While you're here, I can also take a few minutes to show you around the school and introduce you to some of the instructors. If you'd like, you can spend a few minutes actually seeing what a class is like. Would 6 o'clock tonight be a good time for you to do that, or would 7 o'clock be better?*

Prospect: *Well, er...I could come by later this evening. How about 6:30?*

Instructor: *That would be fine. We're located at Main and 5th Street, directly across from Wal-Mart and next door to the Videodrome movie rental store. Do you know where that is?*

Prospect: *Yes. In the Stone Creek Shopping Center. I drive past it all the time.*

Instructor: *Great! Let me have your phone number so I can reach you just in case there's a problem.*

Prospect: *It's 555-6574.*

Instructor: *I look forward to seeing you at 6:30, Pete. Take care.*

Did you notice how, in addition to expressing my pleasure at the opportunity to meet the customer, I maintained control of the conversation by answering the prospect's questions with questions of my own? Just because the prospect asks questions, you do not have to relinquish control of the conversation. Remember, *you* must be in control.

When you speak to any potential customer on the telephone, make a habit of writing down any pertinent information on a "customer survey sheet." This habit will give you an edge. When the prospect comes to your business, you will have at your disposal all the ammunition you need: name, age, likes, dislikes, and so on.

Always try to close for an appointment.

CHAPTER 70

Over-the-Phone Miscommunication Is Common

The more elaborate our means of communication, the less we communicate.

—J.B. Priestley

Because there is a high risk of being misinterpreted during a telephone conversation, you should always try to be face to face with the prospective customer when you quote prices. The following example makes the reason for this perfectly clear.

You tell a caller your product costs $95. The caller says, "Thanks!" and hangs up because, unknown to you, he had previously called another business that gave him a price of $85. Your competitor, however, failed to inform him that to get that price there is an additional $30 fee to join a "Discount Buyers' Club."

The prospect goes to the first business he called, fifteen miles away, ready to buy at what he thinks will be a lower price. He talks to the salesperson further, becomes excited by the product, and decides to take the plunge. That's when he finds out about the $30 membership fee, but being emotionally charged up and not wanting to spend any more time shopping for this product, he gets out his credit card and seals the deal.

You've lost a sale because you didn't find out more about the caller before you gave him your price. (Later on, this same person will find out that your competitor doesn't stand behind his product when it has problems, and the cost will go even higher.)

The customer discovers too late that you had much more to offer in the way of better services and products, not to mention your overall lower price. Had he met you in person and talked to you further, he would have done business with you.

Some Things Are Difficult to Explain Using Words Alone

Another communication problem arises when your product or service is complicated or very technical. The caller has his own idea of what constitutes good value and, with limited knowledge of what is involved, is unable to grasp just how attractive your offer is. In these and similar circumstances, making a convincing oral argument about the benefits of your service or product can be more or less impossible. You need the prospect in front of you where you can demonstrate and explain at the same time.

For example, suppose you are selling websites. Your prospect is uncertain how easy the site will be to update. You tell him how easy it is to add text. He replies, and adds under his breath, "All I need to be is a qualified computer technician!" If you had him in front of you, you could show him in a few minutes all he needed to know. This would also have the effect of putting him slightly in your debt for taking the time and trouble.

You Can't *See* the Caller's Reactions Over the Phone

Reading a prospect's reactions over the phone can also be a problem. You can't see the nonverbal cues, and this puts you at a disadvantage. For example, when you mention price, the caller may say, "Sounds good to me." In reality, his face may be registering shock or confusion. If he was standing in front of you, you could easily observe that reaction and quickly offer a less expensive option. By interviewing the prospective customer in person, you can gauge his reactions to your sales technique and modify it, when necessary, to complete the sale.

In summary, the key point is that over-the-phone miscommunication is all too common. When the prospective customer is sitting right in front of you and you are able to hand him literature, write down prices, and read his body language, the chances of communicating well are far greater.

Don't write so that you can be understood;
write so you can't be misunderstood.
—William H. Taft

In most retail situations, getting the prospect in front of you is key to avoiding miscommunication!

CHAPTER 71

Handling the Prospect's Price Concerns on the Phone

Most questions focus on the cost of your product or service. By stating numbers over the phone, you give callers the chance to eliminate you on the basis of price alone. Asking them to pay a specific price for something they have not seen is unlikely to be in your best interest—or theirs!

Your price or fee may be higher than that of your competitors, and well worth it because of what you provide, but your prospect has no way of knowing this. It isn't until he listens to you further and actually meets you and sees your product that he will be able to accurately assess its value. Once he has met you and seen for himself, there is a better chance that he will make a decision based on the benefits he will enjoy by buying from you.

Once a person has seen the benefits of your product and decided in favor of it, he will often come up with reasons of his own to justify any price differences. He may say to himself, "So what if it costs me $10 more a month? This salesperson really appears to understand my problems, so his service should be a lot better."

How do you handle questions concerning your prices? Let's listen in on a typical phone call.

The Money Script

Salesperson: *Good morning. Johnson's Photography. How may I help You?*

Prospect: *Hi. How much do you charge?*

Salesperson: *Hi, my name's Andrew. What's yours?*

Prospect: *Mary. How much do you charge for family portraits?*

Salesperson: *Well, Mary, we have many programs suited to a wide variety of needs and budgets. Have we had the opportunity to serve you before?*

Prospect: *No. I'm just calling to find out just how much it will cost me if I decide to do it.*

Salesperson: *Well, we have rates starting as low as $39. The best thing for you to do is stop by our studio and take a look at everything we have to offer. We also have a free brochure that outlines the full range of our services and options. Would you like to stop by this evening Mary, or tomorrow? We're open until 7.*

Prospect: *Can't make it today. Tomorrow maybe.*

Salesperson: *Good! I have some time available at 6 p.m. tomorrow night. If you could come in then, I could give you my undivided attention. How would that be for you, Mary?*

Prospect: *That's fine.*

Salesperson: *Do you know where our studio is located?*

Prospect: *Yes. You're across from the Wal-Mart at 5th & Main.*

Salesperson: *Right! We're next door to the Videodrome movie rental store in the Stone Creek Shopping Center. Mary, what's your number? (casually asked).*

Prospect: *555-6574.*

Salesperson: *Nice talking with you, Mary. I look forward to seeing you tomorrow evening at 6 p.m.*

Notice that when the prospect asks about price, the salesperson answers indirectly and then redirects the flow with a question of his own. In this scenario, the caller returns twice to the cost of services. Therefore, the salesperson, having already indicated that there is a range of prices and services, responds with the lowest price she has to offer. Then she invites the caller to come and see her in person at the studio. She could also have mentioned a limited-time special offer that might suit the prospect's requirements, thus encouraging her to come in and take advantage of a good deal. Had the caller allowed herself to be redirected, the salesperson could have further qualified her without having to name prices on the phone.

The prime objective is always to get the prospective customer to talk to you face to face. You can't make a deal with anyone over the phone; the prospect has to be right in front of you to sign the check.

When it comes to price, ignore the question on first request; suggest more discovery is necessary on second request; then finally quote a range on the third request!

CHAPTER 72

When the Prospect Asks Specifically for Something You Don't Have

This problem is frequently the result of the common desire of many people to buy the latest product or be part of the latest trend which has just caught their attention. Because of advertising, recommendations, or hearsay, people often set their minds on a certain product name. It is important to realize that most people who become interested in a particular product for the first time have little or no idea how it works or whether it will really serve their purpose. They also have little understanding of what makes similar products different from one another.

Suppose a caller wants to buy a video camera, but wants one that records in near darkness. He has seen one advertised on TV that is manufactured by Video King. Ninety-nine times out of 100 the prospect would be unable to tell you any of the slight differences in operation, performance, or price between the model he is asking for and the ones you have available for sale. He wants what he perceives to be solutions to his problems and has simply latched on to a particular product name.

He has found your ad in the Yellow Pages and called because he lives quite close to your store. He asks right away if you sell the Video King camcorder that works in the dark. If you say, "No, we don't carry that make," he will hang up and try somewhere else, and you will have lost a potential customer.

Dig deeper and find out what the prospect really wants. Once you have discerned his true objectives and goals, you can then explain how the prospect's needs can be met more effectively and at a lower price by purchasing a model you do carry—it doesn't matter that it isn't what the prospect asked for in the first place.

Here's how it might go. I'll play the role of the camcorder salesperson.

Prospect: *Do you sell Video King camcorders?*

Andrew: *Hi! My name's Andrew. May I ask what you intend to use it for, Mr. ...?*

Prospect: *My name's Fred. I want to take pictures of nocturnal animals.*

Andrew: *Is there any particular reason that you want a Video King camcorder, Fred?*

Prospect: *Yes, I just saw one in a TV commercial. It was rated one of the top models and works well in very poor light.*

Andrew: *It certainly does, but there are several other low-light camcorders that have other features that might be just what you need and are no more expensive—some even cost quite a bit less.*

We carry five different models. Perhaps one of those would be of interest to you. The best thing for you to do is to come in and see me. I'd be delighted to show you the full range and what each of them can do.

Prospect: *Five models! I guess I'd better take a look*

at all of them before I decide. Where are you located?

Be careful about offering detailed information about products and services before you have found out what the prospect really wants and needs. Many sales are lost by relaying information the prospect doesn't need.

Prospects know what they want the product to do, but they don't always ask for the brand or model that makes the most sense. You must probe and help them!

CHAPTER 73

Dealing with Loaded Questions on the Phone

Often prospects will ask *loaded* questions. A loaded question is one that can be answered in two ways, either of which could be wrong! How can you know what the caller wants to hear without having more information? You can't, of course.

In order to handle loaded questions effectively, find out more about the prospect's desires before you answer. We're not talking about deliberately deceiving someone, only about making sure that your answers are interpreted correctly. Until you are better equipped to respond, your answer should be as noncommittal as is reasonably possible, within the limits of honesty.

Here's an example of a question often heard by martial arts instructors. The caller asks, "Will martial arts lessons make my child more aggressive?"

Answer "yes" or "no" and you have a 50/50 chance of being wrong. Parents of shy children want them to be more aggressive, while parents of hyperactive kids want them to learn some self-control and develop the ability to focus. We'll cover both situations with just one qualifying question.

Instructor: *Is your child aggressive?*

Mom: *No, Aaron is very shy. He doesn't mix well with other children.*

Instructor: *Martial arts training is one of the best ways to build confidence in shy children and give them the assertiveness needed to succeed in life.*

Here's the other side of the coin.

Instructor: *Is your child aggressive?*

Dad: *Gary's a real problem. We're at the end of our wits. He disrupts classes at school, never sits still for a moment, and fights at the drop of a hat. If we can't find a way to calm him down soon, we don't know what will happen. His teacher, Mrs. Lewis, recommended martial arts lessons and referred us to you.*

Instructor: *Mrs. Lewis is right. Martial arts training can benefit your child. We have experience in dealing with hyperactive students and can teach Gary how to channel his excess energy and put it to good use. I can give him all the personal attention he needs to calm him down and help focus his energy.*

The instructor needs to give the parents the answer they want to hear, which isn't hard to do since he can provide both qualities, assertiveness and self-control, in their children's training. The solution to a dilemma like this is to ask a couple of questions before you provide the answer. Once you have evaluated a loaded question and determined the appropriate answer, move on to your prime objective—to get the prospect to meet with you and make a commitment.

Never provide the answer to a loaded question before you know the question behind the question!

CHAPTER 74

Problem #4: Questions, Questions, Questions

An anonymous philosopher once said, "Nothing derails a train of thought more effectively than listening to a person with a one-track mind."

Occasionally, you will encounter a prospect who barrages you with a steady stream of questions. Fielding these questions with lengthy explanations is unproductive on two counts. First, it disrupts the flow of your sales presentation. Second, even if you answer every question, there is no guarantee the prospect will come to your business, or make an appointment to get more information and give you a chance to close.

Answering general questions misdirects the focus of the telephone call from *sales* to *information*. Remember, in most retail situations you cannot get the signature of a new customer over the phone. When you must answer questions related to information and unrelated to sales, don't get into long explanations.

Here are some of the most frequently asked questions. Your answers will obviously depend on your field. Keep them short and to the point.

Question: *What's the difference between the standard and deluxe models?*

Answer: *The deluxe model is larger and has more capabilities. It is, of course, slightly more expensive.*

Question: *Which is the best?*

Answer: *The one that best fits your needs.*

Question: *How much does it cost?*

Answer: *Price varies with styles and fittings. I'm sure we can show you what you need at a suitable price.*

Question: *Do you accept credit cards?*

Answer: *Yes, and we have a number of other payment plans, designed to suit all budgets.*

Question: *When are you available?*

Answer: *What time would be convenient for you?*

By stating your schedule over the phone, you can kill a sale in much the same way that you can by quoting prices. If your schedule doesn't fit in with the prospect's, he may just say, "Thank you!" and hang up. He can't come and see you in the evening — he bowls! Overcoming schedule objections can be as easy as having you and the prospect consider alternatives.

Answer questions briefly and directly. If your response is complicated or long-winded, it falls into the informational category, rather than being sales oriented. As soon as you have answered the question, continue your presentation.

Often prospects will ask about the differences, frequently technical in nature, between individual products and services.

Rather than getting into a long and detailed discussion, close the discussion by answering:

> *Mr. Smith, that is a very good question, and when you come in this afternoon I can show you the difference. What time is best for you?*

Answer questions quickly, to the point, or with your own questions. Then get back to asking for the appointment.

CHAPTER 75

The Caller Wants to Give You His Life Story

Sometimes a caller will try to give you his unabridged life story from birth in response to one of your questions. When this happens, it's time to regain control and get back to making an appointment.

As the caller babbles on tell him you have another call, or distract him in some other way, and put him on hold. This breaks the caller's train of thought. When you resume control of the conversation, concentrate on making an appointment.

Here's part of an epic I heard a few years ago.

Store owner: *International Electronics. What can I do for you?*

Prospect: *Hi, my name is Morris Jones and I want to buy a Blue Ray disk player that will work with my television.*

Store owner: *Have you ever seen a laser disk, Morris?*

Prospect: *My friend had one when I was in the Marines. In Okinawa, we could buy electronics from Japan really cheap, but like a fool I didn't buy one then. When I got back to the States, I bought a DVD player, but the picture quality wasn't good at all. The colors weren't clear, and the picture just wasn't sharp. So then I decided to buy a better DVD player to see if that would help.*

Store owner: *Excuse me. Would you hold for a moment, please?* [Putting the caller on hold helps you regain control. The less attractive alternative is simply to stop talking and listen.]

Morris? Sorry about that. It sounds like you know quite a bit about players. Why don't you come to the store so that I can meet you in person? That way I can show you around the store and tell you about the laser disc players we offer.

Prospect: *Do you think I can buy a laser disc player and still be able to use my DVD. I have lots of movies that I've bought since I moved into my own apartment and now that my roommate moved out, I have a lot of spare time and...*

Store owner: *Excuse me, Morris. Could you give me one more second? I would appreciate it.*

Prospect: *Sure.*

Put the prospect on hold again, put your feet up on the desk, and wiggle your thumbs. The caller can only imagine what important task you have undertaken. Now it's time to take control of the conversation again.

Store owner: *I'm sorry, but things are really hopping around here. I'd like to talk to you some more, but I'm really busy. The best thing for you to do is to come and see me, so I can talk with you personally, say at 5 p.m.? That way I'll have more time to spend with you and explain things. Does that sound good to you?*

Prospect: *Well, I'm still not sure what to do about my old DVD.*

Store owner: *When you come in, I can show you a few options. I'm sure we can work something out. Okay?*

Prospect: *Sure.*

Store owner: *I look forward to meeting you at 5 p.m. We're at 5th and Main, directly across the street from the Wal-Mart in the Stone Creek Shopping Center.*

Prospect: *Oh, yeah, right next door to the Videodrome. They rent the neatest classic movies. Did you ever see "Casablanca"? It was about this guy...*

Store owner: *I'll see you at 5, Morris.*

Hang up at this point. Time is money!

Putting the caller on hold is a last-ditch effort to allow you to regain control of the situation.

CHAPTER 76

Closing for the Appointment—the Confusion Close

The confusion close enables you to deal with prospects who continually probe for a price before you have had a chance to establish the value of the product, which can, of course, be disastrous. As always, you are seeking to have them come and see you.

A sample confusion close might go something like this:

Prospect: *Can you tell me how much you charge for karate classes?*

Salesperson: *Certainly. My name's Andrew. What's yours?*

Prospect: *John.*

Salesperson: *John, are these classes for you or for someone else?*

Prospect: *For me.*

Salesperson: *Have you ever studied martial arts before?*

Prospect: *No, but I've been interested for a long time.*

Salesperson: *Good. The best thing for you to do is to come to the school. Then I can show you around and introduce you to some of the staff. I'll also give you our free eight-page information kit. It will answer all of your questions. At the same time, I'd be happy to give you a free trial lesson, so you can get a feel for what karate is all about. Would tonight at 6 be good, or is tomorrow better?*

Prospect: *Can't you just tell me the price?*

Salesperson: *We have quite a few options available. To give you an exact price I need to know which course you're interested in. Which course would you like for me to price for you, John?*

Prospect: *What courses do you have?*

Salesperson: *We have Brown Belt courses, Green Belt courses, Blue Belt courses, private lessons, group lessons, 6-month courses, 12-month courses...Would you like information on one of those?*

Prospect: *I don't know. I didn't realize their were so many.*

Salesperson: *I understand, John. That's why the best thing for you to do is to come to the school. Then I can carefully explain each of them, and you can decide which one best fits your needs. Would today work for you, or is tomorrow better?*

Prospect: *Today is fine.*

As is the case with any phone appointment, before hanging up, the salesperson will make sure the prospect knows exactly where the office or shop is located, and sincerely assure him that he is looking forward to their meeting.

The confusion close must be used carefully but works well

when you are dealing with people who know little about your product or service. When you overload them with options and then ask exactly what they want, they grasp the idea that it makes a great deal of sense to come and see you and find out just what you have to offer. In this case, the prospect had no previous knowledge, so he was given choices that meant little or nothing to him. Notice that I did not mention a black belt course to the caller, since that is the one thing he might have recognized and latched onto during the conversation.

Depending on your product or service, the confusion close can be an easy way to get appointments.

But use it with care!

CHAPTER 77

The Information-Kit Appointment Close

When the prospect calls looking for a wide range of information, you may lose the sale if you try to answer his questions without a demonstration or face-to-face meeting. One efficient way to deal with this particular problem is to have first-class printed backup material.

The most effective form of backup material is the information kit. This kit is composed of a cardboard presentation folder containing a series of loose-leaf sheets, with each one cut a little shorter than the previous one so the headlines on each page are visible. You can customize each kit by inserting material such as recent testimonial letters or removing material such as a sheet that contains information about a service you no longer offer.

"Wait a minute," you say. "That sounds just like a brochure." Well, it is like a brochure with important differences. A brochure briefly describes benefits. It emphasizes the call to take action—to buy. The information kit is larger and contains much more detail. It is designed to *help* the prospect reach a decision by making him comfortable with you and your business. It can also be customized and modified while a brochure can't.

When a prospect calls and asks for information about your product or services, you have two choices. Depending on your product, you can mail or email the information and rely on it to do a lot of the selling for you, or you can ask the prospect to come in and get the information. Resist the temptation to email information until you have made a determined effort to make a personal appointment. When asked to send out information by email, it is best to reply, "We can serve you so much better if we show you in person what we can do for you." When the prospect accepts the latter option, you can also include a demo, consultation, or some other type of inducement to serve as additional motivation.

In the scripts and dialogues I have described already, you will have noticed some basic structures. You have probably also noticed that I have emphasized one key phrase:

The best thing for you to do...

When someone tells you in an enthusiastic, knowledgeable, and friendly way what the best thing for you to do is, what do you do? The chances are high that you do what they suggest, because they have assured you it is in your best interests. These words are the key in persuading a prospect to meet with you. I have used them successfully in the karate business, the advertising business, a consulting business, and a host of other businesses for clients and friends. You can easily adapt this concept to your particular selling situation.

It doesn't matter precisely *which* close you use in your phone presentation. Use the one that works best to persuade your prospect to come in person to listen to your sales pitch.

Use your information kits as a way to convince callers to let you "show them" the difference!

CHAPTER 78

Get Back to People FAST!

Recently, I received a letter from a copier company suggesting that I upgrade my equipment. It sounded reasonable so I called them back to discuss it with them. Three days later, after calling them three more times, I finally got a return phone call. The salesperson apologized and said that he had been busy! I eventually concluded a deal with a more interested competitor of that copier company.

This week, I tried to book 50 rooms for a small seminar at a well-known California resort. It took two and a half days before the sales manager returned my call. He apologized. It seems he had been busy attending several important meetings! I booked elsewhere! I'm busy too!

A few weeks ago, I tried to order 100 paperback books on a business topic as a bonus for participants at one of my seminars. I called twice and NEVER got a call back! I was so mad that I tracked down the author and told him about the incident. He was angry too, but by then the seminar had taken place and I didn't need the books! Many, many times I have bought from a salesperson solely because he was the first person to get back to me! When I'm *ready* to buy, I buy!

There is no excuse for not getting back to prospects within 12 hours, even if it is only to tell them that you cannot get back to them for another twelve hours! Not returning calls quickly is a sure sign to the prospect that he is not important to you and you do not need his business. Prospects do not care that you are busy; they do not care that you are at a trade show or seminar; and they certainly do not care that you have to deal with other people besides them. Impatient prospects like me want *attention,* and they want it right now.

Always check your messages regularly and get back to people promptly. If necessary, call them and tell them when you will get back to them! If you cannot call back until after business hours, call back and leave a message on the voice mail system, or answering device to show prospects that they are *important to you!*

Speed is a strategy!
Be the fastest getting back to people.

CHAPTER 79

Good Times to Call

When is it a good time to call? Over the years I have learned that there are certain times that seem to promote positive results. One occasion that has worked well for me is the customer's birthday. Maybe people tend to be in a positive frame of mind on their birthdays because the people around them are making an effort to be nice to them! Another good time is just after someone has received a promotion or award, especially if you open the conversation with congratulations and mention that the recognition was well deserved.

If you call near major holidays like Thanksgiving and Christmas, the result can go either way. Whether you should call near a holiday depends on the type of product you sell and the people who are buying your product. Some services tend not to do as well at Christmastime because they are intangible, like bookkeeping, for example. For the most part, people are looking for things they can touch, hold, feel, and wrap!

Retail stores, of course, live or die based on the five weeks between Thanksgiving and Christmas, but what about business-to-business sales? For the most part, these people put off buying decisions until after the holidays. Some astute salesmen, however, have found that many of their competitors don't make much of an effort during this period. Therefore, it can be a great time to get a head start by doing a little extra work rather than slacking off for the holidays. Some prospects may even be influenced by the charitable spirit that generally prevails in December and actually give you a chance to show what you have to offer.

When a customer doesn't want to commit until after the holidays, offer him extra inducements to buy. This could be the price increase coming on January 1st or the extra bonus if you buy before December 31st. Some customers with fiscal years that coincide with the calendar year will even want to buy now to take the tax deduction from this year's gross income.

Use birthdays, celebrations, or holiday spirit to your sales advantage.

CHAPTER 80

Weekend Selling Weeds Out the Competition

Some people are morning people, while others are afternoon or evening people. I like to spend my early morning writing, then I work out and go to the office. The best time to call me and get a positive response is between 1 p.m. and 3 p.m., or after 7 p.m. at night. I dismiss almost every sales call I receive outside of those times.

A few weeks ago, I received a call on a Saturday morning asking for a particular manual by Andrew Wood. I told the caller that I was Andrew Wood. Obviously he was taken by surprise for he said, "No way!"

"Who else do you think would be in the office at 7:30 on a Saturday morning?" I asked him. He thought about this for a moment and then agreed that a business owner was the most likely person to be there.

If you are in management, cancel call forwarding or switch off the answering machine on a Saturday and listen to your customers. It can be enlightening, to say the least.

Many of my friends run their own successful companies. They sell carpets, boxes, printing, and computers. They range from operations with just a few employees to multimillion dollar corporations, but in one respect, many of them are the same. Nine out of ten of the owners are in their offices on Saturday morning. Often they are the only ones there! There are no secretaries to screen the calls, no blinking row of lights signaling three other calls on hold, and no pressing appointments. Some even go in on Sunday evening to get things ready for the coming week.

The point is that the top people in almost every business seldom work from nine to five. That is why they became successful! They come in early or work late. They may even go fishing one afternoon a week, then make up for it by putting in twelve hours on Saturdays. If you want to reach the real decision makers, work overtime. That is when you are more likely to catch them. An old maxim says, "The key to success is to work half days, and it doesn't matter whether you work the first twelve hours or the last twelve hours."

In a similar vein, calling at lunch time or after 5 p.m. can pay off for the same reasons. The person who screens calls may be gone, and maybe Mr. Hard-to-Get Prospect will pick up his own phone! One thing is certain: You can bet that most of your competitors are taking their leisurely lunches, killing time before their next appointments, or going home early.

Calling at odd hours reaches hard-to-get prospects on the phone!

And you win more sales!

CHAPTER 81

From Hot to Cold

At a recent trade show, I picked up stacks of literature about trophies and awards. The products of two companies stood out and I spent half an hour or more at each of their booths. I took their literature, and the salespeople took my name and said they would call me when I got back to my office.

Reps from both companies called at times when I couldn't take their calls. When I went to retrieve their messages, I found they had not left their numbers or the names of their companies. I could not locate the product brochures I had picked up. Of course, none of this really mattered because they would call me back—wouldn't they? I waited a week. No calls. I waited another week. Still no calls. Eventually I went online and ordered 300 award plaques for my company's annual convention in Las Vegas.

I liked the two salesmen I met at the trade show. They played golf! Their prices were very competitive, and I really wanted to do business with one of them. If only they had taken the trouble to make a follow-up call.

Often, when you make a follow-up sales call to a seemingly hot prospect like me, you get a cool response or even the cold shoulder. Why? Maybe I just got a traffic ticket, had an argument with my wife, or the kids might have kept me up all night. Perhaps my 800-number lines are ringing off the hook with complaints about a product I don't even sell!

The point is that even if you ask the prospect if it's a good time to talk and he says yes, in seconds it can turn to no. It may be that his secretary is motioning to him that he has calls on two other lines or that a hot prospect just walked into his office. Don't let a prospect discourage you the first time you call. It just may not be a good time!

Don't let the cold shoulder stop you from calling back!

Cunningly Clever Presentations

CHAPTER 82

Defining TRUE Communication

Brilliance without the capability to communicate it,
is worth little in enterprise.
—Thomas Leach

When you talk and the prospect listens, that's not necessarily communication. There are four steps that must occur in order for communication to actually take place during your sales presentation.

1. **A message must be conveyed.** Too often salespeople ramble on, enamored with the sound of their own voices, speaking volumes of text and saying nothing. Before commencing any presentation, you must have a clearly defined message that you want to convey. The simpler the message, the better—like "Buy now and this product will save you money!"

2. **"10-4 good buddy." A message must be received.** On CB radios, truckers and others signal to each other that a message has been received and understood using the code numbers "10-4." Salespeople are not as fortunate as there is no such recognized response from audiences to indicate that a message has hit home. But hit home it must or communication has not taken place. We've all listened to someone for minutes on end, only to have no recollection five

minutes later of anything we just heard. That's not communication.

3. **A message must be understood.** I was on a plane once with a woman who was flying to meet her son who had recently moved to Fayetteville. Unfortunately, when she called to find out why he was not at the gate to meet her, she learned from her daughter-in-law that they had moved to Fayetteville, Tennessee not Fayetteville, Arkansas. Your message must not only be heard but also understood. The old acronym KISS, for Keep It Simple Stupid, can never be put to better use than when presenting.

4. **There must be some reaction to the message.** What is it you want the prospect to do after hearing your message? Whatever reaction you hope to stimulate—like BUY NOW—should be spelled out loud and clear!

Unless your sale presentation is conveyed, received, understood, and acted upon, it has failed!

CHAPTER 83

Sales Secrets from Hollywood, Broadway, and Television

It's a fact that your success, not just in sales but in life, will be based largely on your ability to communicate with others—those above you and those below you, those on your team, and those you wish to attract, those you serve, and those who serve you. Master the skill of communication and the doors of opportunity will be flung open to you.

Ignore this fact at your peril.

Contrary to popular belief, not all great salespeople, speakers, or leaders start with strong communication skills. Winston Churchill, perhaps the greatest orator of the twentieth century, stuttered badly as a child and took speech therapy even as an adult. During one of his early performances at the podium he was so afraid that he actually passed out!

Great movies, no matter how good the performances of actors and actresses, are always based on great scripts!

Great comedians always have great gag writers!

Great speakers always have great speechwriters!

All of the great performers are backed by painstaking practice, tweaking, testing, and repetition until the lines flow to the audience smoothly and effortlessly from the tongue!

Many people think that giving a great sales presentation requires a gift of gab or a certain type of personality. Not so! Great presentations are in fact the product of planning, practice, and refinement. Like great performances on stage and screen, the best sales presentations are honed and tweaked over time. Sometimes the addition of a single line, testimonial, or disclosure can mean a huge jump in sales success. This is why testing should always be part of your presentation until you get it just right!

No matter how long you have been in the game, you can always improve your results by refining your sales presentation.

Type your presentation out, then look for areas where it could be made more impactful just as if you were writing a movie script! Then read it out loud—if you stumble over an awkward passage, you'll know it needs further fine tuning. This is a cunningly clever way to improve your sales presentations that few people will do, thus giving YOU who will do it an even greater edge!

Great sales presentations are always the result of great planning, scripting, practice, and repetition!

CHAPTER 84

Learning the Universal Language of Sales Success

You have people in front of you and you have their attention. But each and every prospect you encounter secretly harbors the very same unasked question: Why should I listen to you?

Your opening statements should always offer a clear benefit for the prospect. Your opening is, in effect, your ad for your sales presentation. Tell them quickly why they should give you their undivided attention for five minutes, fifteen minutes, or perhaps even an hour.

How will they be healthier, happier, richer, more effective people after listening to you? Will you show them the path they should take to increase their social standing, wealth, and happiness? Will you save them time, money, or effort?

Do you know the call letters for the world's favorite radio station? They're WII-FM, What's In It For Me?

The basic motivating force that drives nearly everybody is "What's in it for me?" You must understand that peoples' decisions are often exercises in positive selfishness.

The more wants you can satisfy, the more problems you can solve, the more needs you can meet, the more you can show what's in it for the prospect, the more successful you will be!

Look at the text of your typical sales pitch or record a couple of your presentations and listen to them. Are they written or spoken in the universal language of sales success?

All great salespeople speak "Benefitese," the universal language of sales.

CHAPTER 85

Anticipating Objections and Heading Them Off at the Pass

The objections section discusses the benefits of dealing with possible objections in advance. If you *know* that certain concerns will be in prospects' minds during your presentation, you are usually better off dealing with them as part of the presentation. Otherwise, prospects will tend not to listen to *your* points as their minds wander and they think about their own questions.

For instance, price is often a concern, so acknowledge it. Then show how the value your product or service provides far outweighs the cost. For example:

> *Mr. Prospect, if you are looking only for the cheapest product, then I'll be up front—we are not the right choice for you. You'd be better off with Company X or Y. However, if you are looking for the best value product, the one that will last the longest, print the fastest, and ultimately cost you less, we are definitely the right choice for you!*

Or

> *As I am sure you are aware, there are a number of developments around here that have gone bankrupt. That's why I think it's important to point out that our owner is extremely wealthy and has zero debt on the*

entire property. When you invest here you will have no worries about completion of the project!

A little negative disclosure not only removes unspoken objections, allowing the prospect to focus on your presentation, but also builds credibility by the fact you addressed the issue up front!

Don't be afraid to address typical prospect concerns in your presentation, in effect heading them off at the pass!

CHAPTER 86

Hit 'em with Both Barrels—Then Send in the Troops!

Charles Revlon, the great cosmetics magnate, once said, "In the factories we make perfume, in the stores we sell hope!" Of course, you'd come up with some pretty clever stuff too if you were sniffing perfume all day. But the fact remains that to sell anything, you must take basic features and turn them into something wonderful, desirable, and magical.

Organize your sales message around your most compelling points. Hit them with both barrels right away. If you don't capture your prospects' attention and interest with your first few points, it's almost certain they will be mentally adrift by the time you arrive at the last few. Arrange your benefits around your core story and clearly spell out each benefit so there can be NO confusion.

The basic building blocks of your sales pitch are the benefits of your product or service. These are the foundation of your presentation. The first lesson in almost every study of advertising starts, and often ends with, this point. You must list your product's benefits, not just its features. And you MUST know the difference.

Simply put, features are your product's basic qualities—for example, on a car, the size of the engine, miles per gallon rating, type of brakes, cargo space, and so forth.

Benefits Are Prospect-Centered

Benefits are the positive things people derive from your features. Highlight benfits in your presentation. For example:

> *With a V8 engine you will have plenty of passing power, while our Brembo brakes will bring you to a stop faster than any vehicle in its class. It has the industry's top safety rating and has enough cargo space for a family of five to travel in comfort and style!*

Make your sales presentation prospect-centered instead of product-centered.

Organizing Your Key Benefits

A great way to organize your benefits in a logical manner is to write all the key benefits of your company's offer on index cards, one card per benefit. Then simply arrange the index cards in order of importance and you will have a competent, ready-made sales presentation. You can then add details to each card as you enhance the presentation with the concepts in the chapters that follow.

Don't beat around the bush. Start your presentation with the strongest, most-compelling benefits you have. Then back up these with sub-benefits!

CHAPTER 87

Leave Nothing to Chance—Spell Out ALL Your Benefits in Detail

Stand in front of a large group of people and hold up a picture of a large group of people standing up and you know what happens?

Nothing. I've tried it!

Ask those in the audience who feel like it to stand up and a few people shuffle in their seats but rarely does anyone actually get up.

TELL everyone in a room to stand up, and to the last man, woman, and child, they all do!

What works with a live audience works the same way in a sales presentation. Show people a picture without an explanation and they will all draw different conclusions.

Provide wishy-washy instructions or benefits, and you'll get a wishy-washy response.

Expect people to finish off your benefit sentences for you, and it won't happen.

Assume your readers will take your features and turn them into benefits in their heads as you speed on your way to the next sentence in your presentation—it's simply NOT going to happen!

Let's take the feature statement: "Our country club is close to the freeway."

What did the salesperson want that sentence to mean? Or to put it another way, what image did the salesperson expect the prospect to see in his head?

a) The club is noisy and smoggy because it's near the freeway?

Or

b) The club is a quiet refuge but with convenient freeway access, cutting down his travel time so he can spend more time playing, not driving.

When salespeople get lazy and fail to spell out exactly what they mean, there's no way of knowing what conclusions prospects will draw. Saying your club is near the freeway is open to all kinds of interpretations, and not necessarily the one you want.

Spelling out what you mean, as is done in "option b" above, leaves absolutely no margin for error.

This is the way in which you must approach each feature, each fact, and each benefit that you wish to imprint in the minds of your prospects. Here's another example:

a) Our apartment complex has excellent fitness facilities.

IS NOT THE SAME THING AS:

b) Our apartment complex has excellent fitness facilities with state-of-the-art equipment to help you be in the best shape of your life!

The first assumes the reader knows what comes next; the second does not leave it to chance.

And, another example:

a) Gate-guarded community

IS NOT THE SAME THING AS:

b) A gate-guarded community, so private and serene that most residents rarely feel the need to lock their doors!

The second not only spells out the benefit but also adds to the general ambience of the sales presentation.

Can you really make every feature a compelling benefit? Well, if you can't, then don't bother including it in your presentation!

Let's take the fairly mundane features of the community pool and see how we can pack benefits into describing it:

> *Our junior-Olympic-sized pool provides you the luxury of a private pool without upkeep and maintenance hassles. We offer poolside food and beverage service, and our certified lifeguards insure a safe environment for your family. Plus you'll find the pool is a great place for your kids to make new friends—and for you to meet fellow residents and expand your social life!*

Leave nothing to chance or your prospects' imaginations.

The clearer you spell out your benefits for prospects, the more effective your sales presentation will be!

CHAPTER 88

The Incredible Two-Second Sales-Presentation Power Test

If you master the incredible two-second sales-presentation power test and nothing else, your investment in this book will be worth a hundred times what you paid.

That's why this simple test gets its very own page!

It's my age-old test for great copy and for great presentations. It's simply this: After each benefit in your presentation, ask the question, "SO WHAT?"

If the last two to three sentences you have just spoken do not answer that question, then rewrite the benefit because it is not compelling enough to be included in your cunningly clever presentation .

I cannot overstress the benefit of writing out your sales presentation and asking "So what?" after every few lines.

CHAPTER 89

Build Credibility and Reinforce Your Sales Message Using Outside Sources

Once you've made your key sales points, back up your position with logic, proof, independent reports, and anecdotes and testimonials from satisfied customers.

Quote well-known people or other customers who share or endorse your point of view. Give real-life examples of people proving your sales points.

Use magazines, newspaper articles, and reviews—as do the car dealers who always have a copy of *Road & Track* on hand with a positive review of the car you're considering buying!

Use written testimonials.

Use any tool you can find to add believability to your point of view.

For example, here is part of a sales script I wrote for the residential golf community of Black Diamond.

> *"Golf Week" ranks our community as the third-best place to live in the world if you love golf. Of course, I like to point out to people that at neither of the two places they chose above us can you play golf all year round... so I'm not sure how they rank higher since we have perfect weather nearly 365 day a year!*

> *"Golf Digest" rates our Quarry Course as one of the Top 100 courses in the world, and world-famous golf writer Dan Jenkins says our finishing holes are the best five consecutive golf holes anywhere in the world.*
>
> *What's really great, though, is that a lot of our members enjoy our Ranch course even more! Although it gets less publicity, it's really a great track!*

Here in a few short sentences I shared my opinion and quoted respected industry sources: *Golf Week*, *Golf Digest*, and Dan Jenkins. Pretty powerful company there, don't you think? But I also worked in the opinion of other customers and a plug for the other course!

The more different ways you can back up your sales presentation with personal anecdotes, quotes, articles, and third-party endorsements, the greater your chances of proving your point and successfully delivering your message.

CHAPTER 90

Past, Present, and Future Orientation

Undertanding pesonality differences among your prospects allows you to tailor your sales presentations to subgroups of prospects. Many personality systems are used in sales. One that is not covered in other systems is time orientation.

People differ in being past oriented, present oriented, and future oriented. (Past orientation is the rarest.) When you're presenting to each type, you'll be more successful if you emphasize their time perspective. For instance, for past-oriented people you talk about the glorious history of your company, or the battles that were fought around your hotel's location in the Civil War.

Present-oriented people show no interest in the past and don't often think about the future. They're interested in immediate benefits, not future profits. When you ask them about themselves, they focus on the present. When you sell to them you need to emphasize what's going on right now.

Future-oriented people will want to hear about the development plans for the product. They'll be interested in future updates and advancements. They find the present somewhat boring and live for future possibilities. They will not respond as well to descriptions of what's going on right now. They'll be more interested in what's coming down the line.

As you ask questions early in your presentation to build

rapport, listen for time-orientation cues. This allows you to add to what you learned from the prospect to further direct your presentation toward different time orientation styles.

Include references to the past, present, and future in your presentation to make sure you are reaching all of your prospects.

CHAPTER 91

Using Questions to Emotionally Involve the Prospect in Your Presentation

Most salespeople talk too much and don't listen enough. Giving a great sales presentation is more about helping people define what they want than being a great talker. By asking the right questions and being a good listener, you will significantly improve your sales presentation and learn how to adapt your presentation for each prospect.

In the Qualifying section, you learned to ask a lot of questions. The main purpose there was to find out whether prospects *were qualified* (had a genuine interest in buying your product or service and could afford it). Other questions were suggested in the Rapport section. People enjoy talking about themselves to a good listener.

Questions can also be an important part of your sales presentation by getting the prospects involved with your selling points. They can't just sit back and pretend to listen when you ask them questions. Often, even if they wanted to remain detached, good questions will "hook" them into considering your product more seriously:

- What do you like best about our product?
- What do you feel is the most important feature our product offers to meet your needs?

- What do you like best and least about your current supplier?
- What's your biggest challenge?
- On a scale of one to ten, how interested are you in our product based on what you have heard so far?

The more you can get the prospect talking about her wants, needs, and opinions, the more involved she will become in your presentation and the easier she will be to sell!

Ask your prospects questions—open-ended questions that can't be answered yes or no—to get them talking about the features and benefits of your product or service!

CHAPTER 92

Present Your Sales Message With Powerful Words—If You Want a Powerful Response

When giving your sales presentation, it's important that you don't use "wishy-washy" terms. Be precise in your message and your choice of words. Imagine Patrick Henry saying, "Give me liberty or give me death, I think." Changes the whole power of the statement, doesn't it?

Or how about Winston Churchill saying, "I have nothing to offer you except blood, sweat, etc., etc., etc." Would that kind of wishy-washy talk have motivated a nation into action? I think not!

"Take no prisoners!" is a much more powerful image than, "Take as many prisoners as you can and let me know how you did."

Make confident, bold statements; use clear precise wording. As legendary painter Pablo Picasso said, "In painting as in life, one should act with bold strokes."

Saying your resort is Michigan's *most* beautiful golf resort is ten times more powerful than saying yours is *one of* Michigan's most beautiful golf resorts.

Saying you have the *largest* selection in Orlando is a lot more powerful than merely being *one of* the largest in Orlando.

Exact numbers have more power and are more credible. If you can save most companies 27.5% on their energy costs, say so; don't round it up to 30%!

Another way to increase the power of most presentations is the use of repetition. The key theme is repeated over and over again, almost like a chorus in a song. This is where you should be using your Unique Selling Proposition (the one aspect of your product or service that distinguishes it from its competition)!

Always use definitive terms in your sales presentation and repeat key benefits using different words.

CHAPTER 93

How Simon and Garfunkel Can Greatly Improve Your Sales Presentation

Perhaps the most underused tool of powerful presenting is, strangely enough, not speaking at all.

Yes, the sound of silence!

In our efforts to get our points across, we often put forth an almost endless barrage of words without giving the prospect time to think or to let the words soak in.

The deliberate pause gives greater weight to the statement you have just made. It allows the prospect to actually think about what you just said rather than letting it go in one ear and out the other.

To make myself or others do this, I actually write words like STOP and PAUSE into sales scripts!

Remember that great Simon and Garfunkel tune when developing your sale presentation; use the occasional and timely sound of silence!

CHAPTER 94

Too Many Choices Spoil the Sale

Just as too many cooks spoil the broth, too many options spoil the sale!

Complexity is your enemy when making a sales presentation.

On a recent visit to a chiropractor I was given a choice of seven different pricing plans. I took one adjustment and told him I would think about it.

I'm still thinking two months later!

A company bidding for my gardening offered one of five different plans, depending on the level of service I wanted. I chose another company that offered only two levels of service!

A golf club I consulted with in Tennessee had 14—count 'em—14 different membership options!

Too many pricing options confuse your prospects. Confusion causes fear. Fear cause paralysis, not action! Give customers options, but keep them simple and clear in the only place that matters, their minds!

In the karate business, we offered three basic packages.

- a month-to-month no-frills program
- a four-month program that included a free uniform and belt

- a three-year black-belt-club program with a special uniform, patch, card, plaque, extra classes, and private instruction

People would typically sign up for the middle program since it offered the most value without a long-term commitment. They could try out the lessons for a while, then within a matter of four to six weeks almost everyone would step up to the black-belt club. The choices were very clear and obvious.

I sell my Marketing Commander sales and marketing program in three packages. I advise selling memberships, real estate, and just about anything else with three options: Here's a cheap lot, here's an expensive lot, here's a lot with a great view that's moderately priced.

Package in Groups of Three

Take a look at your offerings and group them into three distinctly different programs. If you have a more complicated product with, say, nine options, either simplify the offerings or organize the nine into three distinct categories. This way the prospect is always focused on smaller and easier decisions.

Too many pricing options confuse your prospects. Confusion causes fear. Fear causes paralysis, NOT action!

CHAPTER 95

The Demonstration—Getting the Prospect Involved in the Action

In the martial arts business, one of the most popular promotional events is a karate demonstration at a local school, mall, or fair. This usually involves a team of ten or more students performing self-defense moves, breaking bricks, and kicking through boards. Everyone stops what they are doing and gathers around the demonstration. They point, they ooh, they aah, and they applaud. At most demonstrations, the only thing they don't do is flock to sign up for lessons! Getting two or three new students out of an entire crowd is usually considered a good return. If everyone becomes so excited watching the demonstrations, why do so few buy the product?

Few people purchased after watching the demo because they had no *attachment* to the product. Watching a karate demonstration is like watching *Kung Fu Theater* on late-night TV. It's not real. It's just a show. It doesn't make the watcher taste the sweat. It doesn't make him feel the power. It doesn't make him yell. He doesn't get the thrill of breaking a board with a kick. He just watches the demonstration like a Sunday-afternoon armchair quarterback and thinks, "Maybe I could have done that," or, worse still, he looks at the demonstration and says to himself, "Gee, I could never do that." He is completely detached from the action.

Getting the Audience Involved in the Action

A friend was doing a karate demonstration at the local fair. I suggested that he break a few bricks to create some excitement and get as many people as possible involved in the actual demonstration. As a result, he had fifty children lining up to break boards, men punching padded shields, and women learning how to escape the clutches of an attacker. In short, he had the whole crowd participating. The result was nothing short of astounding. Thirty-seven new students enrolled during the two weeks immediately following the demo. This amounted to an increase of over 50% in his school's income. All of this happened simply because the audience *felt* the thrill of kicking and punching instead of watching someone else do it!

Obviously, if you sell cars, you let the prospect drive the car. If you sell clothes, you encourage the prospect to try on a dress or suit to see how great it makes him or her look. But if you sell computers, do you encourage the prospect to use the machine? Try it. If you are showing a house and you know the prospect likes to cook, linger for a little while in the kitchen. Don't just tell her it would be a good idea to buy the house. Let her feel it, smell it, taste it, hear it, and touch it for herself!

Whenever possible, get the people interacting with your product. Be creative. Find ways to involve your prospect in a demonstration so that it becomes *his own* demonstration.

The more senses you can bring into play during the presentation, the better your chances of making a sale!

Getting the prospect to interact in your presentation will significantly increase his emotional "buy in"!

CHAPTER 96

Quitting While You're Ahead

It seems that one of the toughest things for anybody to do is to quit at the top. The cunningly clever salesperson knows exactly when to stop presenting and start closing. The key is getting the prospect excited about your product. Once that has been accomplished, then close the sale. You must provide logical reasons why the purchase must be *today*. Then close! Continuing to talk after the prospect is ready to buy is overkill and often leads to lost sales rather than successful closing.

The Trial Lesson

The standard practice in the karate business was to give three free trial lessons to prospects and then sign them up. A lot of schools still do business this way, but I believe it hurts sales. First, it takes too much of the instructor's valuable time. Second, the prospect is never more excited than when you first demonstrate your product!

In my karate schools, I changed my free trial period from three lessons to two lessons, and then from two to one. After that, I cut the time it took to do the trial lesson from thirty minutes to about ten minutes. I found that I could get the prospect just as excited in five to ten minutes as I could in half an hour. How long can anyone maintain a high level of excitement anyway?

I had only one hard-and-fast rule about how long the trial

lesson should last: Just as soon as the prospect was kicking, punching, yelling, and laughing, the trial lesson ended. I cut it off right there and the prospect was left like a junkie needing a fix. She wanted more; she *needed* more! That was the time to take her to the office and explain how she could get more.

Finding the "Ridge"

When I lived in California, it was a 300-mile drive from my home to Las Vegas. My wife and I used to drive to Las Vegas regularly to meet friends who had flown in from the East Coast. That has to be about the most boring drive in the world—mile after mile of desert and rare patches of dried-out vegetation as far as the eye can see.

About twenty miles outside Vegas, the land rises and you drive over a ridge. Suddenly you see the glittering neon lights of Las Vegas spread out below you. Your spirits rise. You smile in happy anticipation. You start thinking about million-dollar jackpots, and you become excited and enthusiastic.

The only problem is, that feeling you had on top of the ridge is as good as it's going to get. As you near the city, you start to realize that instead of winning a million bucks, chances are you will actually go home with much less than you arrived with.

Learn how to spot the moment when your prospect comes over his own personal ridge, and then go for the close. Look for the right nod, smile, or gesture, and seize the moment.

Stop presenting when the prospect reaches his maximum level of excitement or interest— then close!

CHAPTER 97

The Yellow Brick Road to Closing More Sales!

You have the prospect captivated with your presentation. You've established your position with proof and maintained his interest with humor and anecdotes. You've used powerful language and he is in the palm of your hand. Now comes the $64,000 question: What do you want him to do?

The greatest percentage of sales are lost simply because people are never actually asked to buy. Lay out a plan of action before your prospects. Tell them the steps you want them to take. Keep it simple. Present them in an easily understood format. You know, 1–2–3, A–B–C. For example:

> *Mr. Wood, I'm going to give you a tour of the facilities. I'll give you a brief overview of what we offer and will get you set up with a course tour and a round of golf. After your round, I will sit down with you, answer any questions you might have and help you select which membership option is best for you and your family. Does that sound okay?*

This is the type of specific information people need in order to make decisions. Showing them a path is not enough. You must help them take the first few steps of the journey.

Explain the Benefits of Taking Action

As we all know people do things for *their* reasons, not yours. Help them by explaining in simple yet vivid detail exactly why they should follow the course of action you have prescribed. What's in it for them? Will they save money? Feel better about themselves? Increase their status in the community?

Ask for some kind of commitment. Challenge them to act in their own best interests. Challenge them to act in the interests of their family. Invite them to buy into the dream because without action, there can be no change in the status quo, and without a perceived need for change, there is no sale.

Provide a clear course of action for your prospect to follow!

CHAPTER 98

Spreading the Good Word

It is a luxury to be understood.
—Ralph Waldo Emerson

I'm sure that as a child you played a "telephone game" at parties where somebody said something in your ear and you passed it on to the next person, who in turn passed it on to the next. By the end of the line, the original message, "A dog called Spot has a ball in his mouth," is transformed into something like "A three-legged camel had spots the size of a baseball."

In many management training sessions, facilitators use similar exercises to show just how fast a simple message can be screwed up beyond belief. At one of the first conventions I had for my own company, I was stunned by the different versions of what I'd said that were circulating around to those who had not attended and I vowed never to let my message get lost again!

The key to making sure your message hits home, not only with your prospects, but also with all the people with whom they will come into contact, is to help them do the job right. Your message (or more likely, some variation of it) could be going home to a spouse or going back to a boss or partner. In the case of younger prospects, it might mean running your offer past their parents, siblings, or friends. Provide prospects with the tools to help them accurately communicate your message.

To accomplish this, you can use tools like an audio presentation to take home, or a carefully crafted handout or brochure. (Note the words *carefully crafted.* Most corporate brochures couldn't sell a nun a candle. (My book *Cunningly Clever Marketing* has lots of great info on brochures.) Other tools could be a PowerPoint® file or an online demo, even handwritten notes or a personalized email follow up. It has to be something more than the prospect's recollection of what they THINK you said!

You cannot afford to let your prospects deliver their versions of your sales presentation to others involved in the decision. Make sure you provide them the right tools with which to pass on your message— the way YOU want them to state it!

CHAPTER 99

Encourage Feedback

Communication is not, of course, a one-way street. You must elicit feedback and encourage dialog at all levels:

- Invite feedback via letters.
- Invite feedback via fax.
- Invite feedback via email.
- Invite feedback in your blog and twitters.
- Invite feedback via phone.
- Most important, invite feedback in person.

Like great coaches, all great salespeople look back on any sales presentation and analyze game performance. From this feedback and from honest personal appraisal, the cunningly clever salesperson realizes what worked and what didn't. Which jokes got a laugh and which ones got blank stares. What you made clear as noted by approving nods, and what must not have been so clear as demonstrated by the number of questions or puzzled looks you got on a specific point.

Where possible, record your presentation so you can go back later and critique your own performance. Using the cunningly clever sales techniques in this section, a few small changes in style and presentation can turn an ordinary sales presentation into an experience that motivates people to action.

Always solicit feedback on your sales presentations and always be looking for tiny tweaks that will make them more effective!

CHAPTER 100

How to Handcraft Your Cunningly Clever and Astonishingly Effective Sales Presentation

Few salespeople ever take the time to develop a professional written sales presentation. Instead they wing it, hitting most key points some days, forgetting a few the next. Even those who know their product inside and out will find that without a written, structured presentation, they miss asking key questions, forget to use important tools like testimonials and take the look of their office for granted because that's the way it is! Because of this unsystematic approach, they fail to reach their true sales potential, leaving tens of thousands of dollars on the table every year!

By focusing on developing a well-thought-out and structured presentation for your business, the payoff will be huge for many years to come!

While you will have to customize your sales presentation to your specific circumstances, you can use the tools in this section to build an excellent foundation for your presentation.

The more structured, professional, and practiced your pitch, the more success you will have.

8

The Lost Art of Storytelling

CHAPTER 101

The Lost Art of Storytelling — Connecting to Your Prospect with Power!

In this section we are going to tackle one of the most powerful secrets in sales—the art of storytelling. You'll discover how to wrap your product or service in a great, spellbinding story—a story that enthralls your prospects long enough to get your benefits and sales propositions across. As with a good book, you just can't put down a great sales story. It should hold the prospect riveted, eager to find out what happens next.

Few companies have sales stories that are anything approaching compelling. Instead, almost all are mind-numbing, boring "corporate speak," designed to appeal to everyone and polarize no one, and therefore doomed to fail.

Products and services with great stories behind them are infinitely easier to sell. If you start to dig, almost every company has the story they need. It's sitting there in an old file, a faded newspaper article, a testimonial from a happy client, in the memory of a salesperson or in the casual remarks from a conversation you once had over drinks with the company's founder. It's a living, breathing story, one that will captivate your prospects' attention and allow you to make a sales pitch that they *want* to hear.

People Love Great Stories!

Since time began, people have loved stories. They painted them on walls of caves before they had the words to speak them. People listen to stories around campfires, at pubs, and 19th holes around the world. They sing them in songs and write them in books. Some of the best stories are handed down from generation to generation. Embellished and retold, they often live on for hundreds, sometimes even thousands of years.

This is true of every culture on planet earth, but it's very often OVERLOOKED by slick salespeople obsessed with style and image over substance and results!

The story is the HEART of your sales presentation. It's what you build your grabber, benefits, and offers around. It's the glue that makes everything else stick.

The best sales pitches I have ever heard were all built around great stories.

The best salespeople I ever saw were great storytellers!

The most successful companies in the world all have great stories!

If you want to sell more, the answer is obvious:

Build your offer around a great story!

CHAPTER 102

Build Your Sales Story Around Feedback and Comments from Customers and Clients

How have customers and clients used your product or service in a successful or interesting way? Very often a testimonial or feedback from a customer can be the basis for a great sales story. Sometimes it might just be a casual phone call that triggers a great story.

The following is an example of one letter from a sales pitch for my software company Marketing Commander that came about as a result of a telephone call I had with a business owner:

How an 80-Year-Old Golf Course Owner Kicked Some Texas Butt on the Internet!

I had a call recently from the 80-year-old owner of a golf course for whom we had designed a website. He told me that while everyone liked the look of the site, it was too hard and too time consuming for his staff to update with specials and promotions on a monthly basis.

He then asked me how we could solve the problem. "Should we," he wondered, "hire someone locally to update the site or pay you extra to do it? I have a staff meeting on Monday and I'd like to know how to move forward."

I asked if he had any computer experience. "Very litle," he replied, although he did have an AOL email account. I asked if he had 5 minutes--to which he replied, "Yes."

After connecting to the Internet through AOL, I had him log into his course's Marketing Commander with my user name and password. It brought up a simple list of every page contained on his club's website. I instructed him to click on the specials page. He did and it opened up a box with the word "headline" at the top. I told him to type "Bring Four, Pay for Three." Next, I had him type a week-long date range and the time (1 p.m. on) during which the special would be honored.

"Okay," I said. "See the little picture of the computer disk in the menu at the top left?"

"Yes" he said.

"Click it with your mouse," I said.

"Okay," he said.

"You have just updated your website."

"SHITTTTTT…Yoouuurrr kiddding meeee?" he said! "That's alllllll it takes?"

"I am not kidding; it's really that easy," I said. "Go take a look at your site."

He did and his special, date, and times were already live on his website. Total time passed since training had begun: 4 minutes and 47 seconds.

"My people were telling me that it takes some kind of brain surgeon to do this!" he barked.

"Well," I said, "with most websites it does, but not with Marketing Commander. Ours are simple to use!"

"Can you show me how to do that one more time?" he asked with just a hint of mischief in his voice, "There is something I forgot to do."

"Sure," I replied.

We logged in again and he went back to the specials page where, he added his INITIALS in block capitals as proof to his staff that HE had updated the website!

I'd like to have been a fly on the wall in that staff meeting!

But that's the beauty of a Marketing Commander site. They are not only the best websites in the world; they are the most user friendly. Anytime, day or night, you can update your site free of charge with less than 5 minutes training. That saves a lot of excuses!

Some of your very best sales stories will come from your existing customers; use them!

CHAPTER 103

Take an Everyday Event and Turn It into a Compelling Sales Story

Here's another example of a sales letter I use that contains a story about an interaction I had with prospects:

Recently I did a sales and marketing seminar to 109 golf club membership directors. Most were from high-end clubs in Naples, Fort Myers, Palm Beach, and other high-income locations in South Florida. Most (108) were women, most were--dare I even say it, middle-aged like me!

Most had been in their jobs for several years, so it came as something of a shock to me when I asked the question: How many of you have ever had any professional sales training?

You might expect to see a lot of raised hands. After all, the job of membership director is to sell memberships and their clubs depend heavily on the income they generate from the fruits of their labor. To earn bonuses they have to sell above and beyond the minimum, so you might think that even if the club failed to provide any sales training (and clubs rarely do), the membership directors might just have gotten the crazy idea in their heads to seek out some training on their own.

But only two membership directors raised their hands.

So I asked another question, a simpler question. How many of you have in the last year or two, read a sales book, any sales book?

Three raised hands!

So out of 109 professional membership directors only five had had any sales training in recent memory and none of them had taken specific sales training on how to sell memberships.

Isn't that INSANE? Their jobs, their clubs, and the lives of 50 other club employees depended on their efforts, yet the clubs weren't providing them with training to help them--training that could easily make the difference between success and failure in a very difficult economy!

In my experience, when most people are given the tools to help them do their jobs better, they gladly embrace them. That's why we created www.cunninglyclevergolfoperator.com, the online sales training program that clubs can use to instantly and effectively train their front-line staff--all their staff--how to sell!

A step-by-step guide, together with video and audios (audios which I might add are guaranteed free of spelling errors!) will catapult your staff to a new level of sales competence, and much more. Check it out!

Take your true experiences and turn them into compelling sales stories. Real stories have the power and believability to motivate because buyers can relate to them easily!

CHAPTER 104

How is Your Product Made—or What Makes Your Company's Service Different?

Is your beer cold filtered, shipped colder in special trucks, or brewed with Rocky Mountain spring water? Do you put it through a 25-point checklist to insure quality, use a secret recipe handed down for over a hundred years, or import choice hops from Bavaria?

Every company can tell the story of how their product is made. Often all it takes to gain a sales advantage is to focus on one key element that none of your competitors are talking about, even if they do the exact same thing as you.

Coors invented lite beer many years before Miller, but Miller was the first to exploit the story of beer with fewer calories.

Hertz was the world's largest car rental company, so Avis exploited their number-two position, with the storyline "We try harder!"

Consider the details of how your product is made. Write down the production process and look for key elements you can exploit in your sales story. It works just the same for services; look at all the elements that go into the service you provide: speed, experience, and guarantees, and write them all down. Very often key elements that don't mean much to you may mean a great deal to your prospects.

How did you come by this knowledge of your profession? What got you interested? Why is cold-filtered beer better? All it takes is one key idea to get an edge.

He who tells the story first, of why their production process, materials, or methodology is superior, usually enjoys a stronger position in the minds of customers!

CHAPTER 105

What Is Your Company's History? Who Started It and Why? What's the Story Behind the Story?

Very often the driving force behind a product or service and why it was created is a great story in itself. For example, Black Diamond Ranch is a high-end golf real estate development in Northern Florida, the centerpiece of which is a number of holes designed around the 100-foot rim of an abandoned quarry. You don't see a lot of 100-foot holes in Florida!

Here is an anecdote the salespeople at Black Diamond tell as soon as a prospect comes in the gate and looks at the magnificent quarry holes:

Isn't it spectacular?

The funny thing is that when the developer Stan Olsen first looked at this property back in the mid-Eighties, the man who owned the 1600-acre parcel of land didn't want him to see the 80 acres that made up the quarry in case it soured the deal. The seller thought it was useless land and he tried everything to steer Olsen away from that part of the property.

Once Olsen secured the deal he began using this "throwaway acreage" as the centerpiece of the Quarry Golf course and developed the world's finest golf community around it.

It's an interesting story that really gets people thinking about the genius of the vision and design.

What's the compelling story behind the story about your company, product, or service?

CHAPTER 106

What's Your Personal Story? Why Are You Involved with the Company You Sell For?

People buy from people they like. People they trust. People they think may have had the same problems and frustrations that they've had.

Kevin Strom who works for the golf division of my ad agency, Legendary Marketing, tells prospective customers the story of how my books and tapes tripled his income as a golf professional. Eventually he became so fascinated with the power of good sales and marketing techniques that he left his job as a golf professional to go and work for this company that had changed his life! It's a true and powerful story that resonates with the golf professionals and club managers that he talks with on a daily basis.

Here's a powerful sales story from world-famous horse trainers Linda and Pat Parelli. When Linda told me this story, I knew it would resonate with horse owners and I helped them craft it into a story that they now use in their marketing pieces.

> *After struggling with my thoroughbred for over two years, I was advised by a local trainer to "Put a bullet in his head!"*
>
> *Had I not met the end of the road with my beloved horse, Regalo, I would NEVER have met Pat Parelli!*

I would never have discovered that there is another way for you to get Astonishing Results from your horse—any horse, no matter what your problem!

A way that doesn't involve more chambons, martingales, draw reins, nose bands, or twenty different bits!

It's a better way...

A natural way...

A fun way...

And a way in which you and your horse will enter a SPECIAL NEW relationship that will change every aspect of both your lives for the better!

Today I ride the "hopeless case" without reins, without fear, and with JOY in my heart!

It all started 11 years ago, when, at the end of my rope with Regalo, a girlfriend talked me into buying a ticket to a horse "celebration" seminar run by a cowboy named Pat Parelli. Holding an English passport, I didn't have much hope that some Western-style rider was going to change my horse's behavior.

He didn't!

Instead he changed my entire world!!

No matter what type of problem you have with your horse, the Parelli method offers you rapid and lifelong improvement...

My Story

To read the story I have used for over twenty years to sell my sales and marketing knowledge, see *Cunningly Clever Marketing* or visit the www.CunninglyCleverMarketing vault section.

Personal stories that demonstrate why you are involved with a particular product, service, or company are among the most power sales stories!

CHAPTER 107

The Hidden Sales Secret of the Chinese Dragon

Telling a story is a good way to relax prospects, engage their full attention, drive home the selling points in a memorable way, and overcome objections and price resistance.

One fine California day two decades ago, I arrived at my karate school armed with a dozen new patches I had purchased from a martial arts supply store owned by my good friend David Miller. (The students sewed patches on their uniforms to personalize them, and the patches were always especially popular with the children.)

These particular patches featured a golden dragon on an orange background, and were about the size of a dinner plate—much larger than the majority of patches we sold. Ron, my assistant instructor, asked how much the retail price would be, to which I replied off the top of my head, "Fifteen dollars."

He asked how much I had paid for them. I told him they had cost me three dollars and sixty-five cents each. He shook his head and clucked like a chicken. Then he informed me that no one was going to pay fifteen dollars for a three-dollar patch no matter how large it was! Now that's just the type of challenge I happen to thrive on, and I quickly picked up the gauntlet. I made a small wager with Ron that all twelve would be sold by that very evening.

I put the patches up on the lobby wall where they would have maximum visibility to the students as they came into class. Just to make sure, as the first class entered for the day, I pointed out the new patches to a number of the kids. After class I was immediately approached by a mother on the subject of purchasing a dragon patch for her son.

"How much are the new dragon patches, Andrew? Peter would like one?"

"They are only fifteen dollars each, Mrs. Slater," I said, as I started to remove one from the wall.

"Fifteen dollars," she gasped! "For a patch?"

"Mrs. Slater," I said in mock indignation as I pointed at the dragon. "Do you know what this is?"

"It's a dragon," she said.

"Mrs. Slater, this is not just a dragon. In China the dragon is a symbol of good luck for an entire village. When Peter has this patch on his back, the dragon's luck will follow him to tournaments, to belt tests, and, of course, home where the entire family will benefit. This is a magical dragon patch."

As she started to laugh, I added, "On top of that, ten little ladies in China probably spent a month stitching this entire patch by hand." At this, she thumped me on the arm and said "All right, all right! Give me the patch." She paid in cash!

In retrospect, it may have been one of the best values she ever got for fifteen dollars. Her son was ecstatic and every time she came in and saw one of those patches her face blossomed into a smile. Incidentally, by the end of the night all twelve of the magical dragon patches had gone, and I made an additional $20 on the side from a wager with a certain assistant instructor.

The dragon certainly brought me luck—I'm not sure about the rest of the village!

There is a point. Although this whole incident was less than deadly serious, the fact remains that you can bring even the dullest, highest-priced widget to life by putting a little pizzazz in your presentation. The more personal the story, the better. Tell a prospect how the set of dishes you are selling changed your life. Tell a prospect exactly how a book, seminar, or video improved your life. Failing that, tell him how your product is specially made or about the special people who make it.

If you don't have a great sales story, make one up; people enjoy fiction just as much as fact!

(Note: I am not saying lie, just have some fun with it!)

CHAPTER 108

Stephen King's Secret to Stories That Sell!

Top-selling fiction writers like Stephen King are masters of storytelling. You can learn a great deal about how to improve your sales stories by using the same secret techniques they use to draw readers into their stories!

There are numerous techniques you can use to "zone in" your prospect on a subject, feeling, or place that will aid you in getting them involved in your sales pitch. Obviously these will vary based on your product or service, but following are a few examples.

Dates

Do you remember:

- the day man landed on the moon?
- the day the Berlin Wall came down?
- where you were on 9/11?
- the day you bought your first car?

Each of these events has very special meaning depending on your age. Few people old enough to remember forget where they were when they experienced each of these events! It zones people into a specific time, a feeling that can be shared by everyone.

This concept can be used simply by talking about the most recent sports event Sunday afternoon, something in the news, or something going on in your industry. Just make sure you can relate it back to the sale!

Feelings

Think for a moment of the song *My Way*. Whom do you see in your mind?

Elvis?

No, Elvis sang the song, as did Sid Vicious and a zillion others. But that song, written by Paul Anka, is forever burned in the minds of millions as Frank Sinatra's theme song. I bet you can see Ol' Blue Eyes right now, alone in the spotlight, impeccably dressed in a black tux and bow tie, giving it his all. When you think of that image and that song, doesn't it make you smile just a little? Doesn't it make you feel just a little more powerful? No matter what position in life a person holds, that song hits home and brings with it a certain glow, a certain feeling that can't be taken away.

Humor

Humor is another way to reach out and touch prospects, but it shouldn't be used just to get a laugh. It must connect to the presentation you are about to make. It also helps if you aim the humor at yourself. Self-deprecating humor makes you more human, more real, and avoids the possibility of insulting anyone.

For example, in the series of seminars I do for the Professional Golfers Association, I usually start off by saying,

"All I ever wanted to do was become a golf pro. Unfortunately, lack of talent held me back!" Then I go on tell how my career in sales and marketing grew out of my love of golf!

Use the proven techniques of master storytellers to enhance your sales story and gain your prospects' emotional attention!

CHAPTER 109

The Fine and Profitable Art of Painting with Words

Legendary storytellers, salesmen, and statesmen paint pictures with their words to make their stories come alive with power and emotion. If you study any of the great speeches of the 20th century, you will find them alive with imagery—images that people can relate to and see with a clarity that makes them real.

Winston Churchill did not merely say, "We will fight in Europe." He said, "We will fight them on the beaches, we will fight them in the hills, on the landing grounds, and in the air." He painted a very clear picture of all the places we would fight in order to gain victory!

Martin Luther King, in his "I Have A Dream" speech, did exactly the same thing to bring people together by touching on different parts of the country in his address. Instead of saying, "We have to pull the country together," he described landmarks in several different states, involving people on a much more individual basis.

Think for a moment of:

- the Statue of Liberty
- the Eiffel Tower

- the pyramids
- Big Ben

In the briefest of moments, we all mentally visited New York, Paris, Egypt, and London. Visualization is a powerful force in building rapport and gaining the full attention of your prospects.

While you speak in words, your prospect thinks in pictures. Employ images the prospect can relate to and they will quickly tune in to what you are saying.

To get a more vivid and powerful connection with your prospect, always paint with words when telling your sales story!

9

Cunningly Clever Deals: The Art of Win-Win Relationship Selling

CHAPTER 110

Creating the Perfect Sales Experience

The last thing I intended to do in Athens was buy anything other than a postcard. Although the cruise had been fantastic, I had started with a wallet full of money and had already had to hit American Express twice for more cash. What I had in mind now was a pleasant tour around the city in a cab and then back to the hotel to rest!

We saw the Acropolis, Olympic Stadium, and Temple of Jupiter. Despite lingering at our first stop over an hour, it seemed that we were quickly running out sights to see! But the driver had an idea. "Why don't we go downtown and look at some of the stores?" he suggested. "Athens has great shopping." Like a lamb to the slaughter, I agreed.

The taxi made a beeline to the center of the city and pulled up next to an expensive-looking store with Greek vases, gold jewelry, and assorted gods in bronze. The driver assured me that the owner was his best friend and to prove it promptly walked into the back room and returned with two cans of Mythos (Greek beer.) It was only 11 a.m., but what the heck, I was on vacation. So I took one, as did my wife. Then an attractive young woman appeared from nowhere with two glasses. The kids were each given a soda and moved to a quiet sitting area to play with their Gameboys™.

We gave a casual glance to the bronzes, statues, and vases. An attractive middle-aged woman came over and introduced herself; she was an American from the Midwest. After a pleasant conversation, she left and a handsome man appeared. Out of courtesy we asked him the price of a couple of items. The beer was just about gone and we were contemplating leaving when, suddenly, as if by magic, another two beers appeared. We started to move towards the front of the shop when Alexander introduced himself. He was the owner and just wanted to show us one piece of jewelry before we left. He brought out a gold chain in a Grecian style. It looked nice around my wife's neck but I had absolutely no intention of buying it.

Alexander was in his early fifties, handsome, charming, and spoke perfect English. He asked where we were from; we both said England. (We discovered early in the cruise that being English saves you at least 30%. Every merchant knows that English people are poor; it's the Americans who have all the money—at least that's the perception.)

Instantly upon learning we are English, Alexander skillfully and subtly changed his sales approach. He praised the taste of Europeans and brought out a beautiful gold necklace that he said was hand made that very week. Sensing that my wife was falling under his spell, I quickly pointed at a pair of gold earrings featuring the face of Alexander the Great.

As the conversation continued, Alexander asked me what I did for a living. I told him I teach people how to sell. He laughed and adjusted course again—now we were really bonding. He placed the earrings on my wife as he talked. He had six stores and his girls were at private school in England. No mention of price was made; in fact, price was very carefully avoided. He invited my wife to look in a mirror. I glanced around looking for the kids; the cab driver and the young brunette had them busy in the corner. He asked what I thought about the pieces. I said they looked great but that I didn't know the first thing about jewelry. He offered up an instant education.

Finally I asked the price; he took the code number and calculated the price. Inexpensive he said—$2,900 for the necklace $500 for the earrings. Not exactly my idea of inexpensive! Nobody said anything. My daughter appeared; she was bored—ah, the perfect excuse to escape!

Thinking quickly, Alexander gave my daughter an inexpensive trinket in a nice case. Having painlessly dispatched a potential sales robber, Alexander turned his attention back to us but said nothing.

By then I was hooked on the whole experience. The store looked great, the beer was cold, and the people professional. All were skilled in building rapport, and Alexander himself was a master salesman. I actually appreciated it. I sprang for the earrings, then asked him how much the taxi drivers get for bringing in their rides. He swore he pays them nothing, but gives them only the occasional good deal. That I didn't believe, but I didn't care!

I knew I'd been set up and sold, but it was all done so professionally that I actually enjoyed it!

Be a pro—allow your prospects to enjoy the sales experience. Products are products, but the experience sells!

CHAPTER 111

Realize What's Important to the Seller!

Last year, before setting off on a seminar tour, I went to a small local tailor to supplement my wardrobe. The shop was run by a family of Persians who loved to barter and loved to sell. I tried on some suits, picked out a couple of shirts, some ties, a pair of shoes, and several pairs of socks. Then we started to negotiate the price. As we were getting close to a price that I liked, the woman I believed to be the owner told me they had just sold the store to the Chinese couple that did the tailoring. She was just staying on to help for a few days. She then told me she could not go any lower on the price. She did agree, however, to do all the alterations free of charge. I paid and left.

A few days later, she came to my house to deliver my purchases. She immediately apologized, saying that she had to charge me an extra $95 for the alterations. I was a little annoyed. How could anyone come back after I had already paid in full and ask for more money, even if it was a small amount? She quickly offered to throw in a couple more shirts if I would agree to pay the $95. The value of the shirts would more than cover the extra charge, so I agreed.

I asked her what had changed her mind about the alterations. She explained with some embarrassment that the Chinese couple who now owned the store had been tailors for thirty years and could not bear the thought of doing alterations for nothing. They had no problem with discounting the suits or giving away $180 worth of shirts as long as the alterations were paid for. That was what was important to them.

What's important to you? Do you ever let that block you from making a deal? If so, you might want to reconsider.

Work to uncover what's important to your prospect.

You have to realize what's important to each party in the transaction in order to make the best deal possible for everyone!

CHAPTER 112

Going Up, Up, Up in Price Until You Get a Deal!

When the bottom fell out of the real estate market in 2009, many new developments were caught between a rock and a hard place. They still needed to drive prospects to their sales offices with their marketing and at least keep things ticking over, but they had little or no money to do it!

Two deals stick out in my mind and while both took nearly all year to complete, persistence and creativity paid off in the end. Both were very similar deals—I started with a $150,000 advertising and marketing proposal that was heavy on the digital side since that is the cheapest way to drive more traffic.

Both were turned down due to cost.

Rather than cutting the size of the deals as many salesmen might have done, I did exactly the opposite. I increased one plan to $250,000 and the other to $500,000, made them all encompassing, and offered to spread the payments out over 12 months.

The first was turned down at once, while the other lingered for a couple of months without an answer either way.

Now it was obvious that both places needed my marketing services and Legendary Marketing was a good fit, but I just couldn't get them to move forward with anything other than a website. Finally I came up with another idea and offered each a three-year plan, one at $250,000 the other at $1.2 million! But instead of cash I offered to take dirt, as dirt was the only thing they both had plenty of!

They both agreed instantly to the deal and I picked up four lots at one place and several premium lots at the other. Now dirt is not as good as cash, but it ain't a bad second. The last time I did this, the lots I took in trade increased in value by over 1000% in just five years before I eventually sold them. That just might have been the best sale I ever made!

Sometimes offering more is an easier sell than offering less!

CHAPTER 113

How the "Down Sell" Hooks a Prospect for Life

The first lesson I ever received on the benefits of selling for the long term occurred when I was about 12 years old. It took place in the golf professional's shop at Lilleshall Hall, a club in Shropshire, England. I was standing in the pro shop when a middle-aged man came in and started to look at golf clubs. The professional, Gwyllam Hardiman (a dear friend of mine to this day), enthusiastically greeted the man and asked if he could help. The man had just taken up the game a few days earlier and wanted to buy a set of Ping golf clubs. At that time, Ping clubs were in great demand in England and were very expensive compared to other major brands.

Gwyl asked the customer why he wanted Ping clubs, and he said he had been told they were the best. Gwyl agreed that they were very good clubs but suggested that since the customer had just taken up the game, it would make little difference to him what clubs he used initially. Instead of buying a new set, Gwyl suggested that the customer start with a used set, take some lessons, and play a few times to make sure he really was going to enjoy the game and continue to play. Then, when he had improved to the point that he could benefit from top-of-the-line clubs, he should come back and see him. In this way he would not waste a large amount of money on clubs he might never use.

I sat there hardly able to believe my ears as Gwyllam successfully talked a customer out of spending several hundred dollars. The customer ended up leaving with a set of used Wilson clubs purchased at a fraction of the price he would have spent on a new set. At best, Gwyl made forty dollars on the deal. I couldn't wait for an opportunity to ask him why he had done such a thing.

Gwyl smiled at me and said, "That man will spend more money in this shop in the next twelve months than any other three members combined." He was right. Although he had not even mentioned the possibility of giving the customer instruction, the man came back the following week to sign up for a series of lessons with Gwyl because he liked him better than the pro he had been taking lessons from at the driving range. While he was there, he bought a pair of golf shoes and some socks and shirts. Later he bought a new bag, golf balls, a cap, and a couple of swing training aids. When he signed up for a second series of lessons, both he and Gwyl were convinced he was hooked on the game, and Gwyl took back the used set he had originally sold him. Gwyl even gave him at a few dollars more than the original selling price as he traded them in on a new set of Pings.

The customer's game improved quickly and it was easy to see that he did, indeed, spend more money during the course of that year than any other three customers. Gwyllam treated everyone that way, so he had a very faithful clientele. Even though he did not give big discounts, or have a huge inventory or an easily accessible location, people came from far and wide to buy golf equipment and take lessons from him. Because of his attitude and his honesty, he had developed an excellent reputation and was the most financially successful golf pro in the area.

I think Mark Twain summed it up best when he said, "Always do right...that will gratify some people, and astonish the rest!"

CHAPTER 114

How the Down Sell Can Make Profits Rise

One of the products marketed by the Business Information Division of my martial arts company was a computer software program for school owners that cost about $900. Almost all of our prospects asked for a demo disk so they could try out the program before purchasing it.

As soon as a prospect asked for a demo disk, I would inquire how many students he had. If he said 150 or more, I either sent him a demo or tried to sell him a program directly. If he told me he had 50 or 60 students, which made his business a break-even operation at best, I tried to dissuade him from buying the computer program.

Why did I do this? The computer program would certainly have saved him time and trouble, but with only 50 students this instructor had plenty of time on his hands anyway! His biggest problem was shortage of cash! It made far more sense to sell this customer one of my business manuals for $150 because I knew it would quickly increase his business and his profits. My manuals were full of ads, flyers, sales scripts, and proven techniques for success. In the short term I made $750 less in gross sales, but let's take a look at the long-term effects of this strategy.

Effect #1: The customer is amazed and delighted that I have talked him out of spending $900 and persuaded him to spend only $150. It creates an excellent bond of trust.

Effect #2: The manual works and the customer calls back very quickly to order other more advanced manuals in the series at a cost of $150 each.

Effect #3: Before long, the customer has so many students that he really needs the computer program. And now he can even afford to buy it!

Considering the customer's best interest is not always a good short-term sales strategy from a financial point of view, but combined with the appropriate follow-up, it is always the best and most profitable long-term strategy.

The world's best salespeople help others make decisions that are good for them!!

CHAPTER 115

Name Your Price

Because my business consulting company was the first of its kind in the martial arts field, I often encountered instructors who had never attended a business seminar and could not conceive of the idea of spending between $595 and $1595 to go to one. In cases like these, to establish my own credibility and confidence in my product, and to disarm and relax my prospects, I let them set the price.

> *Let me do this, Mr. Prospect. I am so sure you will receive thousands of dollars worth of information, I am prepared to offer you a very special deal. Come to the seminar and listen to the information I provide for helping your business and your income grow quickly. At the end of the weekend, write me a check for whatever you believe the information to be worth to you. If you feel it is not worth the price I have set, then I will trust you and accept without question whatever you write on the check. There is only one stipulation. If you, as I believe you will, find the information is worth far more than the $595 I am asking, I expect you to make out the check for the higher figure. Does that sound fair to you?*

What can a prospect say except yes. You are asking him to set the price. It's a no-lose proposition for the prospect and a chance for him to benefit from your knowledge. In all the time I have used this close, I have only been stiffed once, and I was only paid less than the advertised price of the seminar on two occasions. In every other case, I received full compensation and moved on to an even more profitable relationship with the clients I had won over with this approach. I am still waiting for a client to pay me more than I asked for, but I'm sure it will happen eventually!

Most of the sales I made in this manner would not have been completed had I not shown such faith and confidence in the product I was offering. As it happens, the prospect often signed up at the regular rate after seeing how confident I was.

A couple of days after I wrote this (the power of mental energy, no doubt) I received this unsolicted email!

> *Andrew Wood, how the hell are you? It has been a long, long time, about 17 yrs. I still tell the story of how you convinced me to drive all the way to Dallas (600 miles) for one of your seminars, and if I was not satisfied at the end, I would pay you nothing. You also promised that with the things I learned at that seminar I would make my seminar fee back in one, yes, one, week! When we sat down to dinner I paid you. I returned home and made my seminar money back that week!*
>
> *Thanks,*
>
> *Larry Lockhart*

**How much do you believe in your product?
Enough to make an offer like this?**

CHAPTER 116

The Golden Anchor

Always ask for a deposit. In sales, any type of commitment you can persuade a person to make is a hundred times better than no commitment at all. When I first started to sell martial arts lessons, I was like a pit bull when I asked the prospect to leave a deposit! As I became more skillful, I was a lot more confident and did not have to work so hard at it.

Once I looked after a friend's studio for a week while he was on his honeymoon. It was in a much less affluent area than my own school and therefore I had to deal with a very different clientele. A lady walked in with a child of nine or ten. It was mid-morning and I was free, so I gave the child a trial lesson on the spot.

He did well, had fun, and his mother was pleased, so I took them both into the office and made my presentation. I could tell right away that maybe we had a problem with the investment. She said she would get back to me on Saturday. I told her that I could not guarantee a place for her child later in the week and that in order to get a free uniform you had to sign up on your first visit. At that point, I told her if she left a deposit, I would make an exception and guarantee both a place in class and a free uniform.

She took a coin purse out of her handbag and opened it up. It contained a dollar bill and some small change. She poured the coins on my desk and counted out one dollar and ninety-eight cents in coins—for a grand total of $2.98. She looked at me hopefully and asked if that would be enough. I took the $1.98 in change and handed the dollar bill back to her. (Never take a person's last dollar; it's bad luck.) "That will be just fine," I said. With that, I stuck a tag with the child's name on a uniform and made a big production out of putting it in my desk drawer so it would be there when he came back to sign up. Sure enough, on Saturday they came back to pay the balance. Over the years, I have taken all kinds of down payments but this was the lowest.

This technique has worked successfully over and over again. In all the times I did this, I can recall only once or twice when a prospect who left even the smallest deposit did not return; and you must concede, $1.98 is a pretty small deposit!

Because she left a deposit, she came back. Her child enjoyed the benefits of the school, and my friend enjoyed the benefits of the income.

Always ask for a deposit. Any commitment is better than no commitment!

CHAPTER 117

The Merchant of Florence

A few years ago, just before the euro was adopted by Italy, my wife and I visited the ancient city of Florence. The place was amazing: churches, cathedrals, plazas, and streets a thousand years old in better shape than Highway 200 near my Florida home! And shops, lots of shops. Florence is famous for it's leather goods and it was only a matter of time until my wife fell under its spell and just had to take something back home to remind her of the visit.

My hopes that a T-shirt with "I've been to Florence" on it might suffice were quickly dashed. So too was the hope that a handbag or leather belt might do! Both were in great supply and at very reasonable prices. By coincidence, the hotel my wife had picked was just one turn away from the street market that wound in and out along the ancient streets for miles.

We wandered for hours down the twisting stone streets that reeked of history. I must admit that I too fell under its spell and after street upon street of leather jackets, belts, handbags, and T-shirts, I finally stopped at a stall selling leather belts.

Once I had purchased my belt, the die had been cast and my wife, sensing the spending moratorium that I had established early on in the trip was already broken, started looking at the area's leather goods with renewed interest. I suggested a belt or perhaps a nice leather handbag, but it seems a leather jacket had caught her eye.

I had made the mistake this particular day of wearing a bright yellow shirt embroidered with a Ferrari logo. As we walked on, a young man spotted it and immediately told me in English that a better deal waited beyond the stall for anyone who would wear the Ferrari name with pride. We fought our way through the leather coats in the stall into the store behind. The young salesman had assumed we were Americans and started speaking English. He told us how all the stuff you could find in the market was the same but that inside the store of Rosso the goods were truly one of a kind and still at incredible prices.

Now let me digress. Before embarking on this trip, my wife—as with most women, embodied with a keen shopping gene—advised me about Italians. I was not to accept the price they offered but instead was to hem and haw, plead poverty, and keep asking for a better price no matter what they said. To help me in my quest for a better deal, my wife quickly found a peach-colored leather jacket that was exceptionally nice. Once she saw it, she announced that she liked it. She tried it on found it felt wonderful. To "help" my negotiating stance even further, she went into a monologue about how as soon as you see something that looks like it was made for you, it's bound to be a match made in heaven.

I unenthusiastically asked the young salesman for the price. He responded with a laugh and a smile and brought out his calculator. It seems that Italians don't believe in price tags. He came back with a figure of 500,000 lira which, of course, was quite unacceptable, even though it was half of what it would have cost in any American store. (A cup of coffee was 8,000 lira back then!)

I told him that I could never afford such a price, whereupon he laughed at my predicament and pointed at my Ferrari shirt (I knew I shouldn't have worn it). I said I needed a better deal. He instantly offered discounts for not using American Express and for using cash. "Come on, you can do better than this. I can buy this in America for that price," my wife said with all the conviction of Barney accepting a free vacation in Jurassic Park.

The astute young man asked if it were not so that we were English. We explained that we were but lived in America, and thus still qualified as poor Brits, not rich Americans. At this point he decided to hand us over to the owner, Rosso, a charming, handsome man in his late forties with every bit the finesse of the nice Greek gentleman who sold my wife the $500 Roman earrings while the taxi driver babysat my kids with a bottle of ouzo!

The calculator magically appeared in his hand again, and picking up on what he had already heard, he delivered the price in pounds. (Which I had to calculate back into dollars in my head to avoid more confusion.) He had lowered the price by 16,000 lire—the price of two cups of coffee, a fact that I quickly pointed out to him. "My friend," he said, "the jacket is one of a kind; it's the only one of its color in all of Florence. It is handmade and a very fair price. You don't care about the discount any more than I do. But because it's the marketplace, you want to haggle. It's expected, but we both know that at this point the price is really not important."

I laughed out loud; I love a professional salesperson. I gave in on the spot and the truth of the matter is the price was already very fair. My wife, of course, was delighted with her purchase and we adjourned to the nearest restaurant for lunch, where frowning, she asked, "Why didn't you beat him up for a better deal?"

Cunningly clever salespeople realize that there are customers for whom you don't have to cut prices. Understand these customers and they'll appreciate a good deal without grinding you down.

The fact of the matter is, when the deal is right, the price really doesn't matter!

10

Cunningly Clever Ways to Deal with Objections

CHAPTER 118

Sales Alchemy—Turning Objections into Gold

Objections are a necessary part of the sales process. Learn to overcome them and you will massively increase your closing rate and income! Unfortunately, many salespeople take objections personally and their ability to complete the sale is adversely influenced by these negative feelings. They allow themselves to become flustered and upset by the prospect's rejection, attitude, or tone.

Top salespeople realize that objections are a natural part of the sales process. While we would all prefer for prospects to come in with check or credit card in hand, it's natural for people to have questions or concerns in any major purchasing decision. These concerns are generally expressed as objections.

To start improving your techniques, re-frame in your mind how you think about objections. Think of objections not as rejections but as stepping stones taking you across a river. By placing one stone in front of the other you can get to your final goal without getting wet!

An objection is nothing more than a question in the mind of the buyer that has to be defined and answered. It gives you the chance to clarify or improve your presentation.

A large proportion of prospects will procrastinate about making buying decisions by raising objections. You must overcome these "delaying actions." Some objections mask a real or perceived problem (often associated with money) that the prospect will try very hard to conceal. Learn to recognize these "smokescreen" objections and isolate the underlying problem by asking questions. Others may not be qualified or do not have the authority (have to ask the spouse or boss). More difficult is when they don't want to tell you that they don't know you well enough (you haven't built trust) or they don't think it's worth the money (you haven't built value).

Some objections arise as the result of nothing more serious than a lack of understanding. In these cases, it is necessary to further define and explain the benefits of your product in clear and simple language. Use your brochure as the excellent business tool it is. Put it in front of the prospect and check off the listed benefits, giving a short explanation of each benefit as you go. When features and benefits are there in black and white, any misunderstandings should soon vanish. As Oliver Wendell Holmes said, "Every person's feelings have a front door and a side door by which they may be entered."

Above all remember this when dealing with rejection:

Objections are not personal. Prospects are turning down your current sales proposition, NOT you as a person!

CHAPTER 119

5 Steps to Successfully Dealing with Objections

I never learn anything just by talking. I only learn things when I ask questions.
—Lou Holtz

There are five important steps to remember when dealing with objections.

1. Listen carefully to the objection. Resist the temptation to jump in before you have heard the full objection. Use active listening techniques like nodding in understanding to show you are fully engaged in what your prospect is saying. Sometimes the prospect will talk himself out of an objection before you even say a word.

2. The first thing you should do after an objection has been voiced is thank the prospect! This changes the tone of your interaction from adversarial to cooperative. It shows that you're not defensive or trying to avoid the objection.

For instance, you could say:

- "I'm glad you brought that up."
- "Thanks for asking that question. It gives me the chance to explain..."

3. Never argue with a prospect. Remain calm and pleasant. They may just want to be listened to.

4. Isolate the objection. If the objection is unclear, as in, "Well, I have to think about it," then ask more questions to isolate the real objection. You must attempt to get the prospect to voice his objection in tangible terms like, "I think the price is too high," "I must get approval from someone else," or "Your competitor made a lower bid." When there are several objections on the table, many times most of them are minor. Don't be distracted with secondary objections. Focus on finding the major wants and the major objection.

5. Counter the objection with an inescapable solution. When you have all the information you need, you can deal with the root of the objection using carefully thought out and scripted answers that clearly demonstrate a benefit to the prospect. Remember there can only be one perfect answer to any question!

Use this five-step process to effectively clarify, then eliminate, objections.

CHAPTER 120

Anticipate Every Objection—Then Develop a Systematic Way to Deal with Each of Them!

The best way to escape from a problem is to solve it.
—Brendan Francis

Many objections can be dealt with in the sales presentation by bringing them up and solving them before the prospect does. This neutralizes the objection before it is even voiced. Objections that can't be dealt with during the presentation should have been anticipated and a perfect answer scripted out as the response. In a good sales system, there can only be one perfect answer to any objection.

The answer to each objection should be carefully crafted to be the best answer possible, then learned and used exactly as scripted by everyone on staff. This is the type of approach used by Disney, Ritz Carlton, and the world's best companies for a simple reason: It works!

This may sound very rigid, but if you think about it, it's true at least 95% of the time. Sure, intuition and experience can come into play 5% of the time, but 95% of the time a well-orchestrated approach will produce better results. That's why movies have scripts. That's why comedians have scripts and practice them so they don't sound like scripts—95% of the jokes you ever heard delivered, from Johnny Carson to Jim Carrey, were scripted, rehearsed, practiced, and timed to be delivered to appear that they were told spontaneously.

Let me give you an example of a scripted response to an objection. Suppose a membership prospect at a golf club asks the simple question, "How long does it typically take to play a round of golf at your club?" (Four hours would be typical, but way slower than I like to play.)

Now let's look at how three different people could choose to answer that simple but deadly question.

A) It takes about 4 hours and 30 minutes.

B) It depends on what day you play: sometimes it's fast; sometimes it's slow.

C) We are committed to a pace-of-play policy that ensures maximum enjoyment for all of our members.

All of these are possible answers to the question but only one is actually the very best answer. The answer that does NOT turn off the prospect mentally IF he happens to be like me and hates slow play! The best answer, C, will produce better results for you than either of the other two answers or an off-the-cuff answer every time.

Here are some other examples where C is always the best answer of the three:

What kind of gas mileage does this car get?

A) 18 in the city.

B) 34 on the highways.

C) It gets the best mileage in it's class.

How long will it take me to lose twenty pounds?

A) 12 weeks.

B) 6 weeks.

D) Our program allows you to lose weight as fast or as slowly as you are comfortable.

How much do you think my property will appreciate in the next few years?

A) I really don't know.

B) I'm not allowed to say.

C) All I can really tell you is what's happened in the past, and in the past, the appreciation in this development has always been substantial.

What if, when I get home, my spouse doesn't like it?

A) I'm sure she will...

B) I don't think that will happen...

C) Our 100% money-back guarantee removes all risk; if for any reason she's not delighted, simply bring it back for a full, no-questions-asked refund.

Now this doesn't mean that some people won't follow up with a more probing question that you have to answer more specifically, but 80% of them won't! What's more, you will make more sales by giving answers that do not exclude your prospects from buying because the specific answer was not what they wanted to hear!

Often many of the questions people ask are not that important; they ask so they seem like intelligent consumers. It's expected that they ask questions. Many are irrelevant to their main wants and needs, but answer them wrong and you blow the sale!

You can take a teenager and turn him into a sales genius by providing scripted answers to every question. If you are already a sales professional, this exercise can dramatically increase your income. But remember there is only ONE perfect answer to any question: Find it!

You must anticipate every objection, and write the perfectly scripted answer for each!

CHAPTER 121

"Fast Forward" Your Prospects to Help Them Understand and Get Emotionally Involved in the Benefits of Action

The biggest problem in the world could have been solved when it was small.
—Witter Bynner

To overcome an objection, it's very helpful to involve your prospects emotionally in how their lives will improve from the moment they agree to your proposal. This is particularly true when dealing with money issues. By "fast forwarding" your prospects into the future, you can help them see how different their lives will be if they buy your product or service.

> *Mr. Prospect, on average a Marketing Commander website increases our customers' database of leads by 300% in six months or less. How do you think that would affect your business? How much extra money would you make next year with three times the leads as you had this year?*

Let them think about the future and answer the question, then expand on their positive response further.

Prospect: *If I got 300% more leads, I'd certainly expect to get some business.*

Salesperson: *Sure, you'd get whatever closing percentage you have now on a lead, but you'd have triple the leads. That sounds quite exciting to me. What do you think?*

* * *

Salesperson: *Ms. Prospect, if you were to join our club, a club with over 500 active members, how much business do you think a sharp lawyer like yourself might pick up, even by accident, in your first few months of networking with your fellow members?*

Prospect: *I am sure if I joined the club I could pick up some business.*

Salesperson: *Some business! I'd be shocked if you didn't pay for your membership in the first couple of months alone!*

* * *

Salesperson: *Mr. Teenage Prospect, what do you think your friends (girlfriend) will say at your graduation party when you show up in this red convertible?*

Prospect: [Beaming wildly] *It would be awesome!*

* * *

Salesperson: *Mr. Prospect, if you invest in this audio program, how much more fun will your trip to Spain be next year knowing that you can speak the language?*

Prospect: *It would certainly solve some problems.*

Salesperson: *Not only will it solve problems, but with additional language skills you'll be able to negotiate better deals on everything, easily covering your investment in our product.*

Fast forward your prospects into a future that helps them see, hear, feel, and live the benefits of your product or service!

CHAPTER 122

"Fast Forward" Your Prospects to Help Them Prevent the Loss Associated with Inaction

Fear is the most powerful of all emotions. People are far more likely to work to avoid a loss than to obtain a gain; therefore, there are many times when you must "fast forward" your prospects into seeing what will happen if they do *not* take action.

Salesperson: *Mr. Prospect, you already realize that the technology you have is antiquated and not providing the results you want. If you don't invest in new technology now, don't you feel you will continue to lose productivity and put yourself in an even worse position down the line?*

Let him think about the future and answer the question, then expand on his negative response further:

Prospect: *I suppose that might be true.*

Salesperson: *I assure you it is true. By acting now you can avoid a host of bigger problems down the line.*

* * *

Salesperson: *Ms. Prospect, you have already said the car you are in now is unreliable. What will happen if it lets you down in the middle of nowhere or late at night? Don't you worry about that?*

Prospect: *Yes, I do.*

Salesperson: *We can eliminate all that worry by simply going ahead with this deal. And you'll get a five-year warranty with free roadside assistance included.*

* * *

Salesperson: *Mr. Prospect, if you don't enroll in our program to increase your skills and marketability, do you think it will be any easier to get a job six months from now, with no additional qualifications?*

Prospect: *It's really tough to find work right now!*

Salesperson: *I hear you, but I assure you that learning another language and adding "bilingual" to your resume will give you an edge in many interviews. Let's do it!*

* * *

Prospect: *I think I might wait until next year to buy.*

Salesperson: *Mrs. Prospect, if you leave it until next year, you'll have one year less to enjoy it. The best time to buy is when you need it—which I'd say is now—wouldn't you?*

* * *

Salesperson: *Miss Prospect, we all know that prices go up. If you wait until next year, you'll almost certainly be paying at least three to five percent more. Why waste that money by procrastinating?*

Prospect: *Do you really think the price will go up that much?*

Salesperson: *That's been quite typical. The cost of raw materials keeps going up. Investing now will be like money in the bank.*

Fast forward your prospects into a future that helps them see, hear, feel, and live the negative consequences of not buying your product or service!

CHAPTER 123

The Feel-Felt-Found Solution

One of the most powerful objection busters in the business is the Feel-Felt-Found solution. It can be adapted to handle many different types of objections.

When the prospect raises an objection, you listen attentively then follow up using these three agreeable steps:

1. "I understand how you FEEL." This statement avoids being argumentative and takes prospects' objections seriously. It tells them you were listening and shows that you do indeed have their best interests at heart.

2. "Many of our clients FELT that way before they invested in our services. For instance, Mr. Miller is in your line of work [church, age group, or other category]." This shows prospects that their concerns are valid and the fact that you name other customers they can relate to who had the same concern builds trust in you. "He worried about that but..."

3. "What he FOUND was that... [your answer] there were lots of people with [concern]. However, his family enjoyed the club facilities, the contacts were valuable to his business, etc."

Here are some examples that put all three steps together:

> *I understand how you **feel** about our company having a $5,000 set-up fee while others do not. In fact, last year we were working with XYZ company from your*

> *state and their marketing director* ***felt*** *exactly the same way as you do. However, he* ***found*** *that being able to track the effectiveness of his ads by using our Marketing Commander solution saved him twice that much in the first month alone. And ten times that amount over the first year. As you know, no one else in the industry offers the ad- and phone-tracking features that we do. How much do you think you would save if by using our Marketing Commander technology you could cut out the 50-60% of your ads that are not effective?*

Or

> *Dr. Smith, I understand how you* ***feel*** *about the cost of membership. In fact, just a couple of months ago I was talking with another prospective member, Dr. Johnson, and he* ***felt*** *the same way you do. However, what he* ***found*** *was that on joining the club he instantly picked up more patients, easily paying for his yearly membership in the first couple of months alone!*
>
> *Don't you think that a golf club might make an excellent source of business for a chiropractor like yourself?*

Or

> *I know how you* ***feel*** *about the cost of upgrading to our silver or gold levels. A lot of people* ***felt*** *that way before they changed. But what they* ***found*** *was that the additional convenience of receiving the instructional information on audio and in manual form more than makes up for the additional investment.*

The feel-felt-found approach has been proven for over 50 years as a good way to respond to almost any objection. It allows you to take your winning story from current customers and create a personal solution that your prospect can identify with.

The feel-felt-found solution is one of the strongest techniques for dealing with objections. Add it to your repertoire!

CHAPTER 124

Using Testimonials to Let Your Customers Help You Solve Objections!

Written testimonials can be invaluable in helping you solve all kinds of objections. Nothing is quite so powerful as a letter from a satisfied customer that addresses the very issue that is holding your prospect back from making a decision. You can tell him of another customer's success, but nothing beats that customer telling his own story in good old black-and-white text on his company's letterhead!

If it's in print, on letterhead, it has to be TRUE!

Gather a portfolio of letters from your satisfied customers. Together they should address all the objections that your prospects will have. Ask satisfied customers to address particular issues when you request testimonials. Failing that, write the testimonial out for them based on your interactions with each customer and then ask their permission to use them.

Your portfolio of testimonials will be impressive by itself. You could have them framed and hung in the lobby area or in your office. You could have them in a three-ring binder on a coffee table. My dentist does this to great effect!

By organizing your testimonials according to type of objection, you can use them when specific objections are raised. For instance, after you have answered a couple of objections, as a change of pace you might say, "Instead of my answering that question, why don't I let one of our current customers do it for you?" Then bring out the relevant testimonial from your file, drawer, briefcase, or laptop with the relevant passages highlighted! For example:

> *Why don't I let one of our customers answer your concern? This one here is from Ashley Martin, CEO of ACME Corp. "I can't tell you how excited everyone is now that we actually have a way to track all our print advertising. Using Marketing Commander is saving us a small fortune every month by clearly showing us which ads make the phone ring and which do not!"*

This works for all kinds of businesses involved in face-to-face selling and can even be used over the phone by quickly emailing a prospect the relevant testimonial as a PDF file. You can also email several testimonials prior to your call to build credibility before you even start talking.

Testimonials are one of the least used yet most powerful tools for handling objections. Get yours in order, ready for action!

CHAPTER 125

Third-Man Objections

An obstacle is something we see
when we take our eyes off the goal.
—Anonymous

A key decision blocker that is often overlooked is how other people's feelings and views may affect the buying decision of your prospect. Where most large personal purchases are concerned, the question is often expressed as, "What will your buyer's wife, husband, or partner think about the buying decision?" Sometimes, but by no means always, this question is verbalized as an objection. However, often a man's ego may not allow him to tell you that he must consult with his wife before making a buying decision.

The significant other for teenagers or young adults may be their parents, a boyfriend or girlfriend, or their peers. At this age, what others think is of major importance to the buyer. In many cases, what others think may actually be more important than what the prospect thinks!

Anytime a third person is brought into the sales decision, your presentation must take them into account. You need to give your prospect the ammunition they need to "sell" the spouse or significant other—or make sure the significant other is involved in your presentation. This third person's objections should be answered first, since once their objections have been handled there may be no more.

If another person is in the room, try to establish the relationship to the prospect. The prospect brought them along or included them for a reason. Make sure you greet them, bond with them, and look at them as you present—they can make or break your presentation.

In most cases you won't want to do a sales presentation unless both decision makers are present. If that's not possible, try these solutions.

Objection: *I need to talk to my wife.* [uncle, father, etc.]

Solution: *I understand you want to talk to her and get her approval. There are a couple of ways we can go. One, we can go ahead and make this purchase contingent on her approval or, two, we can surprise her and show her a decision has already been made. Which way should we go?*

Objection: *I need to talk to my husband about taking martial arts lessons.*

Solution: *Wouldn't your husband be pleased and relieved that you are learning to defend yourself? Of course he would...*

Objection: *I need to talk to my accountant.* [lawyer or other professional]

Solution: *A client of mine once told me a story when he was asked if he felt he should get his accountant's approval on purchasing the property he was examining. He said, "My accountant probably makes $100,000 per year. I make considerably more than that. He is not paid to tell me what I* *can and cannot do. He is paid to tell me how to structure the things that I tell him I want to do.*

Objection: *I'm not sure that my sons are going to like it.*

Solution: *That's why I suggest that you initially sign them up for one month and see how well they do. In my experience, children take one lesson and can't wait to come back for more.*

Objection: *I need to talk to my boss.*

Solution: *Let's call him now and I'll explain all the cost-saving benefits to him!*

The "third man" can make or break your sale. Make sure you address and include his concerns in your solution.

CHAPTER 126

No One Ever Got Fired for Buying from IBM—Dealing with Boss Objections!

In a business-to-business situation, the other significant party to the deal tends to be the boss or department head, although in some cases, it may be a colleague. Buying a no-name computer system that saves the company $100,000 is a risky proposition for the purchasing agent. If the product works out well, he gets a pat on the back. If it doesn't work out, he is blamed, chastised, and may even be fired for making such a dumb decision. It's no wonder that the opinion of others can be of paramount importance to your ability to close the sale.

In business-to-business sales, removing fear and getting approval from multiple parties is the key to success.

Objection: *Making a big purchase like this is a bit risky!*

Solution: *Risky? What exactly do you mean? What could I do to make you feel more at ease with your decision?*

Objection: *I have never heard of your company.*

Solution: *We may not be as big as some of your other suppliers but our size allows us to respond quickly to your needs. That's why we've been chosen by companies like…* [name some in their industry] *to be their supplier.*

Objection: *I'm not sure head office is going to like it (approve it).*

Solution: *That's why I suggest we get everyone involved in the demonstration. In my experience, after your executive officers observe everything our product can do, they'll have complete confidence in your decision.*

Objection: *It's all very confusing; I don't want to make a big mistake. I'd prefer we get someone else involved in the decision.*

Solution: *I understand. Who else should be involved in this demonstration?*

Removing fear is the biggest hurdle in business-to-business transactions.

CHAPTER 127

Destroying "The Price Is Too High" and Other Money Objections

While it doesn't always come down to money, for most salespeople, overcoming price objections is often at the top of their list. Let's look at some typical—and cunningly clever—ways to deal with this issue.

You've given a first-rate presentation and your prospect showed many signs of interest along the way. But the first response is: "Your price is too high!"

You can reply:

> *I understand how you feel. Prices today are certainly higher than they used to be in the past and will no doubt keep rising. But what we are talking about here is far more important than just a few dollars, Ms. Miller. We are talking about your life here and whether or not you are going to enjoy it to the fullest.*

Or

> *Too high compared to what, Ms. Miller?"*

Wait to see if the comparison she has is "apples to apples," then say:

> *If you look at the convenient location, the superior clubhouse, and the quality of the course, what other*

clubs can really compare at any price? In fact, we are one of the least-expensive top-rated clubs in the country!

Or

Compared to what? Wouldn't you agree that the price is a minor concern if we can increase your business by 30% using Marketing Commander?

Here are some additional ways to deal with objections to price:

Objection: *Your price is too high!*

Solution: *Mr. Prospect, as I mentioned at the start of our conversation, if you are looking for the cheapest website solution, we are not going to be the product for you. However, if you had a website that could triple your database of leads and automatically follow up on all of them, substantially increasing your income, then price should not really be the issue, should it?*

Objection: *I don't have enough cash to buy right now.*

Solution: [Pause for a moment.] *No problem, we don't need all the money today. What kind of deposit can you leave today?*

If he names any reasonable amount, accept it. Better to accept less than the full price than risk losing a sincere customer. Work out terms for the balance and close the deal. If you do not get a deposit, chances are you will not see the prospect again. Ask for an initial deposit; when prospects leave money, it's a surefire guarantee they will be back!

Or

No problem, just leave a small deposit and I'll hold it for you until your next paycheck.

Or

Well, if I can arrange it so you don't have to put up the full amount, are you ready to move forward now?

Objection: *I can't afford it!*

Solution: *You really can't afford not to! Look at the money this product will save you. It won't actually cost you anything. In fact, you'll be making a profit!*

Objection: *Is this land a good investment at this price?*

Solution: *It's hard to predict the future value of anything but I always liked what Will Rodgers used to say, "The reason I love investing in land is that it's the only thing they aren't making any more of!"*

I discovered an interesting way to deal with price early in my sales career and have used it very successfully ever since.

Objection: *How can you possibly charge this price?*

Solution: *You're right! When you look at the years of research and development that went into this product, and the amazing time-saving features it incorporates, you'd expect to pay a lot more, wouldn't you?*

What do you think we should charge—20, 30, or 50% more?

The prospect of course has no intention of paying more, but I have found this approach is a good way of breaking a stalemate. This little tongue-in-cheek response always gets them talking again.

The more problems you solve in life, the more successful you will be. When you ease the pain associated with problems, people will pay you for doing so. When you don't solve problems, there's no reason for your services and no reason for anyone to pay you!

Price is rarely important—if you can clearly demonstrate value!

CHAPTER 128

Time Objections— Make the Right Time NOW!

It isn't that they can't see the solution.
It's that they can't see the problem.
—G. K. Chesterton

Time objections are often masked by the sale killing words "I want to think it over." This is your classic objection but one that you, as a cunningly clever salesperson, should have removed earlier in the sales process by use of the pre-pitch agreement and by handling most common objections in your presentation. Nonetheless, for most salespeople, it's a stall you should expect to hear often.

To deal with this stall, you must pin the prospect down to a more specific objection in order to deal with the true objection.

Objection: *I need to think it over.*

Solution: *I agree that a decision such as this should be thought about carefully. May I ask—is it the location or the price that you are thinking about the most?*

Probe and close on the issue that is causing the procrastination.

Objection: *I need to think it over.*

Solution: *What exactly is it that you need to think over? You told me this is something you have always wanted to own. I know you like the benefits we discussed. Is there a money issue?*

Objection: *I want to think it over for a while.*

Solution: *When people say that, it usually tells me that I've left something out of my presentation or that there are questions I haven't answered thoroughly. What other questions do you have?*

Objection: *I want to shop around for a while.*

Solution: *I understand. That's exactly what I would do myself. That's why I always carry a price sheet from my two biggest competitors. As you can clearly see, we offer not only the best product, but the best price too.*

Objection: *I'm going to wait until next quarter before buying the product.*

Solution: *I understand you wanting to wait until September to buy, but if you do that, you'll miss out on our summer discounts. Also, if you wait until fall, I won't be able to guarantee availability; it's our busiest month.*

Or

Let's go ahead and take care of all the paperwork now. Then I can ship it to you as soon as September rolls around.

Objection: *I'm an executive for the XYZ Corporation. I'm very busy and often out of town for several days at a time. My schedule is very erratic.*

Solution: *I can see you are a very busy person. That's why I suggest you take private lessons. That way you can schedule private classes whenever you like or whenever you're in town. Individual instruction also helps you progress faster than those who only take group classes. If you are out of town one week, we'll make up your private lessons another week.*

Most people are procrastinators. Great salespeople are experts at overcoming procrastination.

CHAPTER 129

Left-Field and Red-Herring Objections

Sometime prospects offer a string of unrelated objections, none of which are really important. They ask because as an "intelligent" consumer they feel they should ask something! At other times prospects will ask off-the-wall questions just to see what you will say. Still others may have a hidden agenda and so ask red-herring questions. The key with any of these left-field questions is to simply provide an answer and move the sales pitch back to it's proper place as quickly and professionally as possible.

The Worrier: *Who will I be dealing with at your office? What if you disappear or leave the company?*

Salesperson: *I will be dealing with you personally but I'm also excited about introducing you to our service team as they really do most of the work!*

Accounting Type: *We don't have the budget for it this year.*

Salesperson: *Certainly I realize that everyone has a budget, but everyone also has a bottom line. Our product will clearly help you where it counts the most—in delivering profits to your bottom line!*

The Skeptic: *You sales guys are all the same: promises, promises, promises.*

Salesperson: *You must have a reason for saying that. Have your current suppliers not lived up to their promises?*

The Know-It-All: [Demonstrates an intimate knowledge of your product and those of your competitors. There is little or nothing you can tell him he doesn't already know.]

Salesperson: *Wow, I'm impressed. You have certainly done your homework and know the products—which is why I am sure you realize that our reporting tools are far superior to anything on the market and can quickly save you more money than any of the other solutions you are already familiar with!* [Play to his ego!]

The Gossip: *I hear your sales manager* [CEO, designer, etc.] *is leaving. How will this affect the company?*

Salesperson: *I'm really not sure about Ms. Young's plans, but I do know that our company has been in business for over 25 years and that it's success doesn't depend on any one person.*

Answer red-herring objections quickly and concisely and get back to your place in the orchestrated sales process.

CHAPTER 130

Product Limitations—Answering Objections Is Not Solving Every Concern

While I give you a lot of ammunition in this section with which to answer objections, some objections can't be eliminated. For instance, maybe the condo unit you're trying to sell doesn't have a tennis court, a pool, a gym, covered parking, or whatever. You can't change that. You can only suggest to prospects that the missing feature is not crucial. You'll add to your rapport and credibility by being frank about things you can't change. At the end of answering objections, you and the prospect may agree that there are a couple of points about your product that are not perfect, but that it still compares very favorably to competitors.

Nothing is perfect. Help your prospects make a decision anyway.

Objection: *It's too far from where I live* [work/travel].

Solution: *You know, it's funny you should say that. We ARE 60 miles from Tampa's airport. But I had a couple in here the other day from London who live just 15 miles from Heathrow. And do you know what they told me? Because of the new highway here, they can get here from the Tampa airport far quicker than they can get from their home to Heathrow, sitting on the M-25 for two hours moving at a crawl!*

Objection: *Why don't you have a gym* [pool, or any other type of amenity]*?*

Solution: *A gym might be nice, but most of our residents feel that the quality of our development, location, and price more than make up for not having one. We do have a beautiful pool. John Prince park is just 5 minutes walk, less if you jog, and there are three gyms within a 10-minute drive.*

Objection: *Why doesn't your software offer this feature?*

Solution: *That might be a nice additional feature and certainly one we'd consider adding in the future, but our core competency is the ability to collect and sort data in a way that significantly increases profits for our customers.*

Objection: *I've never heard of your architect* [product, designer, etc.]*?*

Solution: *Certainly Carlos Redo may not be as well known as many people, but he's a real up and comer and it won't be long before everyone knows him.* [Offer proof in the form of magazine articles, testimonials, etc.]

Objection: *This car doesn't have much power.*

Solution: *It's true that it's no race car, BUT it does get 50 miles to the gallon, which will save you a fortune in fuel!*

When answering product limitations, tout the major benefits and downplay the subfeatures that you may not have.

CHAPTER 131

Others Like ME?

Very often when buying a product or service, people want assurances that others just like themselves—Jewish, Catholic, black, young, old, experienced, inexperienced, whatever—have also bought and are enjoying the experience!

Objection: *Are there any other families renting in the complex?*

Solution: *Yes, actually there are lots of couples about the same age as your family.* [Give some examples of real renters.]

Objection: *I don't see anyone my age* [like me] *around the club.*

Solution: *We have lots of members like you and part of my job as membership director is to make introductions. Not only can I think of five people right now who are in your field, but we have lots of people with handicaps like yours. And we can line up games for you with just a little notice.* [Provide sample names here and get back to them with more.]

Objection: *I am really inexperienced with computers. I am afraid this software will be way over my head.*

Solution: *We have lots of customers just like you who certainly aren't techno geeks. One of the key benefits of our product is how easy it is to use, even for first timers.*

Objection: *My English is not so good. Will this be a problem?*

Solution: *No; the manuals are available in seven languages, including Spanish. And the online demos show you graphically exactly where to click to get what you want.*

Objection: *I really want my son to get a private school education, but he's very shy so I'm hesitant to move him to a new school.*

Solution: *I understand. One of the things we do to help ensure a smooth transition is to pair new students up with a buddy to help them get around—so your son will have a new friend on day one, guaranteed!*

People want to know that others like themselves have purchased and are enjoying the benefits of your product or service. Always have examples in various creeds, colors, shapes, and sizes!

CHAPTER 132

I Hear Not All Your Customers Are Happy—the Abe Lincoln Solution

Every problem contains within itself the seeds of its own solution.
—Stanley Arnold

Every now and then you will get prospects who have heard something from a disgruntled customer, the rumor mill, an ex-employee or, more likely, a competing company. They will raise a question about how happy your existing customers are. As with all objections, you don't want a protracted discussion about this; you simply want to quickly and concisely answer the concern and go back to your presentation.

Objection: *I hear not all of your customers are happy.*

Solution: *Really, Bob, I'm surprised to hear you say that. But as Lincoln so aptly said, "You can please all of the people some of the time but not all of the people all of the time." Wouldn't you agree?*

Now think about it, who is going to argue with Honest Abe? By using this well-known quote, you simply help the prospect align with a concept that most people agree is a universal truth.

Abe Option Two:

Objection: *I hear not all of your customers are happy.*

Solution: *Really, Bob, I'm surprised to hear you say that. But as Lincoln, so aptly said, "Most people are about as happy as they make up their minds to be." Wouldn't you agree?*

You can follow up with:

I suppose there will always be people who are unhappy about something at some time but our recent customer surveys show our satisfaction levels are higher than any other vendor in our industry, and we're always trying to further improve our service.

Most of the time either approach will work. If the prospect persists, casually ask for an example of what the prospect means, for example:

Is there something specific you've heard that I might address?

Make Abe your ally in dealing with unhappy people.

CHAPTER 133

How Does Your Company Compare to Your Competitor? Converting "Shop Around" Prospects to Loyal Customers!

Well done is better than well said.
—Benjamin Franklin

Sometimes—especially in a retail situation—you have prospects who want to check out other places or prices. This is a natural reaction and one you should be ready for in advance by doing a frequent and thorough investigation of your competitors' prices, policies, and packaging.

Objection: *I want to check out a couple of other places.*

Solution: *That certainly makes sense, Mr. Prospect. I'd do the same thing myself. May I ask whom you had in mind, as perhaps I could save you a little time?*

Then give your benefits in direct relationship to that competitor.

Yes; those two companies are our closest competitors, which is why I have put together a price-benefits comparison sheet. Let me show you.

If you cannot get the prospect to commit to you, at least get them to commit to asking questions you know will uncover your competitors' weaknesses. For example:

> *That makes sense. When you talk to XYZ company make sure you ask about their rates for service when you need to make changes in the future. While their up-front cost may appear lower, in the long run it will cost you substantially more than choosing us because we include ongoing service in our price at no additional charge.*

Another variation of this is a prospect who will ask you how your product or service compares to a competitor. In this case, it's good to know if the prospect is considering this competitor seriously or just throwing out a name to see how you react. Either way you need some solid, short answers to position your advantages over your top competitors.

Prospect: *How does your product compare to ACME?*

Salesperson: *Have you looked at ACME's product in detail?*

Prospect: *Yes.*

Salesperson: *Then you already know it's older technology, lacking in many of the key features we offer.*

Or

Prospect: *No, I haven't. But they seem to be offering much the same thing you do.*

Salesperson: *Bob, on the surface it may seem similar and I'm sure they'd love you to believe it is...but that is just not the case. Our product has 800-number tracking so you can determine your cost per lead, plus your own digital team to execute your marketing plan for you.* [List any features and benefits your competitors don't have.]

Or

Prospect: *How do you compare to your three closest competitors?*

Salesperson: *There really is no course in the area that offers such a great layout, conditioning, and friendly service. So any comparison with others is really not an apples-to-apples comparison. But, if we had to compare I'd say…*

Houston Lake has a very nice setting, but most people think our layout is more challenging Haverford is a very average course with no real clubhouse facilities.

The Landings has quality courses, although our greens are generally regarded as much better. Our clubhouse and social activities are far superior, and people who have played both places feel that the attitude and service of our staff is generally more consistent!

Know your competition's weaknesses that you can exploit to your advantage.

CHAPTER 134

Using Props to Bury the Competition When You're Compared to Them

In my karate school, and more recently in selling my management and marketing services, I have often used printed tools to great effect.

For example, when pitching karate lessons to a mother, I'd break out the personal-development curriculum for kids we developed, which was 600 pages in a very large three-ring binder. In it were lessons on self-esteem, confidence, persistence, and other traits that all parents want their children to develop. When someone would say they were going to check another school, I'd say:

> *Before you go, Mrs. Smith, there is just one more thing I'd like to show you. It's our school's personal development program. It's written by top educators to help kids succeed not just in martial arts, but also in school and life. We have spent a great deal of time and money perfecting this curriculum and are very proud of the results it produces in our students. So I just want to ask you one thing: When you go to check out some other schools—and there are plenty in the area—all of them are going to tell you about the benefits they offer. Just ask to see their written curriculum and compare what they have to offer with what I have shown you.*

At that point many people just reconsidered and signed up. If they did go to one of the other schools, none of whom had any written curriculum whatsoever, they'd come straight back to us.

I did the same thing to a lesser degree with our full-color 8-page information kit.

> *Mrs. Smith, when you visit some of the other schools, all I ask is that you compare the information and quality of instruction you get from a full-time, professional school like ours to whatever you might get somewhere else.*

A second-rate, photo-copied flyer was what they were going to get somewhere else, at best! By simply changing the focus of what they might compare when looking at the competition we had a significant increase in sales.

In my marketing business, I authored 25 manuals, each about 30 pages (The Guaranteed Marketing Success System). I'd keep them in a hold-all bag while I was making the pitch. Then if the question of comparison came up with another agency, I'd start bringing them out one at a time and say:

> *Most ad agencies and marketing companies talk a good game. They like to talk about brand, image, and impressions. We take it much further. We have developed a complete, step-by-step marketing success system for our partners to follow that guarantees consistent results. Compare this comprehensive approach to what XYZ offers.*

Use appropriate props to solve objections, build value, and change the focus of the prospect to your area of superiority!

CHAPTER 135

Killing the Competition With Cunningly Clever Innuendo

I don't always agree that you should NEVER say something bad about your competition; sometimes they deserve it. You'd be doing yourself and your prospect a disservice by not bringing to light key information that might be considered negative. For example, you may know for a FACT that a competitor is dumping product on their way out of business and thus won't be able to stand behind any of their claims. But even when justified, it's a dangerous game.

Obviously, as a general rule, bad mouthing the competion is something you want to avoid. It often comes off the wrong way, making YOU look bad instead of them, even if what you say is true. A far better way to deal with competition is to praise their strengths but raise subtle doubts about their weaknesses.

If you raise doubts about the competition through subtle questions and innuendo and allow the prospect to come to his own conclusion, it's far more powerful than anything you will ever say. For example:

Objection: *Competitor A charges far less that you do!*

Answer: *Why do you think that is?* [Then just wait for an answer.]

Frequently, when this type of objection arises, and you invite the prospect to guess why the guy down the street charges 50% less, he will. Even if he doesn't respond at once, he is almost always sitting there thinking, "Because his product is inferior." Or "Maybe that's all he's worth!" or "They must use inferior materials."

My friend in Canada, Harold Warden, had a wonderful way of casting doubt on his competition down the street who charged 50% less than he did. Harold owned the most successful karate school in Toronto with well over 600 students in a splendid facility. Then a competitor opened in an industrial location, down an alley on the very next street. In an attempt to gain students, the competitor slashed his prices and parked an old van on the street corner with a large arrow pointing to his school.

People would come into Harold's school first, since he advertised heavily in the newspapers and on TV, but would hesitate when told the price. They would point out to Harold that the school down the street advertised that they charged 50% less. Harold, with a look of utter shock and horror, would reply, "You mean the guy who parks his old van on the street corner who owns the school in a back alley where all the students wear black uniforms?"

They usually sat there in stunned silence, trying to figure out what he meant.

He wouldn't say a word.

Eventually when the silence grew too uncomfortable, prospects would finally ask, "What do the black uniforms mean?"

Harold would look at them thoughtfully and then slowly answer, "What do you think they mean?"

Now prospects had images in their minds of the black prince, the black knight, the black death, Darth Vader, and whatever the latest satanic cult in the news happened to be!

That did the trick. They signed up with Harold, without his ever addressing the issue of price or saying a questionable word against his competition. He merely redirected their focus. (For the record, while the majority of karate schools wear white uniforms, an increasing number use black, blue, or other colors, none of which signifies anything in particular, other than personal taste!)

Another example:

> *XYZ is a fine company, although you probably won't be dealing with the same person for very long. They have had seven sales mangers in the five years I've been working here.*

Now you haven't really said anything negative. In fact, you praised the company. But in a single sentence you told the prospect that if he likes dealing with the same person, which of course most people do, then he'd be far better off dealing with you.

> *ZXY company does have a good product but it's written in an old programming language. At some point in the very near future, they are going to have to do a major overhaul of the product. At that point, their customers will experience all the issues that typically go along with new code. Our product is written in the very latest code, and since it's version 3.0, all the bugs have already been worked out.*

Once again you haven't really bad mouthed anyone, but you have planted a seed about the long-term viability of the product and suggested a universal truth that all new software has bugs—bugs they don't want any part of when there's another solution available.

Casting doubt on your competitors is best done by making a casual comment or phrasing a question in such a way that prospects draw their own—negative—conclusions!

CHAPTER 136

The De Niro Principle

I shall prepare and one day my time shall come.
—Abraham Lincoln

Most people don't like to role play overcoming objections or using various closes; it makes them feel self-conscious, embarrassed, or silly. Because people don't like doing it, most companies don't insist on making it a significant or ongoing part of their sales training. As a result, they NEVER get the best from their salespeople!

Just like any other endeavor, training and repetition increase performance across the board. Robert De Niro did not become a great actor by accident. Like Brando before him, he did it by being in the role mentally and physically for weeks before actually shooting. You must do the same. You MUST relentlessly practice and role play overcoming objections and closing the sale until nothing can divert you from your well-thought-out and carefully orchestrated sales process.

Arrange for people from your office to role play objections with you. Their job is to pretend to be buyers and to raise a series of objections. Give them the list of objections and their categories from this chapter to use as a basis. They should at least raise price objections, facilities objections, and a stall like "I need to think it over." They should also throw in something completely off base to give you the opportunity to steer the sales process back on track.

You are far better off making your mistakes and honing your art in front of colleagues and friends rather than losing thousands of dollars, pounds, or euros on failed sales attempts to real prospects!

Top performers in every field never stop learning, never stop training, and never stop trying to improve their basics through role playing and repetition!

CHAPTER 137

How to Eliminate All Customer Objections

In previous pages, I have addressed the majority of the objections you will ever hear, and shared with you a formula for addressing new ones. Now let me give you the biggest secret of all: how you can actually eliminate almost every objection from your customer's arsenal.

Here's how—qualify the prospective buyer thoroughly:

- Make sure she is the decision maker.
- Make sure she can pay for your product or service.
- Make her agree in advance to make a decision with a pre-pitch agreement.
- Ask questions to make sure there is a need for your product or service.
- Ask questions to find your prospect's hot buttons.
- Build rapport.
- Build credibility.
- Build trust.
- Build value.

- Make a well-orchestrated presentation based around a great story, your key benefits, and the prospect's hot buttons.
- Succinctly answer any question the prospect may have and go back to your presentation.
- Ask for the sale multiple times.

Most salespeople don't follow all, or even most, of the above steps. They take shortcuts, guess at some answers, or delude themselves that their intuition or gut feel will be enough to go on. They present to non-decision smakers and keep unqualified prospects on the hook because dismissing them means they have to go and find more prospects. Cunningly clever salespeople take no shortcuts and thus do not have to deal with time wasters or objections. They go from one successful sale to the next.

Objections can be greatly reduced or even eliminated by rigorously following a carefully orchestrated sales system.

Cunningly Clever Closes

CHAPTER 138

The Fine and Profitable Art of Cunningly Clever Closing

Top salespeople know that the close is their sweet moment of victory, and that without closers, a business will not survive. The most important difference between ordinary salespeople and superstar sellers is that superstars are closers!

All the sweat, skill, and time you have put into your sales effort up to this point mean nothing if you can't persuade the prospect to buy. But cunningly clever closing is not about tricking your prospects into buying; it is simply about helping them reorganize their priorities so that your product or service is next on their must-have list!

Closing is an all-or-nothing business: You either make the sale or you lose. Simply asking your prospect to buy multiple times during your sales presentation will produce better results. Doing it in a systematic, scripted way as detailed in this section will produce astonishingly better results.

These pages contain surefire closes that have been successful for decades. Although you might know some of them by other names, anyone who has been in sales for even a short period of time will recognize at least a few of them. Others will be new to you. There is quite a list of different approaches. The key is to try each close out loud. Practice them, role play them, and adopt the ones that are most suitable to your style, personality, and product. Not all will be right for you or your situation, but some of them will be the missing links that will vault your sales to a whole new level!

Find the ones that seem most natural for you and put them into action at once.

Review, practice, and try out some new or different closes. Sometimes just a small difference in how you word a close can make a massive difference in your sales!

CHAPTER 139

Recognizing Closing Signals

An ounce of action is worth a ton of theory!
—Frederick Engles

All the presentation skills in the world won't help if you don't close. Many salespeople get so caught up in their own sales pitches that they fail to hear or observe that the prospect is radiating all kinds of closing signals. The prospect is ready to buy. But the salesperson doesn't know when to shut up and go for the close and just keeps right on with the pitch. Believe it or not, failing to realize it's time to ask for the order is the prime reason for many lost sales.

Overkill

I was in a client's office, in the middle of a consultation with Jim, the owner of a large manufacturing business. A prospect walked in, and Jim interrupted the conversation I was having with him to make a sales presentation to the prospect.

I excused myself and sat outside, leaving the door ajar so that I could hear the presentation. After hearing the basic facts about the product, the prospect said, "Sounds great to me. Let's do it." After the briefest of pauses, the owner continued with his presentation as if nothing had happened! He talked about how good his product was and how his father had founded the business. He went on at length about how well liked the product was by all the companies that used it and what great customers he had. The prospect listened patiently for several more minutes. Then he announced that he had to pick his kids up from school—and he left without buying. OVERKILL!

I have seen this happen a million times, even with my own salespeople. The temptation is to keep talking, to squeeze in a few more features and benefits, not because the prospects want to hear them, but simply because the salespeople didn't finish their spiels!

Be alert to cues that signal when to stop presenting and start selling!

CHAPTER 140

Spotting Verbal Closing Signals

One of the best times to close a sale is when the prospect is visualizing the perceived benefits. Look back at the sales scripts in the previous chapters and see if you can spot any closing signals. Now let's look at some common closing signals that will tell you the customer is ready to buy.

Signal: *When do I get my uniform?*

Answer: *When you register for classes; your registration fee includes a free uniform and a belt. Let's take care of that right now.*

* * * *

Signal: *Do you have it in blue?*

Answer: *Would you like it in blue?*

* * * *

Signal: *When can I start classes?*

Answer: *Just as soon as we complete the preregistration, you can start right away. Let's go ahead and get that out of the way now.*

* * * *

Signal: *Is delivery included in the price?*

Answer: *That depends on how you want it shipped! Do you want it overnight or regular ground?*

* * * *

Signal: *How soon can I get one?*

Answer: *How soon do you need it?*

* * * *

Signal: *When do new classes start?*

Answer: *We have new classes starting this week. Why don't we enroll you right now so you can join a new class immediately?*

* * * *

Signal: *Can I pay for this over a period of time?*

Answer: *If you give me a deposit now, I can arrange for you to pay off the remainder on a monthly basis.*

* * * *

Signal: *Can I try your service for a month before I make a long-term commitment?*

Answer: *Sure. Let's go ahead and sign you up for a month right now.*

* * * *

Signal: *Do you have any specials if I pay in advance?*

Answer: *If I could get you a 10% discount, would you pay for a year right now?*

* * * *

Signal: *What guarantee do you give?*

Answer: *What type of guarantee are you looking for?*

Answer each question quickly and professionally, and go directly for the close. Ask for the order. When the prospect is on the verge of making a buying decision, the most direct way of closing the sale is to ask how he intends to make payment, "Check, credit card, or cash?" This approach can best be used when a prospect has made the decision to buy but is asking unrelated questions—the kind that prevent him from giving you the order! At this point, "Check or cash?" is the best way to take control of the sale and complete it.

Learn to spot buying questions and turn the answers into closes!

CHAPTER 141

Spotting Nonverbal Closing Signals

You must not only listen to what your prospect says, but also watch his or her body language closely. A large percentage of communication is nonverbal. Below are some of the clues you may observe that would indicate the prospect might be ready for a close.

- The prospect begins to nod in agreement.
- The prospect begins to smile.
- He makes more frequent eye contact.
- Her eyes dilate slightly and her brow is relaxed.
- He raises one eyebrow, smiles, and appears to be imagining himself in the scenario that you have described.
- Her body language indicates she is relaxed.
- He leans towards you.
- The prospect picks up and intently studies your sales literature.
- The prospect takes unusual care in reading the contract.

- The prospect starts reaching for her wallet or fumbles in her handbag, starting to reach for her checkbook or credit card.

Be alert for such signals. When you observe any of them, bring your presentation to a close as quickly as possible. You will find your sales volume increases significantly when you raise your level of alertness to nonverbal signals.

When you observe positive body language, it's time to go for the close.

CHAPTER 142

The Thermometer Test

This simple technique helps you measure the degree to which your prospect has been sold—up to this point in your presentation. Here's how it works:

> *Teresa, we've covered a lot of ground so far, and there's still more to show you. But on a zero-to-ten scale, zero meaning you have no interest in our Marketing Commander solution and ten meaning you have already decided to invest in Marketing Commander, where are you?*

If she says 10, game over. Sign the paperwork and get out of there!

If she's less than a six, you've got a problem. She's agreed with all of your qualifying and review this far and she's less than a six?

> *Teresa, based on what you've told me so far, I don't understand that.*

Whatever Teresa says will reveal deeper pain, new pain, or pain that your earlier step hasn't alleviated. Be patient. Listen. And begin the process again.

Most of the time at this stage of the presentation, the prospect will be higher than six. In that event you say:

Teresa, what do you need to see [hear, understand] to get to ten?

And then, whatever she has to see is what you show her. No more and no less. After you've shown her what she's asked for, take her temperature again.

When your prospect arrives at ten, simply ask for the signed order or credit card number.

The thermometer test takes the guesswork out of knowing how ready your prospect is to close.

CHAPTER 143

The Straightforward or Assumptive Close

They conquer who believe they can.
—John Dryden

Now this close is not going to sound all that cunningly clever—unless you know the statistic that 63% of all sales calls end without the salesperson actually asking the prospect to buy! Always start by assuming that every prospect wants to buy, and that the only variables in the equation are when the prospect wants to take delivery and the desired method of payment.

Never let a prospect get away before you've asked for the sale!

The assumptive close handles the sales interaction as if you are certain that the prospect will buy. You can do this without actually asking the prospect the straightforward question—"Would you like to go ahead and purchase?"—although even that's a better option than not asking.

Here are some ways of asking the prospect to buy:

- "Would you like to take it home with you?"
- "I've already taken care of the paperwork. All you need to do is endorse it and we'll ship it to you within 24 hours!"

- "Will 20 cases be enough?"
- "Let's go ahead and make an appointment for your next visit [session, treatment, lesson] while you are here"
- "Would you like us to begin service right away?"
- "Mr. Miller, I assume you'll probably want to go ahead and fill in a reservation form today to lock in your dates and rates."
- "Mrs. Jones, based on our conversation it seems like our product meets most of your criteria. Let's go ahead and get the paperwork out of the way right now while you are here!"

Always assume your prospect will buy and always ask for the sale.

If you do that and nothing else, your sales will improve!

CHAPTER 144

The Alternative Close

Victory is a thing of will.

—Ferdinand Foch

The alternative close is perhaps the best known of all closing techniques and has many variations, depending on your product or service. Another common name for it is the "either-or" close. This close gives the prospect the choice between buying and buying—between "yes" and "yes." The key is to make the close at the appropriate moment. This close is initiated with questions such as:

- "Shall we put an offer in on this property, or the first property we looked at today?"
- "Which house feels more like home for you, the first one we looked at or this one?"
- "Would you like the free gift or the free month of service?" When you give the prospect a choice of free benefits, it is much more difficult to say no.
- "Would you like to start your Spanish classes tonight, or would tomorrow night be more convenient for you?"
- "Do you want the three bedroom unit or will the two bedrooms be fine?"

- "Do you want to take the six-month program or would the 12-month course and the discount be better for you?"
- "Would you like the V6 or the V8?"
- "Did you want to lease the computer system or purchase it?"
- "Do you want to take it with you or do you want us to ship it?"
- "Do you want us to install the parts or will you do it yourself?"

When the prospect is on the verge of making a buying decision, simply asking, "Will you be using a credit card or check?" is the best way to take control of the sale and complete it.

Each one of the previous alternative closes offers the prospect a choice. No matter which one they choose, they will feel committed to buy once they have made the choice.

Offering alternative positive choices is one of the easiest ways to close a sale without specifically asking for the order!

CHAPTER 145

The Action Close

We shall not be asked what we have read,
but what we have done.
—Thomas Kempis

In the action close, you offer the prospect the opportunity to take some ACTION that signifies acceptance of your terms. I perfected this technique during my years in the karate business. Directly after the trial lesson and following a brief presentation, the instructor would excuse himself and come back into the office a moment later with a uniform. He would hand the uniform to the prospect and invite him to try it on and check to see if it fit. If the prospect accepts the action of putting on the uniform, then he has already mentally signed up for lessons.

There are lots of simple action steps you can create to get this same quick commitment. Here are some examples:

- "Ms. Miller, we like to start all new golf members off with the gift of a logo golf shirt. Shall we go to the pro shop now and pick out yours?"
- "Shall we head over to the design center and decide on carpets?"
- "Shall I get the car detailed for you while we finish the paperwork?"

- "Mr. Miller, shall we go down to the locker room and pick out your new locker now?"
- "It's cold—do you want to wear the coat home?"
- "Can you email me a copy of your logo so I can get your "Quick Site" started?"
- "Mrs. Smith, I've gone ahead and filled out most of the reservation form for you. If you would like to go ahead and approve it, I can get your order processed at once." Hand the prospect a pen and casually slide the agreement across the desk. Once a prospect has accepted the pen, you have a psychological advantage.

Once the prospect performs whatever action you have asked her to take, she has already mentally signed up for the sale.

Think of what subtle action steps you can offer your prospect that if complied with mean she is closed!

CHAPTER 146

The Minutes (or Cents) Close

If you have a prospect who is stuck on price, the best way to handle it is to break it down to ridiculous proportions. When you show people how little your product or service will cost them on a daily basis, it makes it much easier for them to justify, or rationalize, the purchase. This is how life insurance has been sold for decades, but this type of close works just as well selling all kind of products and services.

- "Mr. Miller, when you think about it, your membership at a world-class facility like ours works out to be just $19.95 a day! Wouldn't you agree that's a spectacular value for all the amenities we offer?"
- "Due to the efficiency of this machine, your copies will only cost about one cent per copy. I am sure you will agree the savings this offers easily justifies the investment."
- "This website, with all the features and benefits it offers, comes to just $9.95 a day."
- "Membership in our health club is just a dollar a day. Isn't your health worth a dollar a day?"
- "You can be driving a brand new truck for just $14.95 a day."

- "For just $35 a day, you can have a Marketing Commander website and a fully trained digital team at your beck and call to update your website and execute your email campaigns! Where else can you hire dedicated professional staff and get a world-class website for just $35 a day?"

Depending on the audience and your product, you can also relate the cost to a common item:

- "For about the cost of a single beer a day, you could own this."
- "For the same cost as two cups of Starbucks coffee a day, you could be speaking another language in just six weeks."

When you show people how little your product or service will cost them on a daily basis, it makes it much easier for them to justify or rationalize the purchase.

CHAPTER 147

Closing on an Objection or Question

Very often a prospect's question or objection gives you the perfect segue into closing the sale and you must be alert for such opportunities. This is also called the conditional sale because it sets a condition that if met results in a closed sale. For example:

Prospect: *How quickly will I lose weight on your program?*

Salesperson: *How quickly do you want to lose weight? Obviously the sooner you start, the sooner you will begin enjoying the benefits. Let's get things going now!*

* * * *

Prospect: *Can I break my membership payments up?*

Salesperson: *Would you be ready to join right now if I can arrange to break your payments up?*

* * * *

Prospect: *Do you have it in red?*

Salesperson: *If I can find a red one, do you want to take it with you?*

* * * *

Prospect: *I'm not sure I can get financing.*

Salesperson: *If I can get you approved, do you want to drive it home?*

* * * *

Prospect: *Do I have to sign a three-year contract?*

Salesperson: *If I could get you a shorter [longer] contract, would that make you feel comfortable signing today?*

* * * *

Prospect: *Is the owner willing to hold a little paper?*

Salesperson: *If the owner is willing to hold a little paper, will you put an offer in writing today?*

Make sure your answers to prospects' questions have a closing statement in them, and you will close a lot more sales!

CHAPTER 148

The Giveaway or Puppy-Dog Close

This close is often used when a prospect is hesitant to purchase a product or service because of price. The giveaway close, or "puppy dog" close as it is often called, allows the prospect to enjoy the product free of charge before making a decision whether to buy. The puppy-dog moniker comes from the classic pet shop ploy. A child sees a puppy in the pet shop. The parents are unsure about getting a dog but don't have the will power to say no. Then the owner says, "I'll tell you what—take the puppy home for the weekend and see how he fits in with the family." We all know how that's going to turn out!

Here's an example of a close with a copier machine playing the role of the puppy:

> *Ms. Prospect, we have already agreed that you need this new copier. The speed and sorting capabilities will enhance your business. With your permission, I am going to have a machine delivered to you on Monday and let you see firsthand just how valuable it will prove to be for your business. If at the end of two weeks the advantages are not readily apparent to you, I will remove it with no questions asked. Shall we go ahead and set that trial period in motion for you now?*

I know for a fact that close works—that's how I bought my last copier!

In my digital marketing business, Marketing Commander, between the initial conversation with the prospect and the return of a detailed proposal, we often make a working mock-up of how the new website will look. We tell the prospect that we have already made what we call a "Quick Site." We tell the prospect:

> *It has a single home page and a fully functioning back end for you to collect, sort and email data while we work on the rest of the pages!*

Since key benefits of our Marketing Commander product are the enterprise level data collection, follow up, and reporting, it is usually well worth our four-hour effort to design a custom template because the prospect can't wait to start collecting leads!

In the golf business, we often use a trial month of membership, while in the karate business, it was a free trial lesson. What can you do to let your prospects take the "puppy" home?

Anytime you can remove the risk and let people try your product first, you are more than half way towards closing the sale!

CHAPTER 149

The Insane Close

One of my all-time favorite closes is taken directly from the pages of my most successful direct-mail sales letter—a single-page letter that has made tens of millions of dollars in several different industries, for both me and my clients. (See my book *Cunningly Clever Marketing* for the actual letter.)

The close goes like this:

Salesperson: *Mr. Prospect, my all time favorite quote is one by Albert Einstein, whom I am sure you would agree was a pretty smart chap.*

Prospect: *Sure!*

Salesperson: *Einstein defined insanity as doing the same thing over and over again and yet expecting different results!*

Mr. Prospect, if you don't hire Legendary Marketing to increase your leads and improve your sales process, what do you think your results are going to be next year?

Prospect: *Probably about the same as this year's!*

Salesperson: *And that's not what you want, is it—another year of poor leads and poor sales?*

Prospect: *No.*

Salesperson: *Then let's get started in a new direction, one that will produce dramatically different results than you're getting now! Doesn't that sound like a better idea?*

Prospect: *Yes!*

This is one of the most powerful closes I have ever developed and it works with anyone not getting the results they want from their current supplier!

Is it not insane to keep using products or services that don't get the results you want? Yes it is, so use Einstein to your advantage!

CHAPTER 150

Name-Drop Close

If you have customers who are prominent people or well-known companies, it can often be to your advantage to "drop names." It is also a sound idea to mention the names of present customers if they are friends or acquaintances of the prospect. If your prospect's friends and relatives have bought from you, then your prospect's fear of making the wrong decision is greatly diminished. A typical dialog might go something like this.

Salesperson: *I see that you live on Lakeview Avenue, Mrs. Smith. Do you happen to know the Evans family?*

Mrs. Smith: *As a matter of fact, I do. They are good friends of ours. How do you know them?*

Salesperson: *Brian, their son, bought a car from us last year.*

Birds of a feather flock together. People are happy to involve themselves in the same kind of business relationships and activities as their friends. There is also a law of human nature that says if their friends are using you, then you must be trustworthy!

Often, a prospect will challenge you with a question about who else is using your service or buying your product. Always be ready to drop a few well-chosen names when this happens.

Prospect: *Do you have any other clients in this part of New Jersey?*

Andrew: *Steve Anderson found our Marketing Success System to be a valuable investment.*

Prospect: *Steve Anderson bought your manuals? What could you teach him? He is already very successful.*

Andrew: *Steve, like most other successful people, feels you should never stop looking for new and better ways to conduct your business. I'm sure that's one of the reasons he is so successful. Don't you agree?*

Prospect: *Yes, I guess so.*

Andrew: *Did you want to take care of that with Visa or Mastercard?*

I could just as easily have said that Steve has gotten where he is today by investing in products that save him time and money, or any of a number of other benefits. The key is to drop a couple of names and emphasize the benefits the named people have received. It can greatly reduce the prospect's fear of making a decision. This also works well in conjunction with the testimonial close.

Use the names of prominent people, successful businesses, family members, and friends who use your products and services to build credibility, reduce fear, and close the sale!

CHAPTER 151

The Gift Close

Everyone wants to feel like a winner. Everyone wants to feel that they are smart enough to get the best possible deal from you. Often, as I'm nearing making a purchase, I ask the salesperson for a token gesture to push me over the edge and into my wallet. At the Mercedes dealership where I bought a car for my wife, the salesman asked me exactly what I had in mind. I replied, "I don't know. Be creative." A few moments later, he returned with a set of custom car mats, and I bought. Now, I am not saying that I wouldn't have bought the car anyway, but once the salesman returned with the mats, I was forced to accept the fact that he had fulfilled his end of the bargain.

After spending several thousand dollars with AT&T on a new communications system in my company headquarters building, I decided that I needed an additional cordless phone. I called to get information, and the salesman gave me some prices. Considering the substantial sum I had already spent, it seemed expensive and I procrastinated.

A week later, the salesman called me back and asked me to buy. I was still on the fence, so I asked him for a token gesture on his part to help me make a decision. He told me that this was his lowest price and he had nothing else to offer me. At the time, I might have even made the decision if he had offered an AT&T pen, but instead, I put off making a decision once again. The salesman has never called back, so I guess that puts him in the 22% category of salesmen who only try twice.

In almost any business, the token gesture is a major part of the sales strategy. People love to feel they are getting something for nothing. Don't you?

- "If you buy the car today, I'll throw in the rust treatment, which is worth $695."
- "If you take the phone today, I'll throw in the leather phone case."
- "If you buy the large one, I'll throw in a pair of smaller ones for free!"
- "If you join today, since it's September I'll prorate your fees through the end of the year and give you free carts!"
- "If you sign up right now, I'll waive our normal set-up fees!"

People love to feel they got a deal. Always have a token gift you can add to the sale to tip your prospect over the edge!

CHAPTER 152

The Reverse Close

When I was a karate school owner and instructor, my assistant and I would be so busy teaching class during peak hours that it was hard to find time to talk to new prospects. Occasionally, one would come in and announce right up front that he was not going to sign up today or that he was just looking around for a place to practice. This is a classic "shield," or defensive technique, designed to give the prospect a clean way out if he doesn't hear exactly what he wants to hear. It's used often by prospects looking to buy memberships, real estate, cars, and many other products.

Now is the time for reverse psychology. Thank the prospect for coming in and offer to put his name on a waiting list for a membership tour. Explain to him that you have so many people who are interested in memberships right now that you can't possibly spend time with someone who is not ready to join. Be polite, but be firm; ask the prospect to pick a date for his tour a month from now. For example:

Andrew: *Hi! How can I help you?*

Prospect: *I'm just checking out a few schools. I don't want to sign up today but I would like some information.*

Andrew: *Well, it's lucky you don't want to sign up today because all our classes are full at the moment. We are so busy right now that we have a wait-*

ing list, but I would be glad to give you some information.

Prospect: *How long is the waiting list?*

This ploy never failed to change the prospect's mind about wanting to sign up. The moment the prospect hears he can't have your product or service, you have dissolved away his shield. Suddenly he wants what you are selling. An interesting turn of events occurs at this point. Now the prospect is actually trying to sell you on letting him buy your product!

I would offer to put the prospect's name on a waiting list and say that it takes a month or more to get into class. Obviously the waiting list was as long as I wanted it to be. So, a couple of days later, I would call her and say that due to an unexpected cancellation, we had a space available. Would she like to take advantage of the opportunity?

Or I might allude to just such a cancellation, if she wanted to make a deposit then and there. A side effect of this close is that it automatically builds value and credibility for your company. What kind of restaurants have waiting lists? Good ones!

Removing the opportunity to buy very often creates a desire in prospects to act!

CHAPTER 153

The Challenge Close

I have seen the reverse technique and its companion, the challenge close, used in almost every business in one form or another. I was in a carpet store one day, waiting to be approached by a salesperson, when I overheard another salesman's pitch to a middle-aged couple. The measurements had been figured, the color had been chosen, and now the only question facing the couple was the question of quality.

They had been given three basic choices, $25, $40, or $55 per square yard, and they simply seemed incapable of making a decision. The salesman asked if he had answered all of their questions. He had. He tried a couple of trial closes without success. Then suddenly the salesman, realizing that he was getting nowhere, took a calculated risk. He said to the couple, "If you can't afford the $55 carpet, why not take the $40 one. It's almost as good."

Shocked at the suggestion that they could not afford the very best, the wife immediately chose the more expensive carpet. At this point, the salesman instantly commended her good decision as he placed a completed contract in front of her. He then followed up by going into a monologue about how better quality products always work out to be less expensive in the long run.

This close works especially well with high-ticket items. It is exactly how Tom Hassle got me to put down a deposit on a new

Ferrari. And this is how I frequently sell consulting gigs:

> *Look, if you can't afford $20,000 plus expenses to fly me out to your business, you can visit me at my office for half the fee!*

Another way to do this is to suggest the product or service is beyond them intellectually or time-wise. For example:

> *Maybe you are just not ready to upgrade your technology?* [list key benefits of upgrading]

Or

> *Maybe your business is still too small to benefit from the power of Marketing Commander. Maybe you don't need...* [list key benefits again]

These are very effective closes, but you do run the risk of insulting your prospect. It must be handled with great care and should not be used except as a last resort.

When you challenge the prospect's ego, if you have set the sale up correctly, you will often find that the prospect will rise to meet the challenge!

CHAPTER 154

The Miracle-on-Jeffrey-Street Close

In the classic movie *Miracle on 34th Street,* the store Santa Claus starts sending people from Macy's to Gimbels when Gimbels has a better deal on a particular item. The management at Macy's is just about to fire Santa when they realize that business has doubled because of his well-meaning, good Samaritan act. It was after seeing this movie many years ago that I started using a new technique with people who were undecided.

Once prospective karate students made an appointment to come and take a trial lesson, the great majority of them signed up for lessons. Even so, there are always a few unconvinced, habitual shoppers who just had to check into three more places to be sure they can't get a better deal someplace else. In many cases, these prospects are mothers who want to get the most for their money and top quality instruction for their children. Whenever one of them told me she was going to check out a few other schools, and assuming that I felt the reverse technique was inappropriate, I would give her a little assistance in making a choice.

First, I would commend her decision to check into other schools. Then I would hand her my high-quality, full-color information kit. As I handed her the kit, I would encourage her to use it to compare what others had to offer. After glancing through the kit for a few moments, the prospect rarely clung to her intention of checking competitors. If she did, I was well aware that very few other studios had quality promotional literature, and they would therefore suffer by comparison.

As a final step, I would give her the addresses of a couple of nearby schools, shake her hand, and tell her warmly that once she had a chance to compare our school to these others, I was sure she would be back. To end my presentation, I would add that I was going to call her in a couple of days to see how things went. Then I would ask if she needed directions to the other two schools!

Frequently, prospects walked out, hesitated, then turned around and walked back in again to sign up. They told me, "Anyone who is so confident in his product that he will actually give directions to his competitors must know he offers the best value."

I must admit that if they went to either of the two schools I had recommended, there wouldn't be much comparison. One was open only three days a week from 4-9 p.m., and the other was located next to a hole-in-the-wall bar!

Showing your confidence by encouraging prospects to check out the competition will often work in your favor, but the more carefully orchestrated this process, the better!

CHAPTER 155

The Higher-Price Close

Think like a man of action, and act like a man of thought.
—Henri Bergson

I often had prospects come into my school and announce that they were not going to buy now because they were just shopping around for the best price. Many more times, prospects were thinking these words without saying them out loud. When this happened, I always found it beneficial to point out the negatives. I pointed out, right up front, the fact that my school was more expensive than any other in town, thereby eliminating that particular objection. A sample dialog might go something like this.

Andrew: *I think it's a good idea for you to compare other schools' prices. Let me assure you right now that if price is your only consideration, this school is not going to be the one for you, because we are the most expensive in town. Is price your only consideration or are you also concerned with quality and value?*

Prospect: *Well, of course, quality is important as well.*

Andrew: *Are the lessons for you or for someone else?*

Prospect: *They are for Peter. He's my ten-year-old son.*

Andrew: *Excellent! Now let me tell you why our studio charges more. We are open six days a week, 12 hours a day, so scheduling is never a problem. Our structured children's programs have been endorsed by "Inside Karate" magazine, "Inside Kung Fu" magazine, and by John Smith, the principal at Kingsville Elementary School. Oh, Peter goes to that school, does he? We limit the class size to just 15 students, so that each one receives individual attention in every single class. Unlike many of our competitors, all of our instructors are certified by the California Martial Arts Association.*

On top of all that, we were just honored in "Martial Arts Business Magazine's" list of the top 200 best-run schools in America. Now, if you are looking for the finest martial arts instruction for your son, you have found it. If not, I'll be happy to help you find another school.

It is very difficult for prospects to admit they are cheapskates, especially where their children are concerned! It is next to impossible for them to say that price is the only thing that interests them. They will express concern about whether they will get value from their investment, or whether the product or service will last and provide the specific benefits for which they are looking.

By telling them up front that you are more expensive than others, you completely remove that objection from their arsenal. Using endorsements and testimonials you have received from satisfied customers helps substantiate your claim that you are indeed worth more. Carefully-worded comparisons to nameless competitors position you well above them.

Dealing with price up front saves a great deal of wasted time and often changes people's focus to the more important questions of quality and value!

CHAPTER 156

The Ben Franklin Close

It is a luxury to be understood.
—Ralph Waldo Emerson

The Ben Franklin close is ideal for prospects who are considering a competitor or who are very detail-oriented, and in situations when the sale is more complex. It is so named because it was the method employed by the legendary statesman to help him and others make a decision. It is an excellent way to summarize your benefits and the various positive responses you have received from the prospect during the sales presentation. When written down in black and white, the impact of the words is greater than the spoken word.

Look at the prospect and say:

> *Mrs. Chen, when Ben Franklin had an important decision to make, he'd make a list of the pros and cons and decide based on them. I always think it helps in any important decision to write things down on paper. Let's give it a try and go over the key points again, shall we?*

Now hand the prospect the paper and pencil and ask them to start with the "pros."

> *Why don't you start with the things you like that this home offers?*

Two of the keys to this close are that your prospect states the pros and cons and that you give her lots of help with the pros. After the prospect writes down some pros, prompt her with additional positive benefits for her list:

> *You agreed that this is one of the finest overall developments in the area, right?*
>
> *You said you thought the garden would be great for the kids to play in.*
>
> *You liked the view.*
>
> *You agreed that the kitchen and bathrooms are first class.*
>
> *You mentioned that this location is convenient to most of your family's activities like school, church, work and soccer.*
>
> *And our moving-in package will save you a ton of time and money getting set up.*

Then tell your prospect to write down the negatives. Because she's done the positives first, her mind will have a harder time changing gears to come up with negatives—and you don't help! This is one reason it's important to have the prospect do the writing (unlike some ways this close is taught). You might even say, "Now that you've got the hang of it, list all the negatives you can think of and I'll be right back."

When the prospect is done, she will typically have ten or more items in the positive column and no more than three items in the negative column. This alone gives you a psychological advantage in closing. You may be able to say, "It looks like the positives far outweigh the negatives. I guess that's it," and go into final closing mode. For instance:

Mrs. Chen, it certainly looks like the benefits of this home are in favor of you making an offer today. What do you say we go ahead and complete the paperwork?

If there are any important negatives, you now have the chance to deal with the objection, and then close the sale. It's the hidden objections that create problems. [See the Objections section for more details.]

This is an excellent close for more complex sales situations and helps refocus the prospect on your product's unique advantages.

CHAPTER 157

The Slam-Dunk Close

In order to use the slam-dunk close successfully, you have to set it up in advance by establishing an inflated price and then reluctantly accepting less.

It is often very useful to establish a high price in the prospect's mind so they have the opportunity to do some old-fashioned horse-trading and get a deal they like. How many times have you walked into a car dealership and paid sticker price for a car? Dealers put the sticker price on the car to establish a reference point. From there, they will negotiate about the price so the customer can feel he has gotten a good deal when he buys the car for less. The same is true of buying houses. Except in a very hot market, houses almost always sell below list price. The price merely establishes a starting point from which both parties expect to move.

To establish the higher value first, you show prospects a high-priced lot, house, or car, or at the beginning of a presentation, you might mention a $5,000 set-up fee. This proposition is not particularly attractive to most prospects, but it establishes certain values in their minds. They now have a frame of reference for what it might cost. Then, as you wrap up the presentation, you unveil the far more attractive deal.

> *There is one more house I want to show you. I think it's the best deal in the entire neighborhood. In fact,*

it's almost 40% less than that first property I showed you!

We have a special offer this month that allows me to waive the normal $5,000 set-up fee!

There is one other car I want to show you similar to the one you liked that we just took in on trade. I think I can get it for you about 30% cheaper than the one we just looked at.

If you pay three months in advance, I can waive the registration fee and give you an additional month of service for free! That's a savings of almost $200!

This week only, we are offering buy one, get one free!

(See my book *Cunningly Clever Marketing* for chapters on perfect pricing and developing irresistible offers.)

Establishing a high price in the prospect's mind, then unveiling a far better offer, often makes closing a slam dunk!

CHAPTER 158

The Shame Close

Because I consider everyone a prospect, I always try to get others involved in the sale. For example, when a child was brought to my karate school to enroll, I always tried to sign up the parent at the same time. I did this by inviting the parent to take the trial class along with the child. This would physically involve her in the product. Occasionally, one would say, "Sure," but the majority would smile and say, "No, thank you," or, "The lessons are for Johnny, not for me."

The first step I took to change this dismal success-to-failure ratio was to start assuming that everyone who walked into my studio *wanted* to take karate lessons. After all, the lessons offered benefits for everyone, young or old. When a parent came through the door with a young son or daughter, I would ask both of them to remove their shoes. Then, instead of asking if the mother or father would like to participate in the trial lesson, I would gently place my hand on their backs and walk them into the studio. I would tell them where to stop, and move right into the lesson. At least 50% of the time, neither the parent nor the child said a word, and the lesson went on without a hitch. Often, by the end of the lesson, the parent would be just as excited as the child and would sign up.

In the remainder of cases, the parent would still protest, "Oh, these lessons are not for me. They are for Elizabeth." At this point, I would move closer to the parent and put my hand gently on her shoulder. Then, looking her straight in the eye, I'd say, "But Mrs. Smith, all the other parents take the trial lesson with their children." If you are a parent and all the other parents do a certain thing, are you going to refuse?

If her response was not positive and immediate, I would look at Elizabeth and say, "Elizabeth, don't you think it would be fun if Mom took the lesson with you." At that point, all resistance would melt away. By using first the assumptive close and then the shame close, my studio experienced a dramatic increase in the number of adults who signed up for lessons. Once one parent was involved, it usually didn't take too long to get the other parent to try lessons as well.

Here are a few other examples:

- "Don't you think Elizabeth should have the best, running shoes?"
- "Don't you want to give your kids a head start in life?"
- "Isn't your spouse worth it?" or "Aren't you worth it?"
- "Shouldn't a good looking young guy like you have wheels to match?"

Appealing to the prospect's self-worth or his family's interest is a strong emotional close.

CHAPTER 159

The Van Gogh Close

One must act, in painting as in life, directly.
—Pablo Picasso

The Van Gogh close does exactly what its name suggests. It paints a picture in the prospects mind—a picture so vivid, dynamic, and exciting that the prospect just has to buy!

Late one night I got a call from a small business owner in the Midwest, and I could tell right away that this person was depressed. He started to tell me how he loved his coin business but could not seem to attract enough customers and was ready to shut down. After telling me about his situation for a few minutes, he suddenly asked about one of my marketing success manuals. As I told him how these manuals would quickly help his business, he began to perk up. That lasted until he asked for the price.

"I can't afford $150 for a manual," he said.

"From what you have told me so far, assuming you want to continue in business, you can't afford *not* to invest in this manual," I replied.

"I don't have $150," he complained.

"Let me ask you a question," I said. "If I walked into your business tonight with a gold coin dating back 2,000 years, and you knew it was the real thing and worth at least $10,000, would you buy it from me for $150?"

"Yes, of course," he answered.

Then I asked, "What if you had to come up with the money in the next five minutes? Could you do it, or would you have to pass on the deal, and wish for the rest of your life that you had made the investment?"

"I could find the money," he said. "It wouldn't be a problem."

"Well the manual is worth far more to you right now than the gold coin will ever be. It will show you how to quickly make a good living doing something that you love to do. If it helps you sign up just one more good customer, it will more than pay for itself; and it will continue to do so every day for the rest of your business life if you use the information it contains. On top of that, it comes with a money-back guarantee, so you have absolutely nothing to lose. Now, what address did you want me to ship it to?"

The sale was made. It was made because I took the time to paint a picture in the prospect's mind of both the potential rewards and the overwhelming sense of loss he would feel if he did not make the purchase now!

Top closers are great storytellers. They can quickly draw comparisons that clearly paint a picture in the prospect's mind of a need to buy the product now!

CHAPTER 160

The Limited-Supply Close

The "limited supply" close arouses a prospect's sense of impending loss if he does not act now. The confident salesperson can easily create a sense of urgency that compels the prospect to buy the product.

Salesperson: *I see you are interested in our new convertible. It is our most popular model. I can see why it appeals to you.*

Prospect: *So a lot of people like this car then?*

Salesperson: *You bet. We can hardly keep them in stock. In fact, you'd better let me check to see if we actually have any of them available—they go awfully fast.*

At this point, the salesperson goes to the computer and "frantically" searches the database. In most cases, the prospect will not be interested in the information on the screen. He will be focused on looking at the product. The salesperson can make appropriate noises as though he is having difficulty in locating the desired machine. He returns to the prospect with the news that just one has been located or will be coming in tomorrow.

The salesperson then suggests that a deal be made at once or that a deposit be placed on the one coming in that week because, with such demand, he can't guarantee that it will even be here this afternoon. As the sale is wrapped up, the salesperson should congratulate the customer on being able to purchase such a hot item without having to wait for the typical long delivery.

Try these approaches.

- "Every one wants June weddings! I have just one Saturday left—shall we grab it?"
- "Membership at the club is limited to just 375 members. Often we have a substantial waiting period, but right now we do have a couple of memberships available."
- "We limit attendance at our summer camps to only 50 children. Right now I have just three spaces left—how many children do you have?"
- "This model is very hard to get. But you're in luck—I do happen to have one in stock!"
- "We only accept a handful of new clients a year so we can insure quality."

The more limited you can make the supply, the more likely prospects are to want to buy whatever you are selling!

CHAPTER 161

Closing a Closer

If you don't make dust, you eat dust.
—Jack MacAllister

Every so often, you will have a prospect who is also a salesperson. Not too amazing, really. I mean, we're all people; we buy cars, televisions, and computers just like the rest of the world. But doesn't it put you just a little on edge when you realize your prospect knows your closing techniques as well as you do?

I find myself in this situation all the time. It exists when I sell my consulting services. I hit upon the best way to deal with this problem after a lengthy conversation with a chiropractor in Ohio.

Andrew: *Tell you what. Let's sign you up for our monthly consulting service and I can have the first package overnighted to you. You'll have it tomorrow.*

Prospect: *Well, it sounds good, but I have to talk it over with my wife.*

Andrew: *If your wife thinks it's a good idea, would you go ahead with it right away?*

Prospect: *Yes. You've already got me sold.*

Andrew: *Incidentally, you do give a free exam to prospects who come into your office?*

Prospect: *Yes, I do.*

Andrew: *After the exam, do you take the prospect into the office and make a presentation?*

Prospect: *That's right.*

Andrew: *Then let me ask you what you do in your presentation if a prospect tells you he has to talk to his wife before committing.*

Prospect: [Laughs] *Well, I see what you mean.*

Andrew: *No, seriously. I'm interested in what you do.*

Prospect: *Well, first of all, I pick up the phone and offer to get his wife on the line, so he can get started right away.*

Andrew: *I've enjoyed talking with you and I appreciate your help. Now would you please put your wife on the line?*

He did…I made the sale! The best way to sell a tough salesman is to let him tell you how. Most of them will, as it makes them feel good that you are asking for their advice! The worst that can happen is that his wife will say no. You know that his third-party rendition of your presentation will lose about 80% of it's value, even if he does take the trouble to tell his wife. Columbus took a chance. You can too. Go for it!

Take a chance. Ask the salesperson what he or she would do in your place to close the sale.

CHAPTER 162

The Gardener Close

It is the mark of a good action that it seems inevitable in retrospect.
—Robert Louis Stevenson

Every once in a while, you will run into a real skeptic who demands more than you are willing to give prior to making a sale. The first time I experienced this was many years ago in my karate school. Similar encounters have happened every year and in every business I've been involved in since.

A well-tanned, muscular man about 25 years old walked into my office. I got up from behind my desk and greeted him with the warmth and excitement I extend to all prospective students. He was wearing blue jeans and a dirty, sweat-soaked T-shirt with the name of a local landscaping company silk-screened on the front in neon green.

He sat down and I spent the next four minutes or so answering his questions about the programs that we offered. Just as we were approaching the close, he got up and wandered toward the training area. I followed him and offered to show him around. He turned and said, "Why don't you go out there and show me what you can do? You know—break some bricks or something."

I told him I would be glad to have him participate in a trial class at no charge, but that I did not give command performances. He didn't seem to understand. Then, before he could repeat his request for a dog-and-pony show, I commented on his T-shirt.

"Do you work for Greenwoods Landscaping?" I asked.

"I own the company," he replied cheerfully.

"Are you good?"

"The best in town," he proudly proclaimed. "I get all my business through referrals from happy customers. I don't even have to advertise."

"Do you have a card?"

"Sure thing! Don't leave home without them." He smiled as he handed me a card with the name Brian Edwards printed in the same neon green as the T-shirt.

"Brian, have you ever done any work in the Coto de Caza area?"

"Sure," he nodded.

"Good," I said. "Let me give you my address." I scrawled it on the back of his card. "I've been looking for a new gardening service." I told him. "Do me a favor. Go by my house tomorrow and take a look at the garden. Cut the grass, weed the planters, rake the leaves, and trim the trees. When I come home I'll take a look and, if I like what you've done, I'll sign you up to do my yard each week, and pay you for it in the future. But first, Brian, I want to see you in action."

His face reddened as he said, "Are you crazy? I don't do things like that—I'm a professional. My clients pay me when I work."

"Well, Brian, I'm a professional as well. My clients pay me to do demonstrations and break bricks. That's part of my profession."

The clouds cleared from Brian's face and he broke into a

smile again.

"You know, you're right. Tell you what. I'll sign up right now, just as long as you give me a chance to bid on your garden. Whadya say?"

"Done," is what I said. I needed the work done anyway.

I have used variations of this close many times and have found that if you ask people to treat you as they expect to be treated themselves, they usually will, especially if you can draw a parallel between what you do and what they do.

Turning the tables on prospects and treating them as they treat you is a good way to close when softer tactics fail.

CHAPTER 163

The Empathy Close

If you know how your prospects feel, how they are thinking—if you can really relate to their situations—you are going to be a much better salesperson. That's the power of empathy.

Sometimes I deal with prospects who want to buy my consulting services but are so short of money that they can't manage the $250 a month fee. In these situations, the key to success is empathy and, for me, it's easy. I describe how I started out. I tell them I've been beyond broke. I tell them I can remember when getting back to broke was my goal in life! I have lived in my car and I know exactly how it feels to be over my head in debt. With each new revelation, prospects agree and add comments of their own. When I have finished, we observe an appropriate moment of silence. Then prospects ask how I got out of that terrible bind because it sounds like I was even worse off than they are. They haven't had to sleep in their cars, so far! If they don't ask, I ask if they would like to know how I turned my situation around.

Then I tell them what I did. I read books on advertising. I learned how to sell, market, and promote. I discovered how to improve retention and customer service. In fact, I spent the next two years reinventing the wheel. I also point out that I did such a good job that I live pretty well these days. Then I tell them that if they sincerely want to change their businesses and improve their financial status, they have two options. They can do exactly what I did and spend two years and a whole bunch of money they don't have, or they can sign up for my consulting service. Then, every single month, they will get all the ready-to-use information they need to take their businesses where they want it to go. In order to do this, they have to do just two things. They must come up with $250 a month (just about $8 per day, remember), and knuckle down to some hard work.

I then suggest that if they can't find $8 per day to turn their businesses around, it may already be too late for me to be of any help to them. Nine times out of ten, they will buy. They buy because they know I have been where they have been, faced the same tough problems, and have overcome them. The empathy I displayed for them at the start of the conversation gave me credibility and built their trust in me, which allowed them to make a decision that is good for themselves.

I really do care about their situations. Phony empathy would be worse than none at all. I want them to survive and prosper and I can help them if they will just let me.

Use personal empathy to relate to your prospects' problems, and provide the obvious solutions.

CHAPTER 164

The Testimonial Close

There are two modes of establishing our reputation; to be praised by honest men and to be abused by rogues.
—Charles Caleb Colton

The written word always carries more weight than the spoken one. In this age of skepticism, people are more ready to believe what they read than anything you or I tell them. That is why it is so important to always have a stack of testimonial letters on hand. They can be used for PR purposes in your business. More immediately, they establish your credibility and worth as a salesperson, and reassure customers that the service or product you provide can be relied upon to fulfill their needs.

The best letters are, of course, those unsolicited testimonials that just arrive in the mail out of the blue. If you have a good product and provide good service, these will come, but seldom in adequate numbers or as quickly as you would like. For this reason, you must encourage customers to provide you with written testimonials.

Most satisfied customers will be glad to provide such a letter when they are asked. If the customer doesn't know what to write, ask a few questions like,

- "Why are you glad you bought from me?"
- "What is your favorite feature of our product?"

- "How has our service helped you?"

Provide customers with an easily understood format and most will be more than happy to follow it and write a testimonial letter for you. Some customers will tell you to write something and they will sign it. This takes all the work out of helping you. In this case, request a couple of pieces of their stationery on which you can type the letter and then send to them for their approval and signature. For a fast response, be sure to deliver the letter in person or enclose a stamped, addressed envelope when you mail it to them.

Nothing builds confidence in a prospect more than finding out that others just like her have bought, and been happy with, the product or service under consideration. Testimonials can be the clincher in overcoming objections and closing people who are on the fence.

In order to make the testimonial close effective, you must have lots of testimonials. They must be filed under various topics and within easy access of your desk, so you can retrieve them when you need them when selling face-to-face. Or organize them on your laptop as pdf files for rapid email deployment.

When a prospect comes in and brings up objections that I think I can overcome using testimonials, I empathize with her. It might go something like this: "You know, Katherine, a lot of our customers express concern about the level of service they could expect after the sale." Then I reach into the files and pull out letters from other customers commenting on how much confidence they have in our service after six months of experiencing our company.

Another prospect might come in and mention that he wants Pilates lessons, but he's worried about his bad back. I return to the files, look under "physical problems," and pick out a couple of letters from people with similar conditions. Not surprisingly, it turns out that the stretching exercises they learned in class have actually improved their condition.

Using the feel-felt-found method discussed in the Objections section, you can fire off a bunch of emails of problem-specific testimonials to win your case!

When faced with testimonial evidence from people with the same problems, needs, and desires, the close is never far behind. Start building your testimonial file now. Leave the dates off the letters, and your secret sales weapon will never go out of date!

Written testimonials are a priceless ally in closing sales as they help eliminate fear. Make sure you always have plenty on hand, to deal with and eliminate the most common objections!

CHAPTER 165

The Got-Stood-Up Close

Action will remove the doubt that theory cannot solve.
—Tehyi Hsieh

It's 2:15 and the prospect is already fifteen minutes late for her appointment. Odds are that she will not show at all. What do you do? First you run out and get a cup of coffee so the excuse you are going to give later will be TRUE!

Then you look back at what has happened so far in your relationship with her.

- How did the phone conversation go?
- Did you get the prospect's phone number?
- Did you call to confirm the appointment?

If all this went according to plan, here's what I do next when a prospective client doesn't show up. First, step out and buy that coffee. Then wait until later that evening and call the prospect back.

Andrew: *Hi, Mrs. Smith. This is Andrew at Martial Arts America. I owe you an apology. You had an appointment with me this afternoon at two o'clock, and I stepped out for a while and missed you.*

Mrs. Garcia: *Oh...yes.*

Andrew: *Mrs. Garcia, I'm really sorry I wasn't here when you came. Let's go ahead and set up another time for your son to have his trial lesson. Would tomorrow at two be good, or would four work better for you?*

Mrs. Garcia: *I think four o'clock would give me more time.*

Andrew: *Excellent. I'll put you down at 4 p.m. I look forward to meeting you.*

About half the time the prospect would offer some type of excuse and suggest that they were just about to call me. The rest of the time they let me take the blame without offering any comment, but they often showed up the next day out of embarrassment!

Make a last-ditch effort and you'll pick up lots of sales others would miss!

CHAPTER 166

The Columbo Close

A minute's success pays the failure of years.

—Robert Browning

Over the last twenty years, there have been hundreds of cop shows on television, ranging from *Starsky and Hutch* to *NYPD Blue*, *Miami Vice* to *CSI*.

Few heroes have been less glamorous in appearance and seemingly less skillful than Columbo. Yet he became one of the most popular detectives of all time with his shabby raincoat and his trademark comment, "Oh, just one more thing!" On the point of leaving, he would always turn back at the door toward his suspects and tell them that because he wasn't as smart as they, and didn't have such a good memory, could they just help him go over something one more time so he could understand.

This is also called the "lost sale" or "help me" close. As a last resort, when it becomes clear that a sale is not going to be made, the Columbo close serves two useful purposes. You will see what I mean when you read the following dialog.

Salesperson: *Mr. Prospect. I wonder if you would do me a favor?*

Prospect: *Sure!*

Salesperson: *You see, I truly believe that our software can have a positive effect on your business. I feel so great about what I do that I just don't understand why I fail to get others as excited about the product as I am. I would really appreciate it if you would tell me why I didn't communicate that same feeling to you, so it will help me in the future.*

Prospect: *Sure!*

At this point they will drop their sales defenses because you have acknowledged that they said no. They are now more willing to help you to cushion the blow of their turning you down. Prospects will do one of two things. They will either tell you exactly why you didn't convince them, or they will reveal their hidden reasons for inaction. If they tell you why you didn't convince them, you can improve your sales pitch in that particular area. If they reveal their hidden reasons, then you can answer those objections. In any event, this gives you a final opportunity to provide them with additional information and ask them for a response on the new and improved proposition. In the process, it does not hurt that you have stroked prospects' egos and self-esteem by asking for their advice.

When a sale is clearly lost, reactivate it by using the Columbo close!

CHAPTER 167

The Mentor Close

This approach is a very effective way to make contact when you are new to a specific product, territory, or city. If, after making your best attempt to sell, you tell the prospect that you have just started and you are new to the business and the area, most people will be only too willing to point out your weaknesses.

Once a prospect has decided not to buy and has offered some advice, put it into action. Then, when it pays off, call her and thank her for the advice. A simple conversation like this will pay big dividends.

> *Ms. Prospect, I just called to thank you for the excellent advice you gave me in our last meeting. I just sold two thousand cases of widgets to Mr. Jones up the street, and I really appreciate your help in showing me how I could improve my presentation so I could make the sale.*

Not only is this appreciative message a massive ego boost for the prospect, but she now has a personal interest in your success because she visualizes herself as your sales mentor. Often this prospect will now give you a small order for something, saying she forgot she needed it when she last saw you. Even if this doesn't happen, she will be much more receptive toward you the next time you call.

Now, of course, is a great time to set up your next appointment. Consider using one of the following approaches.

- "Ms. Prospect, I was wondering if I might take you out to lunch and get a few more pointers? You know so much about this business."

Or

- "Ms. Prospect, I will be in the area again in three weeks. You were so helpful last time, I was wondering if I might set up a time to call on you again?"

Does this approach really work? You can bet on it! Very bright people can be threatening to some prospects, who fear the salesperson may be taking advantage of them. When they're the mentor, you are not a threat.

Remember this basic fact of life:
Everyone wants to feel important!

Humble, quiet, and seemingly dumb people who ask for help make prospects feel good and pose no threat at all!

CHAPTER 168

The Calendar Close

The calendar close is your last-ditch effort to keep the sale on track before admitting defeat or being cast into the Never-lands of "I'll call you in a week" [or month]. Some, of course, will call; most will not!

If your prospect is simply not ready to close now, agree to a future date when you can meet to discuss things further. This at least keeps the deal alive and allows you to return to fight another day. It may also be just what you need to regroup and take your proposal to the next step in the deal strategy. Putting a date in the I-phone or Blackberry is easy for the other person and may be agreed to as a subtle exchange for your not pressing harder for a close now.

For example:

- "I can see that you need some time to review this proposal. Can we go ahead and set a follow-up date now?"
- "Obviously on a complex deal like this you are going to want to kick it around a little. Can we go ahead and pencil in next Tuesday for a follow up discussion?"
- "I'd like to give you the chance to consider this in detail. What's the best day next week for me to follow up with you?"

- "While we are both together, let's look at our calendars and see when a good follow-up date would be."

In all of these examples you are giving the prospect a chance to consider further—in fact you are even suggesting it, but at the same time you are also still assuming the prospect will buy!

When all else fails, close on a follow-up call or visit to keep the deal alive.

i2

Cunningly Clever Ways to Build Your Referral Machine

www.CunninglyClever.com

CHAPTER 169

Painless Prospecting—Building a Referral Machine

Ask any good business how they generate most of their sales and they will instantly and enthusiastically tell you they do it through referrals. However, if you ask them to *explain* their referral system, you are very likely to get a blank stare or a shrug.

Only this week I asked the vice president of a major real estate development, the owner of large law firm, and the CEO of a major service company what type of referral system they had in place. All had the same answer: They didn't. Referrals just happen, they say. Well, so does death, but it doesn't mean you should wait around for it!

When my wife bought a truck, the salesman sheepishly pushed a third-generation photocopy of a form in front of her that asked for referrals. Before she even had a chance to respond, he said, "They make me do this, but if you don't know anyone, it's okay."

She didn't bother!

Referrals are the life-blood of any good business. There is simply no quicker and less-expensive way to build your customer base and increase your income than to double or triple your referral rate. It doesn't matter what type of business you are in, referral business makes you more money than any other type of new business. Referrals cost little or nothing to get and they come with the healthy endorsement of a friend or colleague.

While some referrals *will* happen by accident, you cannot build a reliable sales and marketing system on accidents. You have to plan, measure, and implement a referral system that ensures two or three referrals from every single person with whom you come into contact.

The age-old business adage that what gets measured gets done is just as true for referrals as for any other part of your business. Referrals are a far too important part of your marketing strategy to leave to mere chance as most do. If you track sales calls, closing ratios, and up-sells, you should track referral generation as well—it's a great indicator of future business prospects!

The only way you can see whether your referral program is working is to set up a referral system and measure your progress monthly!

CHAPTER 170

Understanding the Psychology of Referrals

Let's start building our referral machine by first looking at the psychology of referrals. Many people are reluctant or embarrassed to ask for referrals. They fear people will think them pushy, or worse still, reject them! Nothing could be further from the truth. People actually LOVE to give referrals; you just have to ask!

Giving referrals involves two contrary impulses. First, people like to give referrals because it allows them to help others at low cost to themselves. It makes them feel good about themselves and be a "hero" to others. Second, people worry about giving referrals because if something goes wrong they get the blame. And if things go right, the thanks they get is usually small. Because of this ambivalence, it's easy to get some people to give referrals and hard to get others to. Even the same people may change their attitudes over time. Clearly, your job is to encourage referrals and also make it safe for customers to give referrals to your business.

People like to give referrals for three important reasons:

1. **Ego**. When people buy a new home, car, or investment, they want their friends and neighbors to be impressed. When was the last time you met someone who bought a new car and told you what a schmuck they were for buying it? It simply doesn't happen—at least not in the first few weeks!

2. **Most people like to feel important; they like to be the center of attention or information.** When the opportunity to take center stage arises, they are more than ready to step up to the plate by giving a referral.

3. **People want their friends and neighbors to share and experience the same things they do!** There are two parts of this equation. The first is the obvious point that people want their friends to share in the joy of the same experience. The less talked about reason is that people want their friends to share the risk! If they are going to spend big money to join the country club, then they want a friend to do it as well. Then if it turns out not to have been such a great idea, at least they are in it together. Few people talk about this side, but it exists nonetheless, the "I'll do it, if you do it" syndrome.

People LOVE to give referrals. Make it easy for them to do by reminding them that you want referrals!

CHAPTER 171

When Is the Perfect Time to Ask for a Referral?

The short answer is anytime; ask early, ask often, ask now!

The very best time to ask for a referral is right after you have completed a sale with a new customer. If they've just purchased from you, they must trust you and so are usually very open to helping you. In fact, they're more open now than they may ever be again!

Over 80% of all referrals in most businesses happen within 12 weeks of making a sale. And the first six weeks accounts for most of that success! This is the time when excitement and anticipation of the benefits of the product or service they have just purchased are always at their highest levels. After that, people tend to fall into their regular routines and face product or service challenges. The new product that was a "new toy" for the first six weeks has now become an everyday thing. The honeymoon, as they say, is over!

When the country club I used to belong to in California first opened, we all promoted the club at every opportunity because we wanted more members with whom we could golf. After a few years, when the club was fully established, we remembered what it used to be like, playing whenever we wanted, and not even needing a tee time. When I resigned my membership, there were 900 members and you could hardly get on the course at all. None of the golfers in my group wanted more members. On the contrary—they wanted fewer. Consequently, they didn't refer anyone. New members, on the other hand, who didn't know what a paradise it was ten years prior, put up with abysmally slow play and still encouraged their friends to join.

You must strike while the iron is hot, while the excitement and expectation of success is high! While your product or service enjoys top-of-the-mind awareness in the customer's mind.

In fact, there is no time like NOW!

The earlier in a relationship you ask for referrals, the more successful you will be in attaining them!

CHAPTER 172

A Simple and Foolproof Way to Get Referrals Without Asking Directly

I first discovered the amazing power of passive referrals in, of course, a karate school. Right after a parent would sign up little Becky, I'd put the check in the drawer and say: "You know, Mrs. Smith, oftentimes when the child comes to their first class it can be a little intimidating, so what I'd like to do is to encourage Becky to bring a couple of her friends to class. That way she'll be real comfortable." Then, looking at Becky, I'd say, "Becky, whose names should I write on these two guest passes?"

That question never failed to get two names and two people in for a trial class. Fast forward twenty years and Dr. Jones has just signed up at the golf club for membership.

"Dr. Jones, I am sure you are looking forward to sharing the club with your friends and colleges. As a special gift to you I'd like to set up a free foursome for you. I have three invitational guest passes here—whose names should I put on them?"

Still works like a charm.

Let's switch to a retail business:

- "Fred, thanks for buying a car with us today. As a special gift to you I'd like to give you $500 discount certificates, good on any new car. You can share these certificates with up to five friends. Whose names should I put on the certificates?"

- "Congratulations, your new diamond looks fabulous. As a special thanks, I'm going to include a couple of friends-and-family discount certificates good for up to $200 off any diamond of $1,000 or more. Whose names shall I write on these certificates?"
- "Madison, congratulations on your new home. Now that you are moving to our development, I am sure you'd love to let your friends know just what a special place this is. Who should I send a copy of our information kits to?"

If you can get your customers to give you names, there is a much better chance they will make the effort to pass on the gifts!

Using gift certificates, guest passes, and invitations is a great way to get guaranteed passive referrals!

CHAPTER 173

How to Ask for—and Get—Referrals Every Time

Many people are bashful or just downright scared to ask for a referral. They don't want to seem pushy, desperate or, heaven-forbid, both. While I assure you that most people really do like giving referrals, you can make the process even more painless: Ask for a referral as a favor or as a personal appeal.

The most important point is that you have to develop a method that you are comfortable with, remembering that it takes a little practice to get comfortable.

You can use the personal appeal:

George, it would really help me if you could suggest two or three other people I could talk to about the membership programs we offer here at Legendary Country Club.

Notice we set an expectation by asking for two or three other people.

You can use a personal favor approach:

George, I wonder if you could do me a personal favor. I'm looking for a few new customers and I'd appreciate it if you could suggest some people who might be appropriate for me to approach.

You can use some humor.

> *Congratulations on your new home, Laura. I've really enjoyed working with you. There is only one bad thing.*

When the buyer asks what that is, say:

> *Now that you have bought a home I have lost my very best prospect! Would you be willing to do me a favor and help me by replacing yourself and giving me the name of a friend whom you think would like to know about our development?*

You can do them a favor:

> *This sale only goes on until Friday. Who else at work would you like to help out by sharing this opportunity with them before the prices go up again?*

Or you can use the friends approach:

> *Sue, you and Andrew are probably like a lot of other folks. Once they get a home at Opulent Heights, they like to have a couple of their friends here too—not necessarily next door but close enough so they can do things together. Which of your friends will you first tell about your purchase? Do you happen to have their addresses handy? I'd love to send them some information.*

If your customers don't have the addresses handy, set a time up to call them for the information.

Reframing referrals as favors, personal appeals, and even as a service makes them easier to get!

CHAPTER 174

Ask New Customers Who Else Might Benefit

It is almost certain that your most recent customer knows someone in her line of work or situation who has similar needs. Everyone is an opinion leader—at least to a few people. A special few are opinion leaders to hundreds, or perhaps even thousands, of people.

> *Jennifer, we're trying to build up our Monday outings business here at the course. It would really help me if you could suggest a few groups you belong to that might hold a golf event. Are you in Rotary or any other group that might hold a tournament for charity?*

If the first answer is no, try a few probes with specific examples.

- "Are you a member of the local Chamber of Commerce?"
- "Do you have any kids in schools that have fund-raisers?"
- "Do you work with any charities that raise money?"

The more you help jog her memory, the more likely she is to come up with some excellent answers,

Some people just come right out and say it, business person-to-business person like this:

> *Juan, just as you probably do in your business, we find we get most of our new clients from existing clients. Who else do you know who would be a good fit for our service?*

Or you might ask Juan if his customers, rather than his peers, could benefit.

> *Juan, I am sure you have some customers who would love to visit our spa. Who do you think might enjoy some treatments?*

Notice above, I asked "Who else?" assuming that they know people rather than "Do you know anyone?" Never ask, "Do you know anyone who might...?" Instead always ask, "Who do you know?" The first generally produces an immediate "Oh, I'll have to think about it"—or worse yet, a no—while the second requires a response of actual names.

This subtle difference creates very different results

Always word your question in such a way that suggests your customer knows people to refer!

CHAPTER 175

How to Use Psychic Debt from Lost Sales to Create a Stream of Great Referrals

Even when a sales presentation has not been successful, there is absolutely no reason why you should not ask the prospect for the name of a person who might benefit from what you have to offer. After someone has told you no is very often a good time to ask, as there is often a certain amount of psychic debt present. This invisible debt is built up from taking up your time, asking questions, and then not buying. Sometimes a prospect will actually offer up a referral without being prompted in order to make up for not responding to your offer.

The landscaper who does my yard dropped by to see if I could refer him to any new customers. He told me that he had contracted to do two new jobs in my area in the last month. Each was worth almost $50,000, and both had come as a result of asking for a referral from two homeowners who had turned his bids down because of the cost.

Simply say to the prospect:

I'm sorry I don't seem to be able to meet your needs today. Who else do you know who might be interested in looking at our type of product or service?

Again, notice that I did not ask if they knew anyone, for that almost always elicits an immediate no. I asked whom *else* they knew, which implies that there must be someone.

Ask Ex-Customers for Referrals

Just because a customer happens to be an ex-customer doesn't mean he or she can't or won't refer people to you, especially if you parted on good terms. Make it a point to stay in contact with ex-customers at least a couple of times a year and let them know you are still in business. I frequently get referrals from ex-customers who have since moved on to other things but still have friends or contacts in the business. And, as a bonus, often ex-customers come back just because you kept in touch!

Prospects who turn you down, and even ex-customers, can often be great sources of referrals out of a sense of psychic debt!

CHAPTER 176

Discovering an Often-Overlooked Source of Diamond-Grade Referrals

One prime area that's often overlooked for referrals is that of your suppliers, both business and personal. You and your company both make purchases. You buy goods and services from others. You are a good customer to them. Those suppliers should be glad to give you referrals as a reward for the business you give them. Suppliers should keep you up on industry happenings, and they also know people who buy what you sell.

In sales, just as in other areas of your life, you won't receive if you don't ask, so be sure to remind your suppliers that you are always in the market for new leads.

Don't Forget Personal Suppliers

You bought a car locally, a home locally, and have relationships with dry cleaners, gardeners, and a host of other personal-service companies. They have your business—have you asked them to help your business?

How about bartenders, waitress, hairdressers, cab drivers? They all come into contact with hundreds of people a week and often have jobs at more than one place. They can be a huge source of referral business.

Get Everyone on Staff Involved

Make it a clear policy in your business that SALES is everyone's job! Remind employees that nothing happens until a sale is made and that the company's success and their PAYCHECKS depend on a constant stream of new business! You can offer a small reward for each referral or sale. The more people on your staff that you can involve, the quicker your referrals will grow exponentially.

Look close to home for referrals from staff and business and personal suppliers.

CHAPTER 177

Catching Bees with Honey—Getting Referrals from Your Competitors

Most business owners would be surprised to learn that their competitors can be a good source of referrals. Before you think that I'm a couple of cards short of a full deck, think about it! Sometimes you get a request for services when you're fully booked or the job is more than you can handle at your company. Or you and the prospect simply don't hit it off! She's from Venus; you're from Mars! In these cases, instead of letting the prospect bounce around to three or four more people, take the proactive approach and refer them to someone who can help them at once. Then call that person in advance to let him know what you can about the prospect.

When you give referrals, others should return them out of courtesy. You can, of course, set up a formal alliance whereby it's agreed in advance that all extra business gets referred. In one case, two of our golf clients in Orlando have this arrangement and give each other a 30% commission for the referral of a golf outing. THINK ABOUT that; on a day when the course is full one client generates 130% of maximum revenue!

Taking Out Your Competition with a Bottle of Dom Perignon

Many years ago when I ran my karate school, an athletic young man from New Zealand made several visits to my school without signing up. Each time he asked for information that bore no relationship to wanting to study and a strong relationship to wanting to open a karate school. Still I treated the guy with guarded respect and courtesy. Sure enough, about three weeks later he opened a school a couple of miles away.

In the karate business, the typical reaction to a new competitor is—to say the least—not very positive. I checked out his school, however, and saw at once that it was far too large and was in a poor location. It had no chance from day one. So instead of being mad I did just the opposite. I stopped by the school and left him a bottle of Dom Perignon and a card wishing him well. He called me later to thank me and express his astonishment about my attitude.

Six months later when he went out of business, he sent all fifty of his students to my school. That bottle of champagne may be the best $100 I ever spent to get business.

While it's not always possible, keeping good relations with your competitors can result in better business for both of you. Why not be the first to reach out? Refer business you can't take or don't want to your competitor, and reciprocity will likely follow. Take a booking fee for your trouble or just keep score on a quid pro quo basis.

You catch more bees with honey than vinegar!

CHAPTER 178

Referring Your Customers to Others

Getting referrals is your goal, but you often have to give referrals to get them. In fact, that's often the best way to generate referrals—and if certain people don't reciprocate, find someone else to refer to!

When you learn that a new customer is in a business that might be of use to you or one of your clients, immediately ask for that person's business card. Ask for several cards, so that you can pass them on to your clients. It will make your customer feel good and it will build your list of resources.

Simply asking a customer the question, "What type of people make the best prospects for your business?" is sure to build instant rapport and good will.

Be proactive by introducing your customers to others, "Joe, this is Scott—not only is he my dear friend but he's the best investment mind in town!"

Offer to swap website links; add customers to your LinkedIn, Facebook, and other social networks. Offer space on your website or a mention in your e-news. Tweet the fact your new customer is in a particular business and generally make yourself an excellent resource. Few others will make that kind of effort, which puts you at the top of the referral pecking order when it comes time for your customer to give a referral to someone in your business.

I recently contacted two companies whose products I felt would fit into the context of my marketing seminars. Both were receptive and both offered some compensation. One I declined and gave him the leads for free; from the other I took a small fee in trade—a classic win-win situation. I built a psychic debt with one company and good will with another.

Being a good source of referrals for others creates psychic debt in your favor!

CHAPTER 179

Make It Easy to Give Referrals and Spread the Good Word

The easier you make it for other people to promote you and your business, the more they will do it. Having a large supply of business cards is just a start; you should also provide free postcards, discount passes, gift certificates, and special promotions for "their friends only!"

Audio seminars have been one of my best producers for over twenty years and I hand them out at every opportunity. People listen to them and then can pass them on with their recommendation. On the CD is a 45-minute presentation that's engaging, entertaining, and filled with sales messages! While people may not like to read or have the time to watch a DVD, everyone has to drive! A 45-minute sales pitch with only one person in the "room" sounds like a great opportunity to me!

Here's another example: At a seminar in Las Vegas, I distributed 200 postcards to attendees and asked them to write down the three most important things they had learned so they could send the postcard to a friend who would remind them to take action on these items. At the next break, I announced that if everyone would drop the postcards up front, my assistant had a bunch of postcard stamps and would take care of mailing them. Ninety percent of the people dropped them off for mailing!

While these postcards weren't your typical referrals (telling others they should take my seminar), they were implied referrals. In any case, it was 180 referrals in the mail at very little cost! Now, to me, that makes a lot of sense.

Show Your Gratitude

Once you have received a referral, whether it works out to your advantage or not, make sure that you thank people. When a customer gives you a referral that results in a sale, make a big production out of the event. At the very least, you should send her a thank-you note. If the amount of money involved in closing the sale is substantial, consider sending the customer who gave you the referral a suitable gift as thanks for her assistance. A book on a subject that interests her or a bottle of her favorite wine will go a long way toward ensuring that this particular customer will continue to refer good prospects to you.

Ask Again for Referrals

Every time you thank a customer for a referral, you have the opportunity to repeat the cycle by asking for another referral. Always end each thank-you communication, whether it's a letter or a phone call, by asking if the customer knows of anyone similar who might benefit from what you have to offer. Remember, the best time to get a referral is right after a sale. The same is true of a referral once a person has started to think about who else can benefit from your offerings. Strike while the iron is hot and ask for more names at once.

Provide your customers with the tools to spread the good word about your business.

CHAPTER 180

The Law of Large Numbers—You Are Who You Know!

The more people you know, the more referrals you get! Now that's a pretty simple concept, isn't it? But far too many people involved in sales fail to take advantage of this simple fact! Join the club or association in your town or industry that will bring you into contact with the largest number of prospective contacts!

So there are already ten people in your field involved in the Chamber who are more established than you are—now what? Before you take the next step, consider this: More than half the members never go to a meeting anyway. Of the half that do go, most either go only once a year, or spend their time in aimless socializing rather than building relationships. As Woody Allen said, "90% of success is just showing up." If you still feel there is too much competition in the local chapters of whatever organizations you have considered, try a jump to left field and change the game. Join a related organization rather than the most obvious. Join the Chamber of the next town over, or instead of the Realtors' association, join the builders' association or the mortgage brokers' association.

Attending conventions is an important part of networking. While I live in hope of going to a convention where the speakers are dynamic, funny, and knowledgeable, it hasn't happened in along time. The real value of such events is actually in the cockparties or in the bar at the end of the day. It's there that you meet people and really get to talk to them. It is there, not at the trade show, that people let down their guard, and relationships can be forged.

The value of networking is espoused in every business. Yet few people make more than a passing effort to meet more people and almost no one puts networking in their marketing plan. That's a shame because networking is perhaps the quickest and surest way to build your business and it doesn't cost very much.

It's a simple fact of life that the more people you know, the more business you will get. The 250 Rule states that the average person knows 250 people well enough to invite them to a wedding or a funeral. People at the pinnacle of success in any business know four or five times that many. When I was active in the martial arts business I knew in excess of 2,000 clients and potential clients by name, sight, state, style of art, and enough other personal information to hold a meaningful conversation with them.

Doing seminars really fast-forwarded this program because each time I did one, I got to spend all day with 50 or so people. That's why seminars are such an incredible way to market professional services, not just because people get to hear what you have to say, but partly because of the sheer volume of people that you can meet.

That's also why golf has played such an important part in my life. Not only do I enjoy the competition, but it's an incredible way to meet new people. Where else do you get to spend four uninterrupted hours with prospects or clients?

Most people get very set in their ways and stop expanding their circles of friends and business contacts almost by accident.

Perhaps now would be a great time to take the other approach from both a business and personal standpoint, and expand your network.

Start actively looking for ways to expand your circle by meeting more people and making new friends; more business will surely follow!

CHAPTER 181

How to Ask for Referrals to Get Them from Every Single Customer Without Fail!

Imagine tripling your referral rate by simply demanding that your customers provide them? Sounds a bit unlikely, I know, but it's actually not that far-fetched at all.

In the karate business, many schools adopted a policy that in order to become part of the school's "Black Belt Club" (the ultimate up-sell), you had to introduce two new students to the school. It was written right into the sign-up contract as a condition!

I frequently write such conditions into my speaking contracts. Sometimes I do it as a bonus based on outstanding performance; other times it's written in as part of my up-front fee.

If it's bonus based, the contract might specify a $12,000 fee and include a clause that says, "provided you are happy with my performance, you will provide two direct contacts within your industry or pay a $3,000 bonus fee!"

If it's part of the general fee, I'll say my fee is either $15,000 or $10,000 plus two personal introductions to someone else who has the means to book me.

After the event, organizers often forget about the bonus fee or referrals provision, but you'd be surprised how quickly they come up with two referrals when faced with the $3,000 invoice on their desk and a copy of the signed contract spelling out the deal!

Why would I give up $3,000 to $5,000 per speaking engagement in exchange for a couple of referrals? Simple. If I can book just one in four of those referrals for a speaking engagement, I've made my money back.

After I speak, audience members fill out a survey rating my performance. In addition, I always request ONE referral to another group they know that could benefit from my program. Most people, because it's a specific request, fill it in!

There are more subtle but equally effective techniques besides demanding referrals. As mentioned earlier, when we sign up a new member at one of my country club partners, we immediately invite the new member to bring three guests.

Set the expectation up front with your customers that if you deliver great products and services as promised, you expect—even demand— their referrals!

CHAPTER 182

Be Specific When Asking for Referrals

Once you are given a referral, make every effort possible to get a little background on the person who has been referred.

When I was selling my consulting services for karate schools, I asked each client to provide me with three referrals. One client in Mississippi faxed me right back with the names of three people.

The first sneered when I mentioned who our mutual friend was, but was nonetheless mildly interested.

The second told me that if this particular client was using me, then he certainly wouldn't.

The third started shouting at me on the phone at the mere mention of my client's name, and went on to tell me what he would do with the "son of a bitch" if he ever got hold of him. I was completely taken aback and called the client to ask him what was going on with these people. He said he had simply referred people to me who he knew needed my services. He didn't know they had to like him!

Whenever you get a referral, try to find the REAL connection between the person referring and the referral. Ask how Joe knows Harry. Ask how long Sally has been friends with Chelsea. Ask what line of work the prospect is in. The more information you have about the referral and the clearer you are about their relationship with the referrer, the better your chances of a successful, new sales relationship.

Find out something about the connection between the referral and the referrer.

CHAPTER 183

The Ultimate Cunningly Clever Million-Dollar Referral Secret

When I first moved back to Florida a decade ago, my wife took a telemarketing call from a group in Orlando that sold organic foods. A few days later, a short, round man in his mid-sixties showed up at my door. He greeted me warmly and commented on "my lovely home." In fact, he asked if I might show him around the downstairs before we got started.

I quickly took him from room to room and finally outside to the pool area before sitting in the lounge to listen to his presentation. He brought out an old-fashioned three-ring binder full of tasty looking food and he started shooting off a string of questions about our family's eating habits.

Some thirty minutes later I'd bought a $2,000 industrial freezer that I didn't know I had needed and a truckload of organic food. After carefully helping me with the paperwork and putting it away in his briefcase, he took out a slick, glossy piece of paper and placed it on his lap.

"Mr. Wood," he said. "There is just one more thing before I go. You have a very lovely home here and a very lovely pool area. But I couldn't help but notice while I was out there that the 'little' Weber grill you have in the corner is really not in keeping with the rest of your BEAUTIFUL home." At this point he started to unfurl the slick-looking black brochure on his lap. It unfolded, then unfolded again and again until he was holding it with both hands stretched out as if he were holding a trophy fish. "This, Mr. Wood, is the type of grill I would want if I was lucky enough to own such a beautiful home as you. And here's the best part: I want to give you this turbocharged, super deluxe, stainless steel, triple decker grill absolutely free. It retails for almost $1,500, but it's yours if you would be kind enough to do me one small favor?"

"And that would be?" I ask like a sheep to the slaughter.

"Simply give me the names, addresses, and phone numbers of 13 of your closest friends in the neighborhood, and permission to use you as a personal reference."

I burst out laughing, explaining that I'd only been in the home for a couple of weeks and didn't know 13 people in the state, let alone the neighborhood!

After various suggestions to get me to commit some names, he finally seemed to take me at my word, whereupon I asked him, one salesman to another, "Seriously, how many people actually write down the names and addressees of 13 people?"

He looked me square in the eye and said, "Mr. Wood, if you don't, you'll be the first person this year!" It was May and—you know what—I believed him! His presentation from start to finish was so professional yet unassuming that I'd just spent $4,000 and hardly even noticed. I had no reason to doubt that he got the referrals every single time, provided they could come up with 13 people in the state!

Ten years later we are still using the service, so figure out that lifetime customer value!

Commit to a simple habit. The most important key to gaining more referrals is to commit to the development of a simple habit that will pay untold dividends over the course of your sales career.

The simple habit that will double, triple, or even quadruple your referrals is this: *Ask for them!!!*

Ask for referrals:

- not sometimes
- not when you feel like it
- not when you are having a good day
- not if you feel the prospect likes you
- but ask EVERY SINGLE TIME in as many different ways as you can until you get what you need.

They say it takes 28 days of constant repetition to develop a habit, so give it a go, starting today! Referrals must be sought from every customer, every client, every contact, and every supplier that does business with you. Furthermore, they must be sought from all your personal relationships, from your accountant to your dry cleaner! Ask everyone!

Make asking for referrals the best habit of your business life!

i3

Time, Goals, and Personal Motivation

CHAPTER 184

Do You Know Your Three Critical Sales Numbers and What They Instantly Tell You About Your Sales Effort?

Do you know your numbers—I mean really know your numbers? Most businesses do not. Even more troublesome, a great majority of sales and marketing people seem oblivious to their value as well. The numbers I am talking about are not found on a lotto ticket—I guess if they were, more people would know them! I am talking the number of inquiries, number of prospects, and number of sales. These three numbers are critical to your marketing success, critical to your sales success, and critical to the success of your company.

In the karate business, I knew the numbers inside and out: 40 inquiries produced 32 appointments, which in turn produced 25 trial lessons, which in turn produced 20 sign ups, 18 of whom made it past the first month. Those numbers, when hit, produced $120,000 a year!!! I always hit those numbers because I looked at them every day and held myself accountable for reaching them.

Selling real estate is no different. I have a Realtor client who turns 6% of her leads into prospects and then closes 25% of the prospects. Good second number, poor first number. By increasing her leads-to-prospects ratio from 6% to 12%, she would double her sales. That's an incredible number. The truth of the matter is, she gets more than enough leads to double her sales, but she fails to convert them to prospects. A low leads-to-prospects ratio indicates one of three things:

- a poor marketing program that generates too many unqualified leads
- a poor sales process or sales training program
- a poor follow-up procedure that allows good leads to slip through the cracks

That's how powerful numbers can be. You can troubleshoot a multimillion-dollar operation with just three numbers!

When I ran a telemarketing operation selling business books and tapes, the numbers once again were key. My staff called 60 people a day, talked to 18, and sold $800 worth of product. If they did not call 60 people, they did not talk to 18, and therefore did not sell $800 worth of product. It sounds simplistic and it is, but, day after day, week after week, the numbers held true. (They could have made more than 60 calls a day if their job descriptions didn't call for them to do other things as well.)

I just hired a new salesperson; his job is to make no fewer than 250 calls a week (and that number could have been 500—see the next chapter on Sales Position Agreements). From that we can extrapolate the number of people he should talk to and the number of sales.

That's the power of numbers: They lead to a logical result.

This last week I was incredibly busy. I had several very large proposals that had to get out and several in-house projects that had to be finished. Because of this I did not send out my regular weekly ezine. By not sending out my ezine, I have thrown off my numbers. Every week that my ezine comes out, I get at least two calls. Not surprisingly, this does not happen when I don't. So now I have to make it up somewhere. I also didn't make my regular five outbound calls a day to warm up a few prospects—another strike against me. But I'll make it up somehow next week because I KNOW if I call 10 people a day next week, it will put my numbers more or less back on track.

The numbers don't care what I do, and the numbers never lie!

Make sure you know what your numbers are telling you!

CHAPTER 185

Throw Away Your Job Descriptions and Draw Up Some Sales Position Agreements!

If you want superior performance from your salespeople, throw away your job descriptions and opt instead for position agreements. A position agreement is *not* a job description. Instead it is a detailed document that quantifies performance at every level of an employee's job. The quantification has both hard measures and soft measures.

A hard measure might be a line that tells a salesperson the minimum dollar amount of sales they should make in a month, but that's not where it ends. It might also state how many calls must be made each day, the number of conversations that should be initiated each day, or how many new prospects should be added to the database daily.

All position agreements should include daily and weekly reporting so that each of these measures can be checked. Make no mistake about it: When the number of calls or conversations drop, there is a corresponding drop in sales!

Why wait until the end of the month when there is no money in the till to discover that calls are not being made? A simple daily or weekly check will expose a problem long before the end of the month. This is true in almost any department at every level of every company, not just sales.

An example of a soft measure would be asking sales to deal with prospective clients in a courteous and professional manner, to display a positive attitude, and so forth.

General expectations such as acceptable clothing, showing up for work on time, and limiting personal phone calls on company time should be included in the position agreement. Also include job-related specifications such as how quickly phone calls from clients should be returned.

The more detailed your position agreement expectations, the more likely you are to get the performance you want. Misunderstandings will be fewer. If the agreement is well written and adequately discussed with an employee early in the process, simply showing the document to underperforming employees is likely to bring an improvement in performance (either that, or they will quit). If the employee doesn't live up to expectations, having a position agreement makes termination easier.

Position agreements work both ways. Employees should be asked for input on what they expect from the company. This might include clean working conditions, fair treatment, and the chance of advancement based on performance. In might include specific holidays, flex-time options, flexibility via the use of personal days, and the company's policy on continuing education.

Failure to live up to the terms of the position agreement should also be spelled out and, last but not least, the position agreement should be signed. Position agreements take a good deal of time to write, but the heartache they can save and the massive increase in performance they can produce is more than worth the effort!

The more specific your position agreements are, the better your sales will be!

CHAPTER 186

Sample Sales Position Agreement

Legendary Marketing
the world's leader in golf marketing

3 Month, Renewable Position Agreement
October 1, 2011

Position Title: VP Sales

Manager's Position: CEO

Results Statement: I am accountable for producing the following results:

I (____Name_____) will grow the company's revenue by a minimum total of $180,000 in new annualized revenue each quarter.

Specifically,

To make at least $60k/month in annualized billing.

WORK LISTING

General

Plan and direct all aspects of the organization's sales policies, objectives, and initiatives. Work with the CEO to develop the marketing plan and be responsible for implementation. Develop and oversee the sales function, ensuring that department employees and sales plan are organized to achieve maximum sales volume. Develop with CEO and oversee the marketing function, identifying key marketing outlets and competitive strategies. Lead and direct the work of others. A wide degree of creativity and latitude is expected. Free to manage own schedule and work outside the office as see fit. Report to CEO; also provide "reports" to executive staff as outlined by CEO.

Entrepreneurial Work

Recommend to CEO ideas for the vision of the company and innovations and improvements within your department and position that are consistent with the company's Strategic Objectives.

Managerial Work

1. Hiring, training, and reporting of all Sales staff, including telemarketing.
2. Develop Sales & Marketing Budget with CEO. [Note that in many companies Sales and Marketing have separate managers.]
3. Work with creative department to design and produce lead-generating marketing campaigns for the sales department.
4. Quantify all areas of your department:

a) Employee performance, leads generated, closed, dollar value of business

b) Marketing performance, web leads, CD leads, letter leads, etc.

c) Cost per lead, cost per sale, average sale

d) Sales cycle; how long

e) Referrals per MSS, per client

f) Identify possible seasonal factors.

5. Ensure that all customer contact is handled quickly and sincerely.

6. Oversee the meticulous recording of projects and tasks in CM.

7. Report results on schedule.

Technical Work

1. Daily calls.
2. Handle information calls and scheduling.
3. Maintain personal event planner.
4. Attend staff training.
5. Plan and lead sales meetings.

Position-Specific Standards

1. Make a minimum of 50 outbound calls per day, 250 per week, logged in CRM.

2. Have conversations with a minimum of 20 prospects per day, 100 per week, logged in CRM.

   $1,500 bonus paid monthly for completing 100% the above tasks.

$1,000 bonus paid for completing at least 80% of above tasks.

$500 bonus paid for completing at least 70% of above tasks.

0 paid for anything less than 70% completion of above tasks.

3. Minimum of 5 first interview presentations per week, logged in CRM.
4. Minimum of 1 Solutions Development logged per week in CRM.
5. Minimum 1 Solutions Presentation logged per week in Salesforce.

   $500 monthly bonus for completing 100% of the above tasks.

   $250 monthly bonus paid for completing at least 70% of above tasks.

   0 paid for anything less than 70% completion of above tasks.

6. Add 5 new targeted emails to the LM mailing list per day, 25 per week, 100 per month.

   $500 monthly bonus for completing 100% of the above tasks.

   $250 monthly bonus paid for completing at least 70% of above tasks.

   0 paid for anything less than 70% completion of above tasks.

7. I will review all competitors' websites weekly and report on any noteworthy changes.
8. I will subscribe to and read all related industry publications.
9. I will oversee the weekly distribution of the LM ezine.
10. I will notify CEO of any issues that cannot be resolved or deadlines that cannot be met within a reasonable time frame before the deadline has arrived.

General Standards

1. All work will be performed according to company policies and standards, as well as in the spirit of the company's Strategic Objectives.
2. Legendary communication is CRITICAL:
    a) All phone calls will be returned within 1 business day.
    b) All emails will be returned the same day.
    c) All useful data on clients' personal situations (birthdays, kids, awards, etc.) will be logged in CM and a 3-deep contact will be achieved.
    d) Status on all other projects will be given by email at least weekly.
3. All clients, employees, and consultants will be treated with respect and consideration.
4. All proprietary information, both of the company and its clients, will be held strictly confidential outside the company.

5. The VP may not work for or provide any service to a competing company in the golf field for a period of three years should he decide to leave Legendary Marketing.

COMPENSATION

- VP will receive $4,000 per month salary plus bonuses
- Bonus for completing standards 1–2, $1,500
- Bonus for completing standards 3–5, $500
- Bonus for completing standard 6, $500
- Plus additional bonus of 5% for generating new annualized revenues in excess of $180,000 in annualized income for the 4th quarter.

This position agreement may be terminated without additional notice at the end of any month where the standards agreed upon are not met, with no additional compensation implied or expected.

To be valid, both Position Holder and Position Holder's Manager must sign. Copies must be distributed to both parties.

Statement of the Position Holder:

I accept the accountabilities of this position and agree to produce the results, perform the work, and meet the standards set forth in this position contract:

______________________________ ________________

SIGNATURE DATE

____

NAME (PRINTED/TYPED)

Statement of the Position Holder's Manager:

I agree to provide a working environment, necessary resources, and appropriate training to enable the accountabilities of this position (results, work, standards) to be accomplished.

_______________________________ _______________

SIGNATURE DATE

____

NAME (PRINTED/TYPED)

Position agreements produce results for both parties, especially if the completion of key tasks is part of compensation!

CHAPTER 187

Success Breeds Success with New Salespeople—So Make Them Successful!

Over the years I have hired hundreds of salespeople for myself and clients. With new salespeople—even talented, motivated, experienced salespeople—I have noticed a very clear trend. If they sell something quickly, they usually succeed. If they struggle the first couple of weeks to put any numbers on the board, they usually fail.

Selling something quickly sends the message: "This is easy; people know this company; they like its products; I've made a good choice working here!"

On the other hand, if they sell nothing the first week or sales are disappointing, they think: "This is harder than I thought; people don't like this company or its products; I may have made a mistake taking this job!"

People are people and, thus, the last person they will ever blame for their lack of success is THEMSELVES!

A cunningly clever way to beat this trap is simply to stack the deck in favor of a new salesperson. Give him a few of the best leads, or better still someone who is really a "lay down." The difference this makes to new salespeople, regardless of their experience, is nothing short of staggering!

There is an exception to this rule. When you hire salespeople from the same industry, they frequently arrive with a spreadsheet full of names of people with whom they have done business in the past. Often, the salesperson's relationships with these customers and prospects was a key reason in the hiring decision. Strong performance is the immediate result as the salesperson works through the "hot list." But you'll also find that once the names on that spreadsheet have been depleted, sales don't slow down, they stop DEAD!

The solution here is the same—you just start providing lay downs when they begin calling a fresh list! Immediate success with new names helps prove to them that their success is transferable.

Early success means long-term success; failure means death.

Stack the deck!

CHAPTER 188

Creating a "Sales Culture" in Your Organization

Walk into most businesses and ask people what business they are in and you'll get an unusual variety of answers. Managers of the golf clubs and resorts I often work with describe their businesses as:

- service businesses
- people businesses
- hospitality businesses

Even in businesses that make the majority of their money from direct sales, catalogs, or the telephone, an astonishingly low number of their employees THINK that they have anything to do with sales or that how they handle a customer inquiry or complaint has any real meaning to the bottom line!

Perhaps the single most important paradigm shift most companies can make is to change the corporate culture they have for manufacturing, service, quality, or hospitality and get everyone from the receptionist to the truck driver to be involved in sales.

Everywhere I have initiated this change two things have happened: Dead wood leaves your employment and sales go up, usually quite dramatically. The dead wood are usually the people who see sales as somehow distasteful. You are better off without these folks!

EVERY employee should think that they are in—or directly connected to—sales.

At a meeting of club employees at a resort I was helping, I let them know that they were now all officially in sales. The chef brought in two meetings the following week from his food suppliers, along with $30,000 in business! Front-line employees started recommending the resort to their friends for weddings. Sales soared.

If the conversation about sales happens only occasionally, very little will happen. Sales training needs to be an ongoing effort. Training for employees in constant contact with customers, no matter what their position, should be a daily event. Fifteen minutes at the start of EVERY day listening to sales audios or watching a sales training DVD will pay lasting dividends.

Failing that, devote 30–45 minutes at the start of every Monday to a specific sales topic. Serve coffee and doughnuts; make it interesting; make it fun. Make it interactive. Help employees connect the dots between sales success, job security, and company success!

Develop a corporate library of books, audios, and DVDs on sales, motivation, leadership, and other key topics related to your company's success. Reward all employees for watching or listening on their own time. Develop an attitude of *kaizan* (the Japanese term for continual improvement).

Make sales your corporate culture—get every employee involved in sales and reap huge dividends!

CHAPTER 189

A Lesson from Wonderland on Setting Goals

If you don't know where you are going,
you might end up somewhere else."
—Yogi Berra

When my daughter was young, I began to reread some of the children's classics I enjoyed in my childhood. Although Lewis Carroll's masterpiece *Alice in Wonderland* is frequently (and mistakenly) considered to be for children only, its pages contain many basic lessons in life. Take, for example, this wonderful little excerpt.

"Is this the right way?" said Alice to the Cheshire cat.

"That depends a lot on where you want to go," said the cat.

"I don't know where I'm going," said Alice.

"Then it doesn't much matter which way you go," said the cat.

How many of us have found ourselves in this situation—walking, talking, working, and getting by just fine, without ever really knowing where we are going? That's how life is for the 95% of people who DO NOT set goals.

Why is it that two more or less equally knowledgeable and talented salespeople will finish at opposite ends of the sales chart? The answer, of course, is motivation—and there can be no motivation without clear goals!

Don't wait around until the staff meeting to set your own goals. Without personal goals you are just passing time wandering from one appointment to the next. Top people in every field, but especially sales, put pressure on themselves to perform by setting specific, measurable, and attainable goals each and every day. Their days are marked not by monumental victories followed by scores of minor defeats, but rather by steady and consistent progress toward a bright future for themselves and their families.

Using the SMART Goals System

Here is a short and simple course on goal setting using the SMART system. (If you want the full Monty on getting ahead in life, read *Cunningly Clever Achievement.*)

Goals must be **specific** in order to be of any use—you can't just say you want things to be better. "Better" is not specific! Pick a specific number of sales, or dollar amount, or quantity of product sold as a goal. You must also pick a date and break goals down into manageable increments. For example:

> *This year I will sign up 60 new clients who each place at least a $5,000 order. I will sign up five new clients a month, one a week.*

Goals must be **motivational.** This means they are challenging, and they must have the emotional power to excite you enough to expend the time and effort necessary to achieve them. Even when you have goals and are doing something that you like, performing the same tasks day in and day out can become a grind. You need to reward yourself for your continuing efforts and results.

Sales goals are measured in money—what will you do specifically with your share of the profits? Each time you make a sale, you make a specific amount of money. What will you do with it? Will you take a vacation? How about buying that new car you have been promising yourself? Will you put the money down on a new house?

Whatever your goal, come up with a clear and specific use for the money you will make from each new sale. Now, as you make an appointment or pick up the phone to call back a prospect, visualize how spending that money will feel. Think how nice it will be to show up at work in a new car, bought in part by your new clients, Mr. Smith and Mr. Jones. What an easy but effective way to motivate yourself toward higher sales! Just connect the end result of each sale to a personal item you want in your life.

Motivate yourself in small ways like taking a coffee break after so many calls, or taking the afternoon off for golf after closing a big deal!

Goals can be ambitious but they must be grounded in reality. They must be **attainable**. Setting a goal like, "Some day, somehow, I want to be president of a major corporation and very, very rich," does not meet the requirements of attainability. A goal that says, "I want to make $100,000 this year by selling 50 memberships," is specific, motivational, and attainable.

Goals must be **relevant** to your ultimate goal. For example, "I want to sell 50 memberships this year and be the top memberships director in the state next year."

Your goals must be **trackable.** You must be able to measure progress as you go along. If your goals are not trackable, you don't know what progress you've made on the road to your goal. Ideally, you should track your goals yearly, monthly, weekly, and daily.

Now do this exercise. I mean it. *Really* do it!

	Steps:	*Example:*
1.	Write down how much money you want to make in the next year, starting today.	This year I want to make $120,000.
2.	Divide the amount you want to make in one year by 12. That's what you have to make each month.	$120,000 ÷ 12 = $10,000. That means I must make $10,000 each month.
3.	Divide the monthly figure by four. That's what you have to make each week.	$10,000 ÷ 4 = $2,500. That means that this week I need to make $2500.
4.	Divide the weekly figure by five. That's what you have to make each day.	$2,500 ÷ 5 = $500. I have to make $500 today.
5.	Divide that daily figure by eight. That's how much you have to make each hour to achieve your annual income.	$500 ÷ 8 = $62.50. I need to make $62.50 in the next hour.

Sales needed to make this income: $1,000,000 based on a 12% commission.

Now what specific steps can you take today to reach that income?

Self-Improvement Steps to Help You Reach Your Goal

- Read a book about sales to improve your closing techniques. (You've made a good start already!)
- Attend a seminar to learn how to overcome objections better.
- Buy an audio program on better communication skills.
- Read a trade journal to keep up to date on new ideas.
- Call a successful friend and ask for advice.
- Take some work home to get a head start on tomorrow.

Sales/Lead Generating Steps

- Call a prospect now and set an appointment.
- Go through all your old business cards and call everyone who's not a current customer.
- Call an old customer and get reacquainted.
- Up-sell an existing customer.
- Write a letter to an old client to put your name back in his mind.
- Ask an existing customer for a referral.
- Send out a sales letter every single day.

- Put out 10 business cards or flyers every day.
- Write a magazine article to promote your company.
- Join a club or networking group to get more leads.
- Attend a trade show to make more and better connections.

Keep your goals close at hand, review them daily, and continue expanding their scope. Break them down from large goals into simple steps that you KNOW will aid you in reaching them. Use your goal to develop a sense of urgency, and each day you will quickly accomplish more of the simple little tasks, the sum of which adds up to giant sales success.

Remember, each and every day you have choices in the things you do. Some of these choices will move you forward, just as surely as others will move you backward. You are responsible for your choices!

Goal setting is the master skill of sales success—
ignore this fact at your peril!

CHAPTER 190

The REAL Secret to Tripling Your Sales Income

Twenty years ago when I had just started out in the consulting business, I was doing a consultation in North Carolina. I sat with the young man who had hired me and asked him what his goals were for his business. He said he had none; he just wanted his business to improve. I followed up by asking him how much money he wanted to make. He simply said that he wanted more than he had right now. With that I got up, took my wallet out of my pocket, and handed him ten dollars.

"Is that enough?" I asked.

He frowned and said, "No."

I took back the ten and exchanged it for a twenty. "How about this much?" I asked.

"No," he said again.

I swapped the twenty for a hundred dollar bill and asked if it was enough now.

"Of course not," he said, somewhat frustrated by my antics.

"Then how much do you want?" I asked.

"Okay, about $30,000 a year," he said. So, I pulled $30,000 out of my wallet (just kidding!). It took just a few minutes for us both to discover that this too was a ridiculous amount since he was already making almost that much.

It's hard to do better if you have no idea how you are doing now, or if you have no clear idea of what "better" would be like. After talking it over for a while, he decided that if he could make $50,000 a year, life would indeed be grand [as in fifty grand!]. With that amount, his wife would not have to work and they could take a well-deserved vacation once or twice a year. On top of that, he might be able to save up enough money to buy the small used plane he'd always wanted. (Up until now, he had just stared at pictures of it in magazines.) I told him it was time to stop staring, and do something. Now, at last we had a goal: a vision of what life might be like if we could make some things happen.

Together we ascertained that in order to make that kind of money as his own personal income, his business would have to gross around $100,000. He loved his work, so working hard was not a problem.

I then asked, "Do you think you can make $100,000 in a single year from your business?"

"NO," he said, very quickly and emphatically.

"Okay," I said, "Could you make $8,000 in a month?"

Again he said no.

"Have you ever made $2,000 in a single week?" I asked.

He shook his head.

"Okay," I said, "Have you ever made $400 in a day?"

"Of course I have," he answered.

Ah, at last a positive!

"Do you think you could make $400 today?" I asked.

He looked at his watch. It was late afternoon. He thought for a moment and said, I don't think so. At least not legally. We both laughed. (Actually, according to *USA Today,* the average take in a bank robbery is just $4,100. If you are caught, and most are, you get ten years. Now I'm not sure what the hourly is on that but at $410 a year it's well below minimum wage! Clear proof that crime doesn't pay!)

Next I asked, "How many hours a day do you work?"

"Ten," he replied.

"Okay, do you think that you could make $40 in the next hour?"

"Yes," he said. "I could call up some old customers or simply go around the shopping center passing out flyers. I could also..."

He came up with seven or eight ways that he could make $40 in that hour.

I then asked if he could make $40 the following hour. He was a little unsure but thought that he might be able to. When I asked if he could make $40 the third hour he said no.

I quickly moved from my side of the desk and pressed two fingers into his forehead right between the eyes as if it were a gun. "Suppose I told you that if you didn't make $40 in the third hour I would kill you—shoot you right between the eyes. Could you do it then?"

"Yes," he said, looking at me a bit apprehensively.

"And the hour after that?" I asked.

"Yes," he yelled.

"And the hour after that?" I asked as I pushed my fingers a little further into his forehead.

"Yes!"

"And how would you do this?" I asked.

"Well, I would do the same things that I told you before, only I would keep on doing more of them," he said.

"And if you did that for ten hours, how much would you end up with at the end of the day? Four hundred dollars, right? And if you did that for a week that would make two thousand dollars, and if you did that for a month, that would make eight thousand dollars. Which, over twelve months would make just under $100,000, which is about what you need, right?"

"Right," he said with a sheepish grin, "I guess I can make $100,000 in a year."

This simple little story illustrates several key points on the road to sales greatness.

First, you can accomplish little or nothing in this world if you think you can't do it before you start in pursuit of a goal. You have to believe that however big your goal, it is doable!

Second, you already have most of the answers you need to take you to the top. You just have to uncover them. You have to ask the right questions of yourself. You know what you have to do in order to become successful. The question is, are you willing to do it?

The young man in this example knew how to make $40 per hour in his business. In order to make $100,000 a year, he did not have to do anything different. Sure, there were many things he could have done to make reaching that goal quicker or easier, but the fact remains that without my help, he could have still made $100,000. All I did was help him uncover the fact that if he knew how to make $40 an hour, he knew how to make $100,000 a year. He had to do exactly the same thing over and over again.

Within a couple of years, that young man surpassed both the $100,000 mark and the $200,000 mark, and he was challenging the $300,000 mark. He also was able to buy his own plane, all because he set some goals and changed his focus from filling time to actually making things happen. Nothing else really changed: He didn't become smarter overnight; he didn't get lucky; he didn't work any more hours; he simply started working his plan.

We all know deep down which things that we do are money makers and which things are just exercises in "busyness." Remember, you're in business, not busyness. What simple steps could you take today to move toward your goals? You can achieve the results you want in your life if you will commit to working your plan and taking small steps every day toward its successful accomplishment.

What small steps could you take today to move toward one or more of your goals? And I truly mean *today*. Right now, after you get done with this chapter. Don't procrastinate, do not make an excuse. Do it right now! What small steps can you implement today to move toward your sales goals?

Most of us know what to do to succeed in sales. The real question is: Are we willing to do it?

CHAPTER 191

Beware the "Demented-Mole" Syndrome

A key factor in accepting responsibility for the successful accomplishment of both sales and personal goals is how you manage your time. Since every salesperson in the world starts the day with the same amount of time, it's the way you use that time that ultimately determines your success.

Treat your work time like gold. Do this and you'll enjoy maximum results in a shorter period of time, providing yourself with more free time. Follow a carefully scheduled plan of appointments and follow-ups, and never fall victim to the dreaded Demented-Mole Syndrome that has struck down so many salespeople in the prime of their careers.

I first witnessed the effects of the demented-mole syndrome at my local golf club when I was a teenager. I was helping a friend who had secured the contract to rebuild the 16th green. At one point during the afternoon we were waiting for the arrival of some gravel trucks. I watched a workman fill up a wheelbarrow with soil, move it to the other side of the green, and dump it. This was a distance of approximately 35 yards. He repeated the process 10 or 12 more times, whereupon after wandering around aimlessly for a few minutes doing nothing, he filled up the wheelbarrow again and moved the soil back to its original position.

There were, of course, a million and one other, more productive things he could have been doing, but this worker chose instead to focus on waiting for the gravel. In his mind, there was absolutely nothing else of importance except looking busy and waiting for the gravel trucks.

There are always papers to be shuffled, mail to be read, reports to write, and desks to clear.

The trained eye can easily spot the afflicted. They plan extensively. Despite always looking busy, they never actually accomplish much. I'll bet if you look around, you'll find someone already displaying advanced symptoms.

Get a day planner, a laptop computer, a contact management program, and a cellular phone. You don't need anything else. You are now armed and dangerous!

Avoid contracting the demented-mole syndrome and stay well away from the afflicted— it's quite contagious!

CHAPTER 192

Maximizing Your Sales Time Maximizes Your Income

Dost thou love life? Then do not squander time,
for that's the stuff life is made of.
—Ben Franklin

Many years ago singer Jim Croce sang about saving time in a bottle. If someone ever does figure out how to bottle time, I'll put my entire life savings into their IPO. In the meantime, all we can hope to do is put our time to productive use by better management of this precious resource!

Many people don't take time management seriously. They feel that doing so makes them too rigid, or that it robs their life of spontaneity. The truth of the matter, however, is that time management allows for far greater flexibility and spontaneity. It reduces (rather than increases) stress because you are so much more organized. Best of all, it massively increases the amount of quality time you can enjoy with your friends and family.

Time management will not solve all your productivity problems. Unexpected things will come up. Visitors will drop in unannounced and "fires" will need to be put out. You might still be a charter member of the Crisis-of-the-Day Club. Yet, with proper time management techniques, it's very possible to gain an additional one to two hours a day of productive work or life! Do you have any idea what that translates to? Don't worry, this isn't a math test. I'm sitting here with a calculator and I can do the math for you.

This translates into an additional seven to 14 hours per week, or at least an additional week of productive time per month, giving you an impressive 12 extra weeks a year! What would you do with an extra 12 weeks a year? I bet you can think of a host of great uses for this time, time that, after applying these lessons, will be yours to use as you wish.

I didn't take time management seriously until I was in my early thirties. I was sure that I was already extremely productive. Instead I was shocked to find that I was just extremely busy, not extremely productive. Having carefully logged all my activities each day for a week, I found that, despite working an average of 10–12 hours per day, I only spent a (shockingly low) 15 minutes per day in the direct pursuit of my major goals.

How do you compare? Try this exercise: For one week, take your smart phone with you wherever you go and note down what you do, in 15-minute intervals. At the end of the week, total up how many of the 168 hours you had at your disposal that you spent in the productive pursuit of your goals.

Most likely it's not enough. By the way, if you came up with a total of less than 168 hours for the week, you're either doing your math wrong, or you're living in a different dimension!

Good time management can get you an extra week every month!

In the following chapters, we'll look at some specific ways that you can maximize the productive use of your time.

Take time management seriously!

CHAPTER 193

Maximizing Your Selling Time at the Office

Do you ever find yourself making your kitchen table your auxiliary office? Have you considered putting a cubicle around it? But seriously, if you get more done at work, you will feel less inclined to take work home and you can mentally enjoy your time off without continually feeling that you didn't get enough done.

10 Quick Tips to Maximize Your Time at Work

1. **Prepare for tomorrow the day before.** Always set up the next day's appointment and tasks in advance.

2. **When you get to work, start work at once.** Don't spend 15 minutes getting ready to work like most people do. You wouldn't ignore the first fifteen minutes of a movie so you could get ready to watch it, would you? To aid in concentration, clear your desk of everything each and every day. Remove all possible existing distractions before starting to work. And make rules to control fresh distractions once work begins.

3. **Go with your natural rhythms.** Some people are morning people, some people are afternoon people—we all have periods of the day when we find ourselves more or less productive. Work with your natural rhythm; arrange your most

taxing work—such as outbound calling or complex proposals—at those times you know you will be at your peak. Save more mundane work, such as returning routine phone calls, filing, or data entry, for those periods when you are less energetic.

4. **If you eat out, take short lunches before noon or after 1 p.m. to minimize waiting time.** Better still, bring your own lunch and eat in. It's cheaper, more healthful, and more productive. Exceptions are when you have a lunch meeting, in which case you can kill two birds with one stone.

5. **Group your appointments and tasks together so you don't constantly have to break your train of thought.** Do all similar tasks at the same time rather than stopping and starting.

6. **Keep your office door closed, or if you work in an open environment, position your desk so you're not looking at potential distractions.** Position your furniture in such a way as to be uninviting to drop-in colleagues. When interrupted by someone walking into your office, immediately stand up and walk toward the person. Stay standing as you are talking. This will bring a greater sense of urgency to any discussion. Want to avoid distractions? Close your office door!

7. **Invite the drop-in to accompany you to get something out of your car or to walk with you to the restroom.** This will quickly bring them to the point, if there is one. (However, don't indicate that the conversation should continue in the restroom. That's how harassment suits start!)

8. **Avoid ambiguity when discussing a specific project.** Assign tasks, quantify results, set deadlines, and get all parties to agree. And repeat back what was agreed upon. Better still, follow up all instructions with a memo and have everyone involved sign off on the agreed-upon actions and deadlines. More time is lost at work from poor communication than from any other cause.

9. **Rather than rushing to fill up every minute of your day, schedule for the unexpected.** Plot two, three, or even four 15-minute slots into your day to take care of unexpected business, visitors, or fires. This is how doctors are able to accommodate sick patients who don't have appointments and you can do the same thing. As a matter of fact, think of yourself as a doctor, preparing for drop-ins by all those people who are sick (or who just make you sick). By doing this you will find yourself less stressed and more able to maintain some flexibility, while still working within a time-management plan.

10. **Review how you used your time each day.** Spend five minutes at the end of each day reviewing how you spent your time and grading yourself on how effective you were on focusing your effort toward those activities that propel you toward your goals. (This is not a test you can study for, and the only way to cheat is to lie to yourself.) Just take a few minutes and be honest with yourself. As with most areas of life, a simple increase in awareness of your habits can often produce significant results.

Few salespeople spend the majority of their days actually selling. Even the addition of 15 or 20 minutes a day to sales-only activities can make a huge difference to your income!

The more disciplined you are in using your time at work to sell, the more sales you will make!

CHAPTER 194

Maximizing Your Selling Time on the Phone

The telephone is a most interesting device. If you control how you use it, you can save time, money, effort, and greatly enhance your effectiveness, free time, and life.

On the flip side—and more frequently in the modern world—the telephone can also control you, intrude upon your work, stress you out, and waste a huge amount of your time. You can reach a point where the sound of a ringing phone is akin to fingernails on a blackboard. With that in mind, here are nine truly efficient ways to massively increase your productivity on the phone and save yourself hours of valuable time per week.

1. **Set a period of time aside each day—sometime in the morning—to make the majority of your outgoing calls.** I make most of my outgoing calls from 11 a.m. to noon. Any later than that and people are usually at lunch. I schedule a time in the afternoon to make follow-up calls. I also ask my secretary to instant message any messages she has, rather than calling me. That way, I can decide whether or not to act on the information without being interrupted by a telephone conversation.

2. **Budget the amount of time to be spent on each call.** Preface your call, especially on incoming or unsolicited calls, by letting the caller know that you only have a specific number of minutes before you have to leave the office or move to another

prescheduled task. That way, they will get to the point sooner.

3. **Always have a written agenda for each call.** Very often, as soon as you start a phone call, the purpose of your call gets lost in a host of pleasantries or an in-depth discussion of last night's game. (How many times have you actually forgotten the reason you called in the first place?) Stay on track by glancing at a brief written agenda as you work your way through the call.

4. **Always set the tone for your call right up front.** Tell the person on the other end why you called, or if it's an incoming call, ask the person at once how you can help them or what they wish to discuss. Setting the tone for the call leads to shorter calls.

5. **Always take notes when you promise to do something, and when others make promises to you.** When others are talking, it's also a great idea to jot down questions that just pop into your head. (Remember, the palest ink is longer lasting than the strongest memory!) You should be using contact management software that actually logs all the calls you make and allows space for notes.

6. **When you find yourself losing control of a conversation or listening to someone's life story, excuse yourself, then ask them to please hold for a moment.** When you come back, apologize and move the conversation back to the business at hand. If they say, "Now, where was I? Oh, yeah, I was telling you about my cousin in Cleveland...," don't be afraid to put them on hold again, and even a third time, until you might have to say, "Listen, you can see things are a little crazy here today. Let's finish up our business, and we can chat later."

7. **When setting up a follow-up phone call, always ask for a specific time to call back.** That way you save time and can tell whomever answers the phone that your call is expected, thus giving it more weight among the blinking lights. Even if they

answer the phone, "Mr. Smith's office," I always say, "Hi, this is Andrew Wood. Jeff asked me to call him at 3:00." It lets them know that I am on a first-name basis with the person.

8. **When you leave an outgoing message on your answering machine, always tell people when or where they can reach you.** That way you will help others save time and allow the people who want to reach you a better opportunity to do so. Better still, forward your calls to your cell phone and keep it on!

9. **Get a headset or bluetooth for your phone.** It frees your hands to take notes on the computer while you're talking, or if you're stuck on the phone with a really long-winded person, you can be paying bills or balancing the checkbook while you're on the call.

The more disciplined you are using the phone as your ally, the more sales you will make!

CHAPTER 195

How to Get 48 Hours Out of Every Sales Day!

Time management is an essential skill for the successful accomplishment of both your personal and sales goals. Maximize your time at work so you have more freedom physically and mentally during your time off. When you go to work, start work at once and remove all distractions from your immediate working area. Have all publications sent to your home. Take short lunches, and group all similar tasks together. Keep your office door closed and greet all interruptions by standing up. Avoid ambiguity in all communications. Scan mail and quickly grade it, dumping all unwanted items at once. When in doubt, throw it out! Schedule several small blocks of time into your day to handle unexpected events.

What's the best use of your sales time? That depends on your goals. They should be used to determine how to make the best use of your time and effort. Your goals will not only tell you how you should be spending your time, but even more important, they should be telling you what *not* to spend your time on.

Include ongoing personal development in your daily plan; never stop striving to get better at your profession. Never be without a book or audio when you travel; always keep learning!

Prioritize your efforts based on the cost and benefit of each. Maintain balance by segmenting use of your time. Develop the discipline not to waste time. Review how you spent your time each day and grade yourself on your effectiveness. Awareness often helps increase productivity.

Last, and by no means least, remember that YOU are in control of how you manage your time! Sure, others may put pressure on you to use your time as they would like you to, but you often have the power to say NO or to at least point out to others that what they are asking for WILL effect your sales!

Top salespeople don't need much management because they set goals, manage their time effectively, and put pressure on themselves to perform!

The Greatest Skill in Selling

CHAPTER 196

The Greatest Skill in Selling—the Power of Persistence

Our greatest glory is not in never falling,
but in rising every time we fall.
—Confucius

Persistence is a virtue that many salespeople overlook. However, the cunningly clever salesperson knows its power and hangs on like a bulldog to any chance of making a sale. He or she simply does not give up!

The Six Reasons You Must Persist

There are six key reasons why you must be persistent if you are to join the ranks of the cunningly clever salespeople at the very top of their fields. Knowing them will benefit both you and your customers.

1. **The customer doesn't always know what's in her best interest at first.** You may have new information for her. You have to persist and educate her before she is willing to buy.

2. **Prospects are almost always reluctant to change.** You must persist and help them realize what the cost will be if they don't change.

3. **Your prospects often have difficulty comparing different products and services and become confused.** Confused people are afraid of making a mistake, so instead of buying, they procrastinate about making a decision. You must persist in your attempt to minimize the confusion and provide them with a clear path to enjoying the benefits you offer.

4. **Prospects have many different priorities.** You must persist and help arrange their priorities in such a way that your offer moves up the list and helps them achieve their goals.

5. **Another reason for sales resistance is the prospects' desire to see how good you are at selling.** This type of prospect is sophisticated in business. They are familiar with most sales approaches. If they have time, they may entertain themselves watching how you sell to them. They may also use resistance as a way to test your sincerity. We sometimes call this *smokescreen resistance*. They throw up obstacles but expect you to overcome them. They reason that if you're willing to put a lot of effort into signing them up, you may be more likely to put effort into making them happy once they buy.

6. **Some prospects are just not ready to buy right now.** They might, however, buy next week or next month. You must persist to make sure you are still in the forefront of their minds when they eventually do buy!

Often, when all the standard sales techniques have been exhausted, the real winners are the salespeople who simply keep trying to make the sale!

As Johann Von Goethe aptly put it, "Perseverance is a silent power that grows irresistibly greater with time."

CHAPTER 197

A Critical Translation of the Word NO: What Exactly Does No Really Mean?

When people says no to your sales offer, what does it actually mean?

It just means no!

- It doesn't mean they don't like you.
- It doesn't mean they don't respect you.
- It doesn't mean they don't like the way you dress.
- It doesn't mean they don't like your mother.
- It doesn't mean your company sucks.
- It certainly doesn't mean that you or your offer are BAD!
- It doesn't mean they will never buy from you. It just means that they have turned down the exact proposal that you offered them at that specific time.

The more times you hear no, the closer you are to a sale. For example, most golf clubs selling memberships only sign up about one in 20 prospects. Some see that statistic as discouraging, but it also means that after 15 prospects say no, your next sale is just around the corner!

The more presentations you make, the more refusals you will get but you will also inevitably get more sales. Here are some statistics that may not surprise you:

- 44% of salesmen give up after the first no.
- 22% of salesmen give up after two nos.
- 14% of salesmen give up after three nos.
- 12% of salesmen give up after four nos.
- Only 8% ask for an order more than four times! These are the Cunningly Clever Salespeople.

Now, which group do you think sells more, the first group or the last?

When all is said and done, it is the enthusiastic and persistent salesperson who wins sales!

CHAPTER 198

Meeting the Master's Challenge

It is a fact of life that many martial arts schools run their businesses in a very old-fashioned way. This in itself should not come as a great surprise, since the vast majority of people in the martial arts business don't know that Bruce Lee is dead! Still who can blame them—he still makes it onto the cover of every martial arts magazine in the country at least five or six times a year. This seems to cause some kind of time warp that sends the average school back to 1973, or earlier, in terms of its business practices, back to the days of 29 cent gasoline and three-hundred-dollar-a-month rents. Perhaps this serves to explain why some studios still feel guilty about actually charging their students for classes, or why they are afraid to leave class for even a moment in case the student feels cheated out of his lesson.

Several years ago on a visit to New York City, I had a free day. I decided to drop in on a few of the local martial arts schools to try to sell them some of my martial arts business manuals. As any seasoned traveler did back in pre-Internet days, I let my fingers do the walking through the tattered copy of the Yellow Pages I found in my hotel room. I quickly learned that a couple of what appeared to be fairly large schools were within walking distance of my hotel. This was good news, since getting a cab in New York is never as easy as it looks in the movies!

The first place I chose was a Kung Fu school. It was located on the second floor of a two-story building. There were no windows on the poorly lit stairs and, although it was the middle of the day, I went up with a little trepidation. The entire hallway was painted black, which neither improved the visibility nor alleviated my fears. At the end of the hall, in large red letters above the door, were the words "KUNG FU." I could tell from the sounds emanating from the end of the hallway that there were indeed people working out. I walked toward the door only to find a handwritten note posted at eye level that said, "Go away, we're teaching class."

Not wishing to infringe on the wisdom of the great master teaching inside, I did as the note suggested, but I couldn't help wondering how many people were actually learning anything on the other side of the black door. This master, however good at his art, was no black belt in sales strategy!

I decided to make a challenge case out of this school, so I mailed a flyer and followed up with phone calls inviting the owner to buy one of my business manuals. After several weeks I finally convinced the esteemed master that he should part with $149.95 for a copy of my first manual, *How to Make $100,000 a Year or More Teaching Martial Arts*. Several months later, I was in New York again and paid the same school a second visit. The same black paint still adorned the walls in the dark hallway and, as before, there was a note on the door. As I read it, I could see at a glance that I was making headway. On it were written the words, "Come back later. I am teaching class." Yes, sometimes progress comes an inch at a time!

Eventually this master became one of my very best clients and went on to run several of the most successful Kung Fu schools in the world. Along the way he bought every single product I had to sell and flew me in for private consultations at his school several times. The notes are gone on the doors now and his studios are painted red, white, and blue. His student body has grown from 40 to several hundred and he has gone from barely making rent to making millions!

In a classic win-win situation, persistence paid off—for both the buyer and the seller! Remember this when you are meeting resistance to your attempts to sell first-class products.

The benefits of persistence are not one-sided. Closing the sale can, and will be, of great benefit to the buyer, even if he has trouble recognizing it at first.

CHAPTER 199

The Copier Man

Many moons ago when I opened my advertising agency in the back room of my karate studio, I needed a fairly sophisticated copying machine. When I looked at the latest models in the Canon showroom, I was shocked at the cost of a good machine. The salesman realized that the new models were out of my range, so he showed me a couple of good machines that had been used as "demos." These were priced far below the new ones, but, at the time, price was still a problem. I decided to put off my buying decision for an indefinite period.

This particular salesman was undeterred and proceeded to call me almost every week for three months. He was pleasantly persistent, and always asked for a sale. Finally, he told me that if I put down a thousand dollars, he would give me 120 days to pay off the balance at no interest. That provided the impetus I needed to push me past the point of indecision and I finally bought.

In the meantime, I had looked at three other brands that offered similar models at a lower price than the Canon. Their salesmen also tried to persuade me to buy. One followed up with a form letter while another even called me back twice, but the Canon salesman was like a bulldog with his teeth in his dinner. He kept calling, kept asking questions, kept seeking solutions to my objections, and finally got the sale. It was a win-win situation. The copier was just what I needed, and he made his commission.

After the sale, he called me to see if I was happy with the machine. During our conversation, I asked him if he was the number one salesman at his office, and—surprise, surprise—he proudly told me that he was.

"Success seems to be largely a matter of hanging on after others have let go."
—William Feather

CHAPTER 200

The Man in the Sharkskin Gi

For years when I spoke in the martial arts industry I was "hard sell," meaning that while I gave a great deal of information in my talks I also linked everything I had to say to whatever I was selling in the back of the room.

Although everyone agreed that what I had to say was very valuable, some people were turned off by the fact that I kept asking them to buy something. Some of my detractors even took to calling me "The Man in the Sharkskin Gi" (a gi—prounouced gee [with a hard "g"]—is the traditional white karate uniform). That nickname wasn't meant to praise my martial arts skills!

As we grew into a large company, my staff said, "Hey, Andrew, now that we are big and everyone knows who you are, why don't you tone it down a little? Be more professional, less brash, more empathetic," and so on. So I did. I bought some new suits, stopped picking on people in the audience, and made a very short but professional reference to my products at the end of my speech, not mentioning them at all during the body of it.

You know what? People liked the new, more compassionate, professional, empathetic, un-sales-like Andrew Wood. There was only one problem, SALES PLUMMETED like the proverbial lead balloon.

I mean NOSE DIVED into oblivion!

The experiment lasted just a few weeks. I simply could not afford to NOT ask for the sale and keep asking for it throughout my entire presentations. If that turned some people off, so be it. I had kids to feed and the difference in my income was staggering!

This taught me a very valuable lesson that I will now pass on to you, my valued reader. And, yes, the principles hold true for any type of sales you do, in any type of business.

Never assume you can make a sale, no matter how well known and great your product or service is without asking for the sale, often multiple times!

Your passionate advocacy may turn some people off, but they won't buy anyway, so why worry?

CHAPTER 201

Things Change: Yesterday's Blow Off Is Tomorrow's Sale!

How many times have you lost a sale to another vendor, only to find six months later when you check up on the account, that the vendor you lost out to has been replaced by another! It happens all too often. People make a decision and then change their minds, but you are not in front of them when it happens because you thought the sale was lost!

Even a cunningly clever salesperson can't expect everyone to make a fast decision, but as long as you have permission to keep in touch with the buyer, you are in the game. Keep in touch for the short term when they're still in the decision-making mode. And keep in touch for the long term in case they either don't make a decision or buy from another company.

Some objections will dissipate over time ("I'm happy with the supplier I have now."). Either their supplier will make a "mistake," or you will use the repeated sales contacts to better build value or trust. When you keep in touch, you build your credibility and sincerity.

Use technology to make your follow up easy. Program an autoresponder to send personalized emails out periodically to stay in touch. For real estate this could be a series of 12 emails over the course of a year. If you are selling a wedding venue, three to four times over six weeks would be more appropriate.

- Ask permission to add prospects to your corporate e-newsletter.
- Stay in touch by snail mail at least four to 12 times a year, depending on your product. (See the discussion of Thunderbolt Marketing in *Cunningly Clever Marketing*.)
- Drop prospects an occasional personal email with a joke, link to an industry article, or something on their favorite pastime.
- Send a clipping of interest in the mail.
- Put them on a tickler list and call monthly or quarterly as the situation dictates.

The key is to develop a strong system that works for your product and to use it religiously with every prospect.

Develop a strong follow-up system that keeps you in touch.

CHAPTER 202

Every Business Has a Perfect-Timing Zone to Boost Sales—What's Yours?

Persistence is very important, but you could be flogging a dead horse if your timing is off. Timing may not be everything, but it's an important factor that's often overlooked by many salespeople. Trying to sell outside the "perfect timing zone" makes your job ten times harder!

For example, January is the best month to sell weight-loss programs, health-club memberships, and personal improvement products of all kinds. After that, New Year's resolutions are forgotten and it gets progressively harder to sign people up, until it's all but impossible by the middle of the summer!

Then after the kids go back to school there is an upswing of consumer motivation!

In the golf business, the majority of clubs do their next year's budgets in October and November, hence they are our two most productive months for leads and sales.

People normally look for a new car about the time they just finished paying for the last one!

Every business has cycles for leads, sales, and upgrades. Some are obvious, many

are not. Knowing exactly what yours are will increase your success dramatically, at no cost!

CHAPTER 203

Breaking Out of the Sales-Resistance Cycle

Sometimes prospects keep you hanging too long. You have no reason to think that a sale will ever happen and you have no reason to think there is a hidden agenda, but you are also going nowhere. In cases like this you have to break out of the sales resistance cycle that can be created between you and a prospect.

You have to step back and say:

> *Ms. Prospect, I've talked to you several times about our service and we don't seem to be making any progress. I don't want to keep bothering you—should I just leave you alone?*

This will often turn the situation around—they'll start to sell you on why you should keep in touch! Or they'll often tell you their true objection, or they will finally give you a real timetable for making the sale.

At some point offering to quit can be the best way to make a sale!

CHAPTER 204

How to Increase Your Reserves of Persistence

Here are six steps to help you increase your level of persistence:

1. **Be over-prepared.** Start each sales presentation with a stacked deck. Be motivated, positive, and persistent. Know your product, know your customer, know your competition, know your job, anticipate objections, and be overarmed with solutions.

2. **Know that things can go wrong.** Realize that things can and do go wrong, so that each lost sale is not a massive emotional "downer." Estimate how many presentations it typically takes for you to make a sale. Then start counting; every rejection is a step closer to a sale. By approaching the situation in this way, you won't allow it to adversely affect your attitude when you lose a sale.

3. **Analyze what went wrong.** W.C. Fields once said, "If at first you don't succeed, QUIT! There's no use being a damn fool about it!" While I can't agree with his sentiment, there is certainly no point in banging your head against a brick wall and hoping to make a dent. After each incomplete sale, analyze what went wrong. Did your prospect tell you things you didn't know about his particular situation? Was there another person involved in the decision? Did you lose to a competitor? Play the presentation back in your mind and try to find the words or solutions that

might have made the difference, knowing what you know now. Keep notes for yourself on good ideas.

4. **Develop a "Plan B."** Based on what you discovered in your analysis, develop an alternate plan. Call the customer back with some information you had forgotten to give him. Call back and offer a demo model or one with a slight scratch that you can offer at an attractive discount. Call him back with financing terms or a better offer altogether. If all else fails, call him back to ask what cost you the sale—what you did wrong. At least you will gain some experience and hopefully avoid making the same mistake in the future.

5. **Stay in touch.** Send interesting articles, cards, newsletters, or clippings about your company's products. The prospect will remember you if his situation changes and will know how interested you are in doing business with him. It's possible he may come across something else he needs that you have. Often timing is everything. By staying in constant touch, you always gain the edge over your competitors. As legendary football coach Mike Ditka says, "You never really lose until you quit trying."

In my book *Cunningly Clever Marketing,* I detail the Thunderbolt Marketing method I use for wearing a prospect down and overpowering him with benefits and logic. After working a list of 130 prospects to death for almost 18 months, I suddenly stopped calling them and started mailing them. I mailed them brochures, teaser letters, video tapes, and product samples every three days for 12 straight weeks. Each letter had a single compelling reason to do business with me, which tied into whatever product or promotional item was in the package. One by one some gave in, until I had convinced 18 people to take down their store marquees and switch to my franchise—business worth over half a million dollars. The cost was $1,500 in postage and a lot of persistence. Persistence will eventually wear down almost anyone. As an interesting footnote, I actually received letters from three people who did not buy, but wanted to commend me for my efforts and persistence!

6. **Try again.** The sixth and final key is to simply try again. As B.C. Forbes said, "One worthwhile task, carried to a successful conclusion, is better than a hundred half-finished tasks."

The very act of persisting with a prospect for more than three or four attempts will automatically vault you past 90% of the salespeople in your industry!

CHAPTER 205

A Conclusion and Exhortation!

I've spent over 500 pages telling you *how* to sell better, and hopefully *motivating* you to apply the cunningly clever approaches detailed in these pages:

- building rapport with your prospects and customers
- creating opportunities for yourself
- qualifying prospects the easy and intelligent way
- using the phone to set sales appointments and close sales
- telling stories about your product or company
- dealing with any objection a prospect can throw at you
- closing more and more sales
- using referals to get more and easier sales
- managing your time so you sell more and have more free time

You have the amunition you need to achieve astonishing results—now it's time to take ACTION! This book covers a lot. You don't have to deal with it all at once. Choose one new idea today and work on implementing it. When you're comfortable with that, implement another. You'll be on your way to becoming a cunningly clever salesperson and can enjoy the benefits of:

- setting your own hours
- determining your income
- enjoying your work
- having more time to spend with family and friends

Here's to your cunningly clever success!

Andrew Wood

Index

Q

R

S

U

V

W

Cunningly Clever Marketing

The Inside Secrets of a Marketing Legend

By Andrew Wood

Out Market Everyone!

Nothing is more important to your business, career and, indeed, survival than to make your marketing astonishingly more effective than any of your competitors! Read ***Cunningly Clever Marketing*** and watch your **marketing's performance soar with innovative strategies for turning an ordinary business into an extraordinary business and immunizing yourself from recession**. It's over 400 stimulating pages jam-packed with powerful ideas, tactics and strategies to **quickly and ethically double**, even triple **your sales**, through superior marketing!

A fast, easy read full of graphics, examples and stories; you'll find **it fun, entertaining, practical and PROVEN!** Get inside secrets from a battle-tested marketing legend along with a bulletproof blueprint for superior marketing success. **Make every dime you spend on marketing count!**

*"**Cunningly Clever Marketing** made me laugh, wince, nod in agreement, howl, point out a statement to my wife, and become wiser in the ways of both marketing and reality. A superb read!"*

Jay Conrad Levinson,
Author, "Guerrilla Marketing"
Over 20 million sold!

WOW Your Audience with the Energy and Wisdom of a Real-World Sales & Marketing Legend!

Andrew Wood Speaks....

If you really want your group to learn firsthand how to improve their sales, marketing, or business strategy from someone who has **really done it** at every level of the business world, there is no better choice than Andrew Wood. Author of over 20 books on sales and marketing, he's an entrepreneur who built a national franchise of 400 units and a multimillion dollar ad agency from scratch. A real-world Sales & Marketing Legend who continually astonishes clients with unheard-of results from the Internet, direct mail, and his out-of-the-box marketing campaigns.

Andrew will electrify and entertain your audience with his business stories and cutting-edge strategies that attendees can instantly use to increase profits no matter what their businesses. **The highest rated speaker at every event he has ever addressed,** Andrew's audiences support his claim as the pre-eminent marketing speaker in the world!

Visit **www.CunninglyCleverSpeaker.com/** for details of Andrew's speaking and consulting programs including keynotes, half-day, full-day, and multi-day sessions on sales, marketing, and entrepreneurial leadership, contact him direct at 352-266-2099, or Andrew@CunninglyClever.com

CunninglyClever.com
Out Market, Out Manage, Out Sell Everyone!

Cunning Clever is a unique website dedicated to providing you with proven **inspiration, ideas, and answers to quickly maximize your business and enhance your life!** No textbook stuff here; it's all street-smart strategies and firsthand advice that actually works. The very information you need to maximize your profits and enjoy your life without the heartache of making all the mistakes yourself!

Our site is divided into the five main categories of success:

- Marketing
- Sales
- Entrepreneurial skills
- Leadership
- Personal Development.

These are the key master skills, needed to grow any business or advance any career!

Fresh and innovative content is provided weekly by top experts in the form of articles, special reports, audio seminars, and video streams. Use whichever method best fits your lifestyle to keep you on the cutting edge.

Just 5 minutes a day on CunninglyClever.com can change your world!

Speed is a strategy—that's why we have all the potent information and strategies you need to succeed in searchable, bite-size nuggets of information.

Marketing – Lead Generation, Direct Mail, Digital Marketing, Advertising, Fusion Marketing, Websites, Copywriting, SEO, e-marketing, and more...

Sales – Prospecting, Building Rapport, Qualifying, Presentations, Objections, Closing, Up-Selling, Cross-Selling, B2B, B2C, Referrals, and more...

Entrepreneur – Business Growth, Operations, Staffing, Avoid BIG Mistakes, Money Management, Service, Building Systems, and more...

Leadership – Creativity, Motivation, Communication, Problem Solving, Strategy, Personal Branding, Building Trust, Handling Crises, and more...

Personal Growth – Goal Setting, Time Management & Motivation, Developing Your Skills, Wealth Creation, and more...

If you are a business owner, entrepreneur, or career-minded individual looking for fast, proven results to dramatically improve response, sales and profits visit...

WWW.CunninglyClever.com
Out Market, Out Manage, Out Sell Everyone!